"Catherine Newman captures p........y, powerfully, and honestly that wondrous roller-coaster called parenting. *Waiting for Birdy* might be the funniest—and most astute—account of a mother's first years with her child since Anne Lamott's *Operating Instructions*. Pure and simple, this book is a laugh-out-loud gem."

—Chris Bohjalian, author of *Midwives* and *Before You Know Kindness*

"I laughed and cried reading Catherine Newman's wonderful *Waiting for Birdy*. Sometimes I laughed *until* I cried. As a book about parenthood, it is smart, funny, beautiful and excruciating, which means it is perfect. You will read it with the profound pleasure and relief of knowing you are not alone. Newman is there. Phew."

—Cynthia Kaplan, author of *Why I'm Like This*

"It has been a long time since I've enjoyed a book as much as *Waiting for Birdy*. Reading it is a little like a pregnancy itself—if you are a parent or about to become one, you'll find yourself laughing out loud, sobbing in public, and literally vibrating with resonant emotion. You know that little instruction manual you wished that your children had arrived with? Here it is—and if it's not filled with answers, then it's packed with joy, love, anticipation, and a heady dose of the knowledge that when it comes to the mystery of parenting, none of us are in it alone."

—Jodi Picoult, author of *My Sister's Keeper*

"Catherine Newman's new book about the rock and roll life of newborn parents is hysterical—in both senses of the word—and so dead-on honest that, as the mother of six, I wanted to have it made into a pillow. *Waiting for Birdy* proved my own grandmother's adage that one is like two and two is like five, and I nodded like a bobble-head doll as Newman described the delicious, neurotic hostage situation that attends the pregnancy and infancy of a child (Is it a cold? Is it cystic fibrosis?) Don't give birth without it."

    —Jacquelyn Mitchard, author of *The Deep End of the Ocean*
       and *Baby Bat's Lullaby*

"Catherine Newman's memoir of the year in which she parented a toddler and prepared for the birth of her second baby (envision Ann Lamott's *Operating Instructions* as written by David Sedaris) is hilarious, neurotic, intelligent, reassuring—and, yes, 'laugh-out-loud funny.'"

    —Andrea Buchanan, author of *Mother Shock*

"With her artful reflections on toddler metaphysics, the anxieties of parental mindfulness and the imbalances of fortune, Catherine Newman turns the fantasy of idealized maternal love on its head. Be prepared to furrow your brow, nod, and to be caught off-guard by your own laughter.".

    —Meredith W. Michaels, coauthor of *The Mommy Myth*

"Frank, hilarious, sometimes agonizing and always delicious, Catherine Newman's account of early parenthood will ring true for all who have been there, and provide rare insight to those on their way. *Waiting for Birdy* is a gem."

    —Claire Messud, author of *The Last Life*

Catherine Newman is the author of the popular child-raising journal, "Bringing Up Ben & Birdy" on Baby Center.com. She is a contributing editor for *FamilyFun* magazine, and her work has been published in numerous magazines and anthologies, including the *New York Times* bestselling *The Bitch in the House* and *Toddler*. She lives in Massachusetts with her family.

Waiting
for
Birdy

A Year of Frantic Tedium, Neurotic Angst,
and the Wild Magic of Growing a Family

Catherine Newman

PENGUIN BOOKS

PENGUIN BOOKS
Published by the Penguin Group
Penguin Group (USA) Inc., 375 Hudson Street, New York, New York 10014, U.S.A •
Penguin Group (Canada), 10 Alcorn Avenue, Toronto, Ontario, Canada M4V 3B2 (a
division of Pearson Penguin Canada Inc.) • Penguin Books Ltd, 80 Strand, London
WC2R 0RL, England • Penguin Ireland, 25 St Stephen's Green, Dublin 2, Ireland (a
division of Penguin Books Ltd) • Penguin Group (Australia), 250 Camberwell Road,
Camberwell, Victoria 3124, Australia (a division of Pearson Australia Group Pty Ltd)
• Penguin Books India Pvt Ltd, 11 Community Centre, Panchsheel Park, New Delhi -
110 017, India • Penguin Group (NZ), cnr Airborne and Rosedale Roads, Albany,
Auckland 1310, New Zealand (a division of Pearson New Zealand Ltd) • Penguin
Books (South Africa) (Pty) Ltd, 24 Sturdee Avenue, Rosebank, Johannesburg 2196,
South Africa

Penguin Books Ltd, Registered Offices:
80 Strand, London WC2R 0RL, England

First published in Penguin Books 2005

10 9 8 7 6 5 4 3 2 1

Portions of this book appeared in different form on BabyCenter.com and in *Toddler:
Real-life Stories of Those Fickle, Irrational, Urgent, Tiny People We Love* edited by Jennifer
Margulis (Seal Press, 2003).

Page 261 constitutes an extension of this copyright page.

LIBRARY OF CONGRESS CATALOGING-IN-PUBLICATION DATA
Newman, Catherine, ——.
    Waiting for Birdy : a year of frantic tedium, neurotic angst, and the wild magic
    of growing a family / by Catherine Newman.
        p. cm.
    ISBN 0-14-303477-4
    1. Newman, Catherine, ——. 2. Mothers—Biography. 3. Motherhood.
4. Child rearing. 5. Pregnancy. I. Title.
HQ759.N54 2005
306.874'3—dc22   2004053401

Printed in the United States of America
Set in Baskerville MT with Lucida Sans. Designed by Heather Saunders.

For Michael,
Patron Saint of Babies

(and of me)

contents

summer

It feels like I'm babysitting in the Twilight Zone. I keep waiting for the parents to show up because we are out of chips and diet Cokes.

Anne Lamott

Operating Instructions

Last weekend, we took Ben, our two-and-a-half-year-old, out to eat at a country inn. There was a hunting trophy on the wall—an enormous antlered head—and while we waited for our baskets of fried chicken, Ben stared and stared at it. His father, Michael, and I exchanged surreptitious grimaces—How would we explain this?—but before we even waded out into the dreary details of hunting and taxidermy, Ben offered his own interpretation. "Hey," he said cheerfully, through a mouthful of dinner roll, "why do you think that billy goat is peeking in through the window?"

That's exactly how it is to be two. But that's also exactly how it is to become a parent: the world is new and illegible, and you scramble to make sense of things as they appear; every sign is loaded with meaning and impossible to decipher. Until it happened to us, I didn't understand that having a baby would feel like falling in love, but like falling in love on a bad acid trip. With an alarm clock—a *pooping* alarm clock. I wasn't prepared to lie awake by the sleeping babe, my heart pounding audibly and so swollen with passion that I could barely breathe. I hadn't realized that my mind would scan constantly for disaster, like a metal detector casting around for the big stuff and turning up endless bottle caps. *What* is *that? Pneumonia? A brain aneurism? Woops, okay, no, just a little cold.*

3

The thing is, friends and strangers had actually tried to brace our expecting selves for the plunge into parenthood: "Kiss your lazy Sundays good-bye!" they'd warned, or "Enjoy your last movie of the decade!" or "*Farewell*, sex life!" Well, sure. That may all be true. But I happen to think that those are the wrong things to warn people about. Not a little bit wrong—like it's really *restaurants*, and not movies, that you'll miss—but categorically wrong. Absurdly wrong.

Maybe you just can't warn people about the real things. "Oh, good luck with the baby! Enjoy eating out, while you still can! And, you know, enjoy your *mind*, before it liquefies. In fact, enjoy your whole life, before it turns into a disorienting blur of love and crushing anxiety." Nobody mentioned the way my heart would be brought to its knees, a thousand times a day, by my love for the baby. What is it Woody Allen says to Diane Keaton in *Annie Hall*? "Love is too weak a word for what I feel. I *luuuurve* you. You know, I *loave* you. I *luff* you—two 'f's." I wasn't prepared for my terror—twinned freakishly with this love—that we would lose him. I was so anxious all the time that I wanted to have the baby put to sleep, but in the *veterinary* sense—just so I could quit worrying that he would die. *You're still here!* was my first thought every morning. *Oh my God!*

So here's the question: Why, now that Ben is two and I'm finally learning to function in this grief-stricken stupor of doting, are we expecting *another* baby? The short answer—and it's one that kind of begs the "decide" question—is that birth control doesn't actually work by osmosis. Run and tell your teenaged daughters! It's not enough to keep some stashed in the drawer of your bedside table—you actually have to *use* it.

I thought I had decided—before this inexplicable round of the unprotected hokey-pokey—that I didn't want to have another baby. Not only because I didn't want my body to turn back into a giant, barfing kiln. Nor because I wanted to deprive Ben of an accomplice when Michael and I become old and impossible with Alzheimer's. Nor because I didn't like the idea of having, how shall I put this, a *back-up* kid. But because I like the relative serenity of raising only one child. I can imagine us up and going somewhere, if we feel like it. I can imagine us being able to afford college one day, should, God willing, Ben actually live that long without being incarcerated. And I don't want to devote my one life on earth to breaking up squabbles over toaster waffles and acne medication. Our family, in short, is working pretty well the way it is. Michael and I like each other. Ben is kind of odd—and, come to think of it, oddly kind—and we like him, too. Aside from the daily bouts of shattering anxiety, life is good.

But Michael has felt differently all along—not that life isn't good, but that it could be even better. It's not that he's performed a statistical analysis, as I have, of the productivity and overall happiness of only children versus kids with siblings. He hasn't calculated exactly how much money we'll need for extra glycerin suppositories and life insurance. Nor does he worry that we won't actually *like* another baby. In fact, he wants another baby for the simple and lovely reason that he wants to feel the love we feel for Ben, but more of it. He just wants more.

But forget what Michael thinks, because Michael comes from a family of, count 'em, six kids. We should all be naturally suspicious of his wish for a bigger brood. "I've watched the super-eight movies," I complained to him. I'd seen all the kids, grainy and silent, with colanders on their heads and couch cushions belted around their shins while they shot hockey pucks in the living room, the Hummel figurines flying off the mantel like bowling pins. Is it wrong to want your life to be more like *Martha Stewart Baby* than like *Eight Is Enough?* When I asked Michael this question, he first suggested that it *was* wrong, and then drew a specious distinction between eight and *two.* Whatever.

Although its happening was no profound mystery, I want to say here that Michael and I were not, in the strong sense of the word, *trying* to get pregnant. (You know, trying—as in "How *trying!*"—when sex becomes as much of a chore as raking leaves or cleaning out the lint trap.) Michael might even suggest that, in the deciding moment, it was actually *my* idea to get pregnant. And, I confess, this may be true. Although "idea" is not quite the right word for what I was having in that moment—the same way you might, say, stand at the fridge spooning Dulce de Leche Häagen-Dazs out of the carton, stopping every minute or two to spray a gob of whipped cream into your mouth from a can, without this being, exactly, your "idea."

Okay, maybe I have secretly wanted another baby. But I'm going to be like one of those old ladies with a house full of mangy, shedding cats peeing on all her good shoes and kicking litter onto the Persian carpet, while she just wanders around, wringing her hands and muttering, "Where are all my *kittens?*" I can picture the pack of teenagers, with their grubby fuzz mustaches or thong underwear, boiling pounds of spaghetti and lounging around sullenly with their sweatshirt hoods pulled low over their foreheads while they clink beer bottles and inject each other with heroin. I'll be the one hiding in the basement, paging through my albums of pink-cheeked babies.

But perhaps I get ahead of myself. I haven't even been to the *doctor* yet! But we are having another baby. This much I know for sure.

I'm addicted to home pregnancy tests. I start them way too early, just to be sure, I guess, that the results will be baffling. "Honey?" I yelled from the bathroom this time. "Do you think I can try this pregnancy test a week before my period's even due?" "What does the package say?" he yelled back. "'Accurate as early as the first day of a missed period,'" I read, and Michael laughed. But I did the test anyway.

Here's a little secret: if your period's not even due for a week and you leave a distinctly negative home pregnancy test in the garbage can overnight, and then you fish it back out in the morning to look again, you might now actually see a very faint second line, like a double horizon through a pink fog. This might give you a creepy hocus-pocus feeling. "Am I pregnant or not?" you might wonder, but calling the 800 number on the box won't help you at all. The customer service representative will sound appalled and incredulous—"I'm sorry? You did *what?*"—as if you maybe tried shoving the entire test stick into your rectum, and she'll counsel you sharply to wait the correct number of days and try again. If you press her, she'll say that you either might, or might not, be pregnant.

But I think it means you're pregnant. And you should buy more tests so you can re-create the moment of frustrating uncertainty. Then swear you won't buy any more tests until the end of the week. Then buy one more pack, but bury the faintly pink-lined sticks in the bottom of the garbage can so your partner won't have you committed. I can't help noticing that even at Costco the tests only come in boxes of four. Where are the two-handled jumbo packs for the real compulsives? If I'd invested all the money I spent on home pregnancy tests, Ben could start college *now*.

I can't help it. I watch the urine creep up into the stick's little window and leave in its wake first one pink line, and then— yes, there it is!—another, paler line, and every time my heart races. I am profoundly excited. Also mildly despairing. What will we do with the baby? Our lives are already so full with this *one* child. But maybe I'm feeling extra moony because we've just returned from a camping trip on Cape Cod, and it was the kind of week where you pray every second that your memory will serve you. I just want to be old one day, in a rocker with a glass of lemonade (or maybe gin), flipping through my mental Rolodex of perfect moments: the way Ben peered into a seashell and screamed in delight over the sudden, complicated face of a hermit crab; the way his bare, sandy self gleamed in the sunset like a ripe peach; the way he squashed an incinerated marshmallow flat between his palms and then scraped it off with his bottom teeth and, it seems, his hair.

Ah, but ask that little kid what *he* remembers best about the trip, and he'll shout, without hesitation, "The Zooquarium!" Michael and I can only shudder to recall it. I mean, *Zooquarium?* What, are the zoo animals *underwater?* But it was a rainy afternoon and we were sick of playing "Guess what animal" in the tent ("I'm black and white and I say 'moo.'" "Um, are you a turkey, Mama?"), so we spent twenty-two bucks to ogle the local offerings: a lobster, a blind seal, and a balding, claustrophobic llama. The main attraction was the hourly "Creature Show," with a lone star of a horseshoe crab. Its big trick seemed to be waving its legs around torpidly. Ben sat very close to me, and sucked his thumb in this kind of delighted terror—which, come to think of it, describes his relationship to lots of things, like swimming, children's music, a miniature poodle named Eloise, and flushing poop down the toilet.

But the truth is that if I weren't forcing myself to write about it, I'd certainly crop the aquarium altogether from my memory, even though it may be, to date, the single biggest thrill of Ben's life. I think that's what the scrapbooking mania is all about—so you can be like, "Look, we were always smiling! It was always sunny! That was such a wonderful trip!" Just use your bubble-letter stamps and your rainbow ink pad to write "Summer-tastic!" above your snapshots, and you'll have effectively pasted over the fact of the mosquitoes, or the way your kid's hot, sandy feet pressed all over you in the tent, or the way the tent itself became an amazing Odor Dome for hours after every diaper change. Or the way Ben became completely hysterical, I mean *deranged* with grief, after a woman jogged by with her two dogs and a Walkman and, thus, didn't hear him when he asked her, in this heartbreakingly polite way, "Excuse me, but do you know what is your dogs' names?" You might think, from his ensuing breakdown, that knowledge of dog names was the God-given key to all of Ben's remaining future happiness. Michael tried gamely to rescue the afternoon: "I think that big one's name was maybe Sparky, and the little one was Priscilla. Want to go swimming?" But Ben just had to cry it out.

It seems so strange to us, the things that send him spiraling into that exuberant kind of toddler grief. I feel like he's such a trooper most of the time—he can trip and recover tearlessly, give his toys over to grabbers, fall asleep in our driveway in western Massachusetts and wake up happily in Brooklyn—but then some ineffable thing, like the sight of a paper cup floating in a sinkful of water, or that mystery of the dogs' names, will just totally set him off. I worried on the Cape when we went to this "Ahoy there, matey!" type of seafood restaurant, the kind where there's a big lobster tank and you, sadistically, get to pick out the one you want to eat for dinner. I worried that Ben would be devastated. But he just peered into the tank and asked if the lobsters were happy swimming in there, and he kind of wiggled his body all over to emphasize both "happy" and "swimming." "I think so," I said.

Then one was plunked in a colander and whisked into the kitchen, and Ben asked where it was going. I looked into his bright face and imagined what he was imagining: the lobster riding a merry-go-round, maybe, or getting a soft ice-cream cone, before being dunked happily back into the tank with his buddies. What could I say? "Um, the kitchen, I guess. But hey— did you see that big *mermaid* on the wall?" Distraction seems to be our current favorite parenting tool. "Can you imagine," my friend Kathy, also mother of a two-year-old, once asked me, "if you and Michael were fighting, and you were furious and in tears, but he was just like, 'Mmm. I know. That's too bad. Hey, honey, look at the blue jay! Do you see the *blue jay?!* Do you want some *raisins?* Here, have a raisin.'"

In the end, we all ordered fish and chips.

The thing is, having a kid makes me want the world to be a

better place. I dread Ben's dawning realization about cruelty—the day when he will suddenly look up from his dinner and ask, "Why is this called 'chicken'?" and the jig will be up. Until then, we can't help enjoying his optimistic outlook: that blind seals and bald llamas and steamer-bound lobsters are as happy in the world as he is. Which, except for those few unpredictable, dark episodes, is pretty darn happy.

Me too. When we got home, I visited my OB, peed on *her* stick, and now I am officially pregnant. In fact, thanks to their preemptive you're-actually-your-own-grandmother style of calculating it from your last period, I seem to have gotten pregnant two weeks *before* we even conceived. Which makes me six weeks along. Yikes! "Let's wait," I told Michael. "Let's not tell everyone right away." And he said, "That's fine, honey. That's a good idea." And then I called everyone we know. I did the exact same thing when I got pregnant with Ben.

And, in fact, the time before that too—the time I miscarried. I know you're supposed to spare other people the awkward fact of your reproductive klutziness. Shouldn't you be encouraged to tell *everybody*—to cast a wide net for support in a time when you will surely need it? Instead it's like a filthy, embarrassing secret. Like you already did some monstrous, counter-maternal thing—harboring an ambivalent thought, maybe, or smoking that one last teeny pipeful of crack—that caused the baby to leap from your womb in dread. I can say this for certain: all that shame and secrecy do not contribute overly much to the healing process. I once sat up late with a friend, enjoying a shot or two of Jäger-meister and imagining a special line of Hallmark cards called "Womanly Thoughts" or, maybe, "Gynecological Moments." These would be designed around moody little watercolors of women with their feet in stirrups, women skulking around ovulation kits at the supermarket, and greetings like "Sorry to hear about your ovarian cyst. / If I had one, I'd be really pissed."

All of which is to say: I'm already gabbing my head off about this baby, who is, officially, the size of a grain of rice. That's what the ultrasound person said, after she circled my belly with the wand a few times and then swooped down on a pulsing little dark spot: "It's about as big as a grain of rice." Why do they always compare the embryo to food? Rice. A pinto bean. A peanut. It *forces* you to imagine eating it.

I had been nervous about the ultrasound—filled with an oddly paired hope and fear that there would really be a little living something in my tum—but now I find myself relieved to have seen it: krill with a beating little peppercorn heart. A baby. It still seems utterly hypothetical, as it did with Ben more or less up until the moment he was born. And it's so long to wait! March sixth is our due date. It won't be born until the very last gasp of winter. And it's only early summer now! Glorious early summer, and I feel great. I was so sick in the early days of my pregnancy with Ben, so I'm predicting, tentatively, that this time it will be different. I have a good feeling about the pregnancy—a strong sense that I will feel well and strong throughout.

———

A few years ago, when Michael and I went to see *Titanic*, there was a tearful woman sitting behind us, just totally overwhelmed by the unfolding drama onboard. When the iceberg loomed up with a sudden crash—I swear this is true—she whispered to her companion, "I'm not sure the ship can *sustain* that kind of damage!" Um, right. It's the *Titanic*.

Living with a toddler is like that—the mundane announcements, that is, not the sinking steamer—only nonstop. Ben averages an epiphany a minute, but many of them are so exuberantly obvious that it just kills us, like "Hey, Mama! Water comes out of the hose!" or "Daddy is a *person!*" Which isn't to say that Ben's learning process isn't fascinating to us—just that it can be fascinating in this kind of dull way.

We went to the zoo one evening last week, for instance (yes, another zoo—but at least this was a real, big-city zoo complete with live, healthy animals), and Ben was just thrilled to see all these beloved beasts from his books and puzzles, but big and in person. So of course he told us about it: "Those are gorillas!" he announced, after a solid ten minutes of staring at them with Michael and me chirping on and on about gorilla this and gorilla that ("Remember Koko, from your book?" "Are those *gorillas*, Ben?"), to which we could only say, "Right."

But I'll admit that we didn't act so clever ourselves. I could hear us sounding just like all the other parents at the zoo—like some race of shrill beings that can only speak in a high-pitched, hyperanimated voice. "Do you see that hippo? Ben? Do you see the *hippo?!*" Like he could miss a snorting five-zillion-pound animal standing a foot away from him. Like, instead of just being little, he's got massive sensory impairments. Or is from another planet. And Ben, if we can just be quiet and let him be, will often notice such truly interesting things. "Why is that blue peacock over there?" he wondered about a bird that seemed to be fenced off away from the group. "He looks so lonely."

I know it's a total cliché that our kids teach us to pay attention, but it's true. Ben is a Zen master compared to Michael and me. He's always present, always fully in the moment. He just wanted to watch the gorillas for ages, but we rushed him around the zoo, hither and yon, thanks to our zero attention span. In fairness to us, this might also have been because the gorillas are so unsettlingly human—but captive—that you can't watch them for more than a minute or two without getting the distinct impression that they, justifiably, hate you. I watched one peel an orange, scratch the sole of his foot, then look me coldly in the eye, and I was ready to get going.

Or maybe I was in a hurry because I could only suffer the smell of any particular animal for, maybe, five seconds, before craning my neck around to locate the best spot to engage in my absurdly prolonged sessions of gagging. Because I was very wrong about not getting sick this time around. Very, very wrong. After an inaugural Moo Shu Tofu incident, I'm now in the thick of terrible morning sickness—"morning" being a euphemism for endless days and nights blurred together. (Note to self: Don't go to the *zoo* if you're looking to avoid strong smells.)

Whatever the real reason for our skittishness, we hurried Ben onto every next thing. "Where do you think the polar bears are?" we asked after a minute. "Where do you think the petting zoo is?" "Where do you think that woman got those french fries?"

Meanwhile, Kahlo, the year-and-a-half-old daughter of our friend Sam, was having one of those piercing, arched-backed tantrums because she wanted to be simultaneously *in* and *not in* her stroller. She did and yet did *not* want the cold tofu cubes with which we tried to bribe her. She wanted to be home *and* at the playground instead. I'm crazy about Kahlo, and I've loved Ben madly every second of his life, but boy, do I not miss that age. Of course, it's not like living with Ben now is some nonstop meditation retreat with spa food and a fountain burbling quietly in the background. But I do feel largely confident that when I, say, close the refrigerator door or brush my teeth, he won't drop to the ground shrieking. Now it's more like "Why are you closing the refrigerator door? . . . Why because it keeps the cold air in? . . . Why because it keeps our food fresh? . . . Why because we live in the modern age? . . . *Why?*"

Or "Why are those big catties going to bed like me and Kahlo?" which was the unutterably lovely conclusion to our evening zoo trip: a cage full of sleepy lions, so close you could hear them purring to each other. Their keeper was trying to hurry us out—I guess it was long past the big cats' bedtimes—but we lingered, in awe. And for a minute, it was like being a kid again: Ben half asleep in my arms, all of us quiet at the breathtaking beauty of the lions. Or maybe that's more like being a parent. I could swear the mama cat purred, licked her grown cub, and winked at me.

***

S ick and tired": the expression has suddenly come to life for me. I really *get* it. This pregnant tiredness is so unearthly. I stagger into work and sit down at my computer, and it's all I can do not to crawl under my desk immediately and go to sleep on the floor. I *crave* recumbency. I long for it. My brother told me a story once about medical school, how he was so exhausted during a chemistry lab that he fell asleep sitting on his stool, face-down, the flat front of his goggles resting on the long lab table. He had goggle lines etched into his forehead for two days. I feel like that.

Luckily, there's the nausea to keep me on my toes a little bit. I am stuck in a terrible catch-22: if my stomach is empty, I get sick, but I'm always *already* too sick to eat. Our refrigerator is full of a million open jars and containers of all of the pale things I *thought* I might be able to swallow: cream of mushroom soup, rice pudding, creamed corn, cream of wheat, white rice, cottage cheese. Forget about it. Michael even tried making me a simple bowl of egg noodles, but the butter was like a little pat of melting barnyard. Suddenly, I can *smell* the cows behind all those dairy products. My caloric life raft seems to be made of Product 19 cereal, canned apricots in heavy syrup, and cold peppermint tea with sugar in it, but no ice. The ice brings with it too much of the secret life of our freezer: as it melts, I can taste that we have chicken legs and pesto in there. I swear this is true.

At least this time it's all a little bit familiar. When I was pregnant with Ben, I felt like maybe I'd been exposed to some kind of radioactive substance and replaced Lindsay Wagner as the Bionic Woman. Every other day I would wake up, sniff heroically at the air like Lassie, and say, "We've got a gas leak somewhere." The gas guy would be summoned and he'd run his little gasometer around the house until, sure enough, it would emit a feeble bleep over some or other minute whiff of gas. "My God!" he used to say. "We should *hire* you to detect gas leaks!" When a new Thai restaurant opened up on our street, I could smell the acres of rotting sea life from which every drop of fish sauce had been distilled. We started to walk blocks out of our way, just to avoid my gagging into the gutter right in front of their bewildered diners.

I remember when my friend Megan was first pregnant, she threw up so much that it became completely boring. I kind of forgot to notice the impact it might have on other people. We had once eaten dinner together in a nice restaurant and I ran into someone I knew from work as we were leaving. We stopped to chat for a moment, until he said, suddenly, "Oh my God, is your friend okay?" and pointed, and there was Megan, framed in the restaurant's plate glass window, vomiting her mushrooms vindaloo onto the sidewalk. "Oh," I said. "She's totally fine."

Everything made Megan throw up. "Oh God," she would cry from her bedroom while the rest of us tried to sneak a snack in the kitchen, "did someone open the fridge?" And then she would barf. Her receptacle of choice was a hollow plastic jack-o'-lantern—the kind that kids use for trick-or-treating. I found this uniquely comical and disgusting. Even now, on Halloween, the sight of kids toting them around full of candy makes me a little queasy.

Currently, I am more than a little queasy. The worst of the culprits seem to be a) the smell of garlic, b) the sight of chicken, and c) my prenatal vitamin. Don't tell the pregnancy police, but I have, shhhhh, *stopped taking it.* Product 19 is loaded with vitamins (I can, in fact, *smell* the iron in it—as if the cereal flakes were toasted in a rusty old skillet), and I do manage the requisite dose of folic acid. But that big, pink horse-choker of a vitamin? Despite the cheerfully expectant mother sketched pinkly on the label, the mother whose baby will surely boast all of its requisite limbs and organs, I can't do it.

Sometimes, during the late afternoon especially, I feel so genuinely rotten that I worry it won't ever end, not even after the baby's born. I worry that I will always feel like throwing up, and that, for the rest of my life, that's all I'll have to talk about. Let me tell you: my personality—along with my skin and my waist—has taken a turn for the gruesome. But also, I can't stand the way I'm already giving up Ben for this baby—and it's not even born yet. I spend most of the day lying around in the cool dark of the upstairs, listening to the clatter of life below. I hear Ben ask, "Can I go visit Mama?" and Michael answers, "Oh, no, sweetie. Let's let her rest." Or he says, "Okay, but just for a minute and quiet as a mouse." When I hear Ben's small toes on the stairs, I try to sit up a little and I test out a quick practice smile. He climbs into bed and presses his eyes up to my eyes and pats me. He sniffs at my hair and exhales into my face. His breath, which has always smelled exactly like a vanilla milkshake, suddenly seems rank to me. This makes me so inexplicably sad that, after he leaves, I cry into my pillow.

Sometimes I really despair. I dial up my OB's office with the vague idea that I will talk to somebody about terminating the pregnancy, and then I hang up as soon as they answer. When our friend Gautam was frustrated by the political science thesis he was writing, he used to select "Delete All," and only when the computer would ask "Are you sure you want to delete all?" would he hit "Cancel." I think I'm doing the prenatal version of that.

But I'm sending that little pinto bean my very best wishes, I swear. Breakfast cereal and good thoughts. I'm hoping that's enough to grow on.

Okay, it's been three days without them, and already I'm nostalgic for diapers. Partly, it's about Ben growing up so fast, even though I realize that potty training at almost three doesn't exactly make him some kind of prodigy (according to our parents, our generation was out of diapers by the time we were eating ground lamb—at, like, two weeks). But also, and I realize this is less motherly of me, I simply miss the mellowness of diapered life: *Gotta pee in your car seat? Go right ahead. Wanna drink a quart of juice right before bed? Be my guest.* Now it's like, "Do you want to pee before we go? Do you want to just try one last time?" or "Did you give him water after dinner? Jesus, honey, what were you *thinking?*"

But Ben's so liberated now, it's as if he's won his own personal political revolution. I'm surprised he wasn't out protesting all summer with a handful of diapers and a lighter. He sleeps entirely "nudie patoodie," which he loves, and he has unlimited access to, you know, all those protrusions and crevices that were previously lost to him under military-grade plastic. Plus, he's just so proud of himself. I remember the very first time Ben ever peed in the potty, last winter, and how later that same day we were at Michael's parents' house, where they still have all the Fisher Price Little People dolls from Michael's childhood. Ben seated one of the tiny plastic figures on the toilet and said, in a perfect imitation of me, "Oh my God! Are you such a big, big kid?!"

But we really *are* proud of him, which cracks me up. It's like when Ben was about six months old, and we were living in

Santa Cruz. All the moms in my beloved new-mothers group were talking about teeth—and the moms whose kids already had teeth seemed kind of smug and pleased with themselves, and the moms whose kids were still all drooly and toothless were getting kind of anxious. Somebody asked me if *I* was starting to worry about Ben's gummy smile, and I laughed and said, "No," which was true. But then I went home and ranted to Michael. "Do you know of anyone who *never* got any teeth? I mean, do you have to be a good parent for your kid's teeth to come in?" Needless to say, though, when Ben's first little gnasher sprouted up, we must have taken fifty million pictures of it to send to all of his amazed and doting relatives. What a big, big kid! That's what I feel like now.

Everyone has their own little potty trick up their sleeve: praise; humiliation; alternating rounds of praise and humiliation; the frank bribery of a bagful of M&M's. Here's ours: no pants. Plus, the potty's in the living room, where all Ben's toys are, so it's not like he ever has to take his little bare-butt self very far. "I pooped!" he cries, sitting right there while guests nibble cheese and grapes on the couch, grimacing. I grew up with the kind of living room where nobody but my father was allowed to eat their Goldfish crackers, and resting your newly showered wet head on the back of the couch would get you shooed out with a newspaper. But at least it was pretty. Our living room looks like the furniture display area of the Salvation Army: scratchy tweed couches draped with flowered sheets, stained navy-blue throw pillows, books stacked two deep in the bookcase and on the floor next to it. Also blocks and little cars and plastic Mardi Gras necklaces everywhere you look. Adding the reeking plastic throne of Ben's potty really didn't make much of an aesthetic dent. Plus we have another potty upstairs, in our bedroom. We are too tired to identify any shreds of our past dignity, let alone cling to them.

But the convenient-potty method seems to be working. "Good job sleeping without a diaper!" Michael crooned to Ben yesterday morning. And Ben, like he's in a sitcom about old people, squinted and said, "When did I do a good job at the *typewriter?*" Then we took him to the mall to choose underpants. Here's my advice: Don't go to the mall. I mean, what devilish things happen behind the scenes there? Do they pump in some kind of gas that makes toddlers completely hysterical? The underpants selection itself went just fine (we picked up three pairs with the Pooh characters that Ben refers to, amicably, as "the friends"), but then there was the riding up and down the escalator (*"Agaaain!"*) and the creepy animatronic turtles (*"Mooooore!"*) and the little coin-operated riding cars ("Why *nooooot?"*).

Truth be told, I only heard about these incidents from Michael, since I was too busy sitting nauseously on a bench by the swampy mall fountain to join in the fun. But I *was* there for the weepfest over not wanting to hold my hand in the parking lot. And because Ben is Ben, we had to talk about it all the way home. "Why did I have to hold your hand? Why am I too short for the cars to see me? Why did I not want to hold your hand? Why because it makes me feel grown up not to?" and on and on. "Can we stop talking about it?" I asked at one point. "I'm kind of sick of talking about it." And Ben said, "Why are you sick of talking about it, but I still want to talk about it?" And on and on.

But when I was feeling lousy again the other day (because our neighbors were grilling burgers and it smelled, to my sorry pregnant self, like someone had set a living cow on fire in our backyard) and I went upstairs to lie down in the dark, Ben crept in, quiet as a mouse, and lay down beside me. He just kind of patted me and lay there—no questions asked. And I really was proud of my big, big kid.

I'm going to go out on a limb and say it: the first trimester is about as much fun as a sharp stick in the eye. Kathy, who is also expecting her second child, and who has managed to up-chuck her way right into the emergency room during both her pregnancies, is starting to wonder what she was thinking. "I mean," she said when we were comparing miseries, "you'd never be, like, 'Hey, that was a really fun car accident! Maybe I'll try making another left on red. . . .'" I'm feeling a little bit like that. How did this happen? Okay, I *know* how it happened, but still.

People talk about pregnancy "cravings," which is funny, because what most women remember is the opposite: the pregnancy *revulsions*. Mine are mostly over foods that are just objectively disgusting. You know, like toast or rice. Or anything green. Or chicken, garlic, and sesame oil. These things are, I now realize, unfit for human consumption. It's not simply that I can't eat them now; it's that I wish I'd *never* eaten them.

I think obsessively about the very foods that sicken me. I'll be sitting at my computer, typing away, and an image will snap into my head before I can stop it: a scallion on a plate; egg salad; this dish we ate at a restaurant with stir-fried watercress in it. I can't help myself. Then I have to nibble some terribly bland thing, like an entire loaf of pound cake, just to cleanse my mental palate. Last night—this is a true story—I ate potato chips and a Yoohoo for dinner. Ben, sitting happily over his plate of grilled chicken and carrot sticks, stared at me with big eyes, but didn't say a word. When I was pregnant with him, and eating the exact same way, my midwife referred to it as the "white trash pregnancy diet," and said, "Hey, sweetheart—whatever gets you through." Of course we were living in California back then— birthplace of *"Whatever."* Here in New England, I'm probably expected to choke down an earnest meal of boiled meat and cabbage every night.

And my new trick is to get a migraine headache every day— like a miniature drunk Italian stomping grapes in my cranium. Mostly, I do not even come downstairs. I get home from work in the middle of the afternoon, blind with sickness and pain, lurching from the car to the house like a wino. And then I have to lie around in our bedroom in the dark, with an ice pack and the back of my hand pressed to my forehead. It's totally *Wuthering Heights*. I should be wearing petticoats and pining to death over an impossible, dark-haired love. Luckily the actual dark-haired love of my life is turning out to be some hairy kind of Mother Teresa. It's not just that Michael takes care of Ben all day and then massages my temples and brings me bottles of grapefruit-scented water. It's that he does it with so much grace, so much kindness. I fear that, if the roles were reversed, I would thrust these things at him, more like "Here, drink up, you bedridden louse" than like "Can I get you anything else, my love?" It's enough to make me want to kill him. But I'm so, so grateful, I swear.

It makes me remember how lucky I used to feel after Ben

was born, when I lived for Tuesdays—the day my new-mamas group would meet for lunch. This was the same group of women that had once been normal pregnant people, stretching together in a prenatal yoga class, but that had since become a pack of howling, deranged wolves. I loved them immoderately. In fact, in those very early postpartum days, those weekly gatherings were my main source of nourishment: besides the great conversation and all of the nice weepy companionship, there was actual *lunch*. Lunch prepared by crazy people, but lunch all the same. One week my friend Cat had made broccoli soup, and when I asked her what made it so delicious, she said—grinning like a total wacko—"It seemed a little thin, so I melted a stick of butter into it." Of course. On a different week, Cat had made an exquisite platter of sushi, and another new mom plunked a box of Wheat Thins next to it on the table, and said, with some hostility, "Well, *this* is what *I* brought, okay?" before bursting into tears. That's what it was like.

In the beginning, we would just sit around somebody's living room, eating and nursing and laughing and crying our eyes out. Ben would usually be completely hysterical when we arrived— the only baby who had not fallen asleep in his car seat on the way over—and eventually, someone would hold him for me while my heart pounded out its code of despair and I shoveled pasta salad and good brownies into my mouth. Later, when they were bigger, the babies would sit around on the grass clapping and chewing on each other's toes while we drank margaritas from paper cups. Still later—and there were about a dozen of them, of us—the babies would crawl around, poking each other's eyes out and crying and giving each other croup and Coxsackie and other weird viruses. Inevitably, I'd get home from the group to a message on the machine: "Zack had a fever when we got home. I think he might have roseola." And by that time the next day, Ben would be red-cheeked and feverish.

Anyways, I remember when the babies were about a month old, and we were all just wasted with exhaustion, and laughing about our milk-drenched T-shirts, kvetching about what incredible pains in the neck newborns were turning out to be. But then this fantastically beautiful, together woman, with, like the rest of us, a moray eel of an infant hanging off of her, told us how her husband had come home from work and complained, "Chicken and yams, chicken and yams. Is that all you're going to cook anymore?" I don't think I'd even managed to pour myself a bowl of cereal by that time. So I was then, as I am now, counting my blessings.

Like, for instance, the irrepressible Ben. He's so scrumptious that when he stands before me, it's like one of those cartoons where Coyote looks at Road Runner and sees a perfectly roasted chicken (except, of course, for how gross chicken is). I look at Ben and see a big, juicy plum, and then I have to torture him with nibbling. He came in the other night to lie with me in the dark, and I asked—rhetorically, I wasn't really expecting an answer—"Why do I *love* you so much?" and he was quiet for a minute and then he said, "Maybe because I'm gentle."

I guess that's my answer to the "What was I thinking?" of starting this again. I am counting my blessings.

When I was pregnant with Ben, I dreamed of sex. This was in sharp contrast to my waking life, where I was so sick that even the nearing of someone's face to mine made me want to cry. For months after my first trimester, Michael teased me for having said once, dispassionately, and with my face buried in the pillow, "Okay, go ahead. Just don't *kiss* me." But my sleeping self was a tramp. My dreams were so outrageous that I walked around embarrassed in the morning, as if strangers could see the pornographic tapes looping through my brain. Over the course of a month of nights, I had conventional sex with a series of conventional movie stars. Not even edgy, dark ones, like Harvey Keitel or Christopher Walken. But just your regular teen-magazine roster of heartthrobs: Tom Cruise. Matt Damon. Leonardo Di Caprio. "Who was it last night?" Michael would tease, "Christopher Atkins from *The Blue Lagoon*?"

When I ran out of movie stars, I moved onto men—and boys—from my long-ago past. Tom Longstreth, the tenth-grade cross-country star whose lanky frame kept me loitering longingly after practice. Kamau Karanja, my first love, who peeled me, sweaty, from an eagle-emblazoned track uniform while Madonna sang "Crazy for You" from the TV. Even Mr. Aune, my twelfth-grade English teacher, who made us read *Zen and the Art of Motorcycle Maintenance*, and was sexy in a ginger-haired suburban-Bohemian kind of way. He probably grew basil and pot in his backyard and strummed "After the Gold Rush" on his guitar. I did not have a crush on him then, but I wasn't surprised to see him in my dream, walking towards me with a bulge in his trousers. "We meet again!" my dream self said, wittily.

Eventually, I seemed to run out of dirty thoughts and people to match them up with, and I dreamed, finally, about the pregnancy, the baby. I dreamed once that I looked down at my calves, and hanging from them in looped clusters were clear, plastic tubes filled with blood. "Try support hose," my dream midwife had offered mildly, shrugging. "Everybody gets a little varicosity." ("Varicosity"!) I had the classic dream that I gave birth to the baby on a bus, and then lurched off at the wrong stop, without him. I dreamed that the nurses handed me a swaddled newborn, and I parted the blankets to see the familiar, whiskered face of Tiny, our cat. "It's just you!" I had cried, terribly relieved. In one dream I sat down to use the toilet, and the baby slid out from a hole under my ribs.

With this pregnancy, though, I can tell that the complexity of my psychic life is truly a bygone phenomenon. All I dream about is food. "My mama dreams about hotdogs!" Ben announced to a friend when we arrived for a play date. (Okay, so maybe it's not *just* food.) In one epic dream I am waiting in a long line at a cafeteria for a piece of Boston cream pie, only once I get the pie back to the table, the plate is empty. "Shit," I say in my dream, and walk back to the end of the dessert line. This happens over and over again—the dream is so endless and repetitive that even my dreamed self is bored—but I return each time, doggedly, for the pie. Eventually the server shrugs, "Sorry, lady, there's only the fruit cocktail left," and I wake up depressed and nauseated. (When I was in the middle of my graduate school examinations, I once dreamed that I completed the written portion of the test, only to arrive at the committee meeting with a plate of pizza slices. "I guess this is all I wrote," I had said, baffled, and handed it to them.)

I also dream a lot that I am uncomfortable, and then I wake up, uncomfortable. I know it will get much, much worse before it gets better. I know that later I will be selling my soul to the devil for one good night's sleep on my stomach. I'll try to sleep on my proper, good-mother left side and then I'll wake up on my back—My back!—convinced that I have cut off the baby's blood supply, as the books promise. I find this chief among the abundant proof that the pregnancy books are conspiring to drive us crazy. How can you be sure you won't sleep on your back when you're *sleeping?*

At least this time I'll know better than to imagine a glorious return to my stomach after the birth. I hadn't realized, before Ben was born, that the first month of nursing would make lying on your stomach about as comfortable as sleeping atop a pair of wet, agonizing boulders. I was crushed.

During my last pregnancy, we were still sleeping on a futon. Not one of those newfangled mattress futons with organic springs and thick foam what-have-yous. Just a lumpy old futon, which a decade had flattened to the depth of a concrete pancake. After approximately twenty-five seconds of lying on my pregnant side, my hip would fall asleep and I'd have to turn over. If you've ever been pregnant yourself, then you know about this "turning over"—the way it involves a great deal of breathless groaning and a moment of being stuck on your back, like a turtle, your turtle arms and legs flailing in the air. And don't forget the obligatory leg cramp, like a knife to the calf. The kind where you curse and scream, reaching hopelessly for your leg around the barrel of your midsection, and then you cry like a baby while your partner massages the rigor mortis from your arched foot.

But really, I blamed nothing on the futon—until we visited my parents and slept for a week on a real mattress. Our first night back home, I lay down on our little monk's slab of a bed and burst into tears. So we wringed a little money from the stone of our bank account, and we bought a new bed. After it arrived at the house, I lay down and, again, burst into tears. "We got a bad bed!" I sobbed to Michael. "We wasted our money. It's totally uncomfortable." "Honey?" Michael said. "I think you're just nine months pregnant." This turned out to be a wise deduction. The bed is a good bed.

But now, the second time around, I don't even expect to sleep—not really—and so I don't crave it the same way. It's so strange, the way you become a parent on some kind of *cellular* level. This is such a profound shift from that first portion of your life when you live for yourself, more or less. During those first couple dozen years, you go to bed at night and you sink righteously into sleep. You don't feel greedy about it, or even especially lucky: you just wiggle around into your most comfortable position, like a dog, and pull sleep into yourself as if it properly belongs to you. And it does.

Sure, maybe you fall in love, and for some number of weeks, or even months, you sleep on a drifting little love-raft, sloshed awake every now and then to watch your lover's face and to inhale his sleeping breath (yum). Maybe you fall out of love, and you wake every now and then to marvel at how perversely *selfish* a sleeping face can look, to inhale your lover's sleeping breath (yuck), and shake your head over such revealing cover hoggery, and how did you never even *notice* before? Or maybe you're an insomniac, and you wake periodically to a little existential crisis—here I am in my bed, in my house, in this city, on this planet, in this endless, infinite universe, and we're all microscopically hurtling towards death anyway—and you get up to fret and make lists of your obligations and assets.

Still, nothing can prepare you for the Sleep of the Parents. If sleep is an ocean, then I used to sleep on the floor of it, a sunken thing among the catfish, bubbles blooping from my dreaming mouth towards the surface. Now I sleep in a little rowboat. In a thunderstorm, during a war, with cannons going off all night long. And also sharks.

I had no idea. You think, after the baby's born, that if you can just survive past the point when they're pooping six times a minute, then you can make it to the other side, and sleep again, and be okay. But you're wrong. My father's children are grown, and still, when we visit—when we're in the house with him at night—he sleeps his old imminent-catastrophe sleep. Like maybe we're going to burst in and shake him awake because our thirty-something selves had a nightmare and are throwing up. When we were little, my dad would fly up if you so much as tiptoed into their bedroom—he'd reach for his glasses: "What? What happened?" Last time we visited, he told me, "I'm okay when you're not home, because I figure, what can I really do? But when you're here, you're just my kids again. You're still my kids."

All of which is to say: I know better than to imagine a future when sleep will return like a prodigal son—"Hey, I'm back!"—and I will again be deeply rested. There will be years of this—first the nursing and the pooping, then the bed-wetting and the bad dreams, the fevers and the vomiting, the knock on the door and the cop standing there, shaking his head while he holds one or another of our pimply teenagers by the collar.

But it's more than worry, I have to confess. It's more than crisis and management. There is also your own pounding heart that wakes you at night. That wakes you to watch your child's face, to inhale his sleeping breath, and to feel luck coursing through your veins like a drug. There is the love that balloons so enormous and breathtaking that it lifts you up, past sleep, into some other kind of place, where joy is immeasurable, and fear is everywhere. Where "bittersweet" is always the flavor of the day.

Babyhood is falling away from Ben in huge chunks. He's like a molting snake, shedding first his diapers and now, it seems, his trusty afternoon nap. Next he will be drinking Colt 45 in the basement and driving carloads of his friends to see The Who. But meanwhile, the nap: this is a great loss for all of us. For Michael most of all, since he's home with Ben full time. I remember when it was me at home with Ben that first year— those naps were like a little Zen space in my day, even if it was a Zen space that I filled with Snickers bars and such compulsive studying of the J. Crew catalogue you'd think I was expecting to be tested on the difference between the colors "stone" and "sand." Michael, inexplicably, uses nap time well: to slog through his freelance grant writing or pay bills or (I'm not even kidding) make gorgeous wooden bookcases out in the garage. If he were less cute I would despise him on principle. But now, about half the time, his day is a nonstop Ben-a-thon. And even if he never complains about it, that's just a whole lotta Ben.

And poor Ben himself is just a weepy wreck by dinnertime. I ran a bath for him the other evening, hoping to relax him a little before bed. But then he didn't want to get in, so *I* got in and relaxed by myself while Ben stood around naked on the bath mat and decompensated. "Are you getting out now? Are you?

31

Here's your towel." At one point he was rooting around under the sink and emerged with a fistful of Tampax. "Hey, Mama," he said, and held them out to me, like a bouquet, "do you need any of these tampons?" But then he lost his grip on them and they dropped into the tub and a complete nervous breakdown ensued. The wrappers were all disintegrating and the tampons began blooming into their wet alien-rodent shapes, and Ben was trying to gather them up, sobbing, "What *are* these? What's *happening?*" Maybe I'll write the good folks at Calgon to see if they want to come shoot some commercials over here.

But last night we took a happy bath together, and Ben patted my belly and smiled that big, dimpled heartbreaker of his. Then he slit his eyes at me and asked, kind of flirty, "Why's your tummy so big? What's in there, Mama?"

And I said, "Do you remember what's in there?"

And he said, "A baby." But then he screwed his face up in what can only be described as existential bafflement, and asked, "Is it *me?*"

"No, lovey," I said, "you already came out."

And he said, "Oh, good." We've been calling the baby "Birdy" as a nickname (and, currently, we're all convinced it's a boy) and later Ben said, "I want to crawl in there with Birdy and give him a snuggle, but I think it would be a pretty tight squeeze." A tight squeeze indeed!

In truth, though, we're trying not to talk about Birdy too much with Ben: for someone who goes nuts in the one second it takes you to pull the top off his yogurt, nine months might as well be a thousand light-years. We did decide to tell him, though, since the other night, when I got off the phone with my mother, Ben said, "Mama? What are we *not telling yet to Ben?*" So it seemed like high time. We had gone to an International House of Pancakes—driven very far out of our way to do so, in fact, since I had this idea that I might be able to choke down a blintz or two—and we told him there. The reasonable part of you knows that your kid's only two and that you should not hope for a spontaneous outburst of joy over the news of a coming baby. But the other part of you is disappointed when you go through your obligatory growing-in-Mama's-belly-just-like-you-did routine, and then your beloved child, the absolute love of your life, says, "Oh. Uh-huh. Is this blueberry syrup made of blueberries or is it just plain syrup that *smells* like blueberries?" But the blini were entirely delicious, despite my being the only person in the restaurant under the age of eighty who seemed to have ordered them. I ate every last bite and felt well all day.

You know, except for The Headache. Nobody seems to have told my brain that the first trimester is officially over. And when I called my OB practice about the migraines, they really didn't muster a whole lot of concern. But you know how it is—you could call and say, "My leg fell off in the supermarket," and they'd be like, "*Of course* it did. That's really common, especially in all this *heat.*" So I went to see an acupuncturist instead, and she made me feel a little less sick, a little less headachey. I have never been to see an acupuncturist before, and I will grant that I was somewhat wary of all the hypodermic hoo-ha. Wary but desperate. And then I liked her right away. Partly this was because she was large and bossy—two qualities I am genuinely drawn to in a health-care provider—and partly because she asked me a million questions about my health, and then said, bossily, "When you get home, cook a big steak and eat it, even if you don't think you want it. Do that."

She asked about Ben's birth, too, and I told her the shortest version of it I could muster—twenty-four hours of labor, an abrupted placenta, the loss of the baby's heartbeat, and an emergency C-section (I skipped the part about how I made this creepy didgeridoo sound for sixteen hours straight, said "Kill me," and then barfed into a trash can)—and she was watching my face really closely, really paying attention, and when I was done she smiled and said, "How wonderful. How incredibly lucky." Which is *exactly* how I feel! I was expecting her to be like, "How awful. How tragic for you." Which is what everyone else always says, and even though it comes from a kind place—and even though, obviously, Ben's birth was no exercise in natural grace—it sort of drives me crazy. In the end, either the baby tears its own way out your yoni or they go into your belly and get it. Not to sound crass, but who really cares which? Every single day since his birth, I look at my beautiful Ben, and I look at my silver crescent moon of a scar, and I think, "How wonderful. How incredibly lucky."

But then I lay around in the dark for an hour, stuck all over with needles like a life-size voodoo doll of myself. I tried to imagine energy flowing in good and useful ways, whatever those ways might be. I wondered if I was the wrong kind of acupuncture patient, and then I wondered if it was wrong to wonder this. I opened my eyes and stared up at a fairy mobile that had clearly been made by a child—acorns and pipe cleaners and silk flowers—and I thought of Ben and felt my enormous love for him well up and beat along with my pulse. My head cleared a little, and then it was over. I went home, grilled up a big steak, devoured it with sour cream and horseradish, and felt, immediately, strong and well. Go figure.

S ometimes I think that there is something seriously wrong with Michael and me. Take tonight, for example. There we were, putting Ben to bed, everybody happy as clams—teeth brushed, clothes shucked, giggling all around—and then, out of nowhere, it's Antietam on the potty. I'm not even sure how it started. We asked Ben to pee one last time before bed (the usual) and then something went slowly awry. First he didn't want to sit on the potty. It's right by his bed, which is right by our bed, which is where he remained defiantly perched. Then he *sat* on the potty but wouldn't try to pee—we could just tell by the way he was jiggling his legs around and chewing maniacally on a piece of dental floss.

So we got into this big power struggle, but it was oddly boring, like nobody's heart was really in it. I, for one, was lying across the bed like the beached elephant seal I have become, thinking about cherry Popsicles and if there were any left, and intoning at regular intervals, "You just need to try." This was followed by "I *am* trying" (Ben) and then an equally droning "I really don't think you are" (Michael). It was a big slow-motion psych-out, like George Orwell's *1984*, but performed underwater by heroin addicts. In the end, Ben didn't pee and we gave up and put him to bed. Maybe next time we could just belt him to the toilet and play Mozart's *Requiem* while we perform a terrifying marionette show about children who wet their beds. Kill me.

Tonight was not, however, as bad as last weekend, when we flew to Saint Louis, Michael's hometown, for his brother Mark's wedding. It wasn't Ben's fault that we left late for the airport. Really, it was *nobody's* fault that I noticed five miles from our house that the only shoes I'd brought were the flip-flops on my feet. Okay, maybe that was my fault. But there we are on the road, late, in the volcanic heat of August, and Ben pipes up cheerfully from the back, "I have to *poooop!*" So we squeal into Friendly's, wrangle with the toilet and Ben's alphabetic obsessions ("Is my poop the letter J?"), and are back on the highway not one minute before Ben chirps, "I have to *peeee!*" We pull over, Ben pees straight up into the air, it rains down on him and Michael, soaking everybody's clothes, it takes them an hour to dig dry stuff out of the suitcase, and then I fall into what can only be described as a *fit* of berating: "Why weren't you watching him? Why didn't you pack more shorts like I asked you to? Why didn't you hold his goddamn *penis* for him?" This was not my finest hour. I worried that Ben would be too anxious ever to pee again (a child should certainly not have to hear "goddamn" and "penis" in the same sentence), but—luckily or not, depending on your perspective—it was only another six minutes before "I have to *peeee!*" rang out like an alarm through a mouthful of Craisins.

Come to think of it, the car has been the site of many a dull-witted parenting moment. Like the time when we drove thirty-five miles on a winding mountain road, only to have Ben ask from the back, with genuine interest, "Why am I in my car seat, but my straps aren't buckled?" Crud. *Because we were too busy splitting a raspberry Danish to notice?*

Do you remember that feeling, when you were first leaving the hospital with the baby, after they'd monitored its every breath and heartbeat for hours on end, and then the nurses were just waving gaily from the door, like, "See ya! Good luck!"?

"Don't they know we have no idea what we're doing?" I asked Michael as we drove away. "Why are they just letting us leave, alone, with this baby?" Sometimes I still feel like that. I want uniformed personnel to come to the house with clipboards and evaluate our caretaking capabilities. I want a copy of their inventory, with checks and X's next to all the appropriate boxes. "Child's teeth brushed adequately." Check. "Child eats appropriate range of foods." Check. "Proper safety devices correctly installed and utilized." X. "Parents act consistently lovingly toward each other in front of child." X. I want to see the big rubber stamp at the bottom: GOOD ENOUGH.

Anyways. The wedding itself was just a total blast, marred only by a tiny episode of me and Ben getting stuck in the hotel elevator: "Why did the lights go off, Mama, and then you said, 'Oh fuck'?" Mark was radiant in that crazy-smiling way of the newly married. Ben got to race around with his cousins—the sons of Michael's sister and older brother. Michael got to eat Ted Drewes frozen custard, *the* confection of his childhood. And we got to share a hotel room with Michael's younger brother, Keith, who happens to be one of my own personal best friends, even though he lives in Denver, which is quite rude of him, it being so far from western Massachusetts.

Keith watched a lot of TV with me while I tried not to throw up my share of the reception buffet. I'm a terrible TV addict. We no longer have one in the house—I quit cold turkey when Ben was born, worried that I'd sit around in a dirty bathrobe all day, nursing in front of sleazy talk shows and guzzling tall boys. (Instead I sat around in a dirty bathrobe all day, nursing to National Public Radio and slugging back diet Cokes.) Back in our hotel room, we watched a PBS show about glassblowing—believe me,

I have stooped even lower than this—and Ben, in his post-wedding-cake derangement, bounced around naked on all the beds and then asked, "Why did Markie graduate?" "No, lovey," I said, "Markie got *married*. He became partners with Katrina." "Oh," he said. "Then why did we get stuck in the elevator? And why do I have to pee again?"

fall

And we are put on earth a little space,
That we may learn to bear the beams of love.

William Blake
Songs of Innocence

The inside of an ambulance is a humbling place. All around us are life-coaxing defribillators, tanks of oxygen, rolls and rolls of bandages, and bags of plastic tubes in a cabinet marked, chillingly, "infant non-rebreathers." *Infant non-rebreathers?* My heart sinks into my stomach at the thought. But because I am the luckiest person on the planet, and despite the fact that we are screaming toward the hospital at a thousand miles an hour and that I have, unfortunately, watched a million too many episodes of *ER*, Ben is not hooked up to a life-support system. In fact, he is sitting up in his car seat, chattering away happily to the paramedics. "Is it so strange to be sitting in the car but looking out the back door, facing backwards? Do you see that guy on his green, green bike?" And, a little later, "Hey, do you hear that siren? There must be a fire truck coming up behind us." This gets a laugh out of everyone. I am sheepish and apologetic about my happy son, who appears to be fit as a fiddle even though, at the moment we dialed 911, he was not actually breathing and had been clutching at his stomach, screaming. He had been wild with pain; I can't even put words to it. He is not normally a screamer.

Now they have diagnosed him, temporarily, with "gas." I am weak with relief. I am also a little mortified. But the capable young paramedics, as clean-cut and gum-chewing as a pair of babysitters, couldn't be nicer. They assure me that we did the right thing to call, confirming that Ben had, indeed, been pale and in respiratory distress when they arrived. "How could you live with yourself if you didn't call, and then it was bad?" one of them asks me, and my eyes fill up with tears at the question. My God.

But now, a minute into the ride, Ben has turned back into his rosy, interrogative self, and I am reminded of a drug-addled college friend who had once ended up in the ER with what she was sure was appendicitis, only to overhear the doctor say to a nurse, "If one more hallucinating kid comes in here with gas, I'm quitting." "Why are you covering me with sticker snaps?" Ben asks cheerfully about the devices that keep him hooked up to a monitor—a monitor that shows his heart thumping away like a healthy, wild colt.

If I myself were hooked up to a lie detector, and they asked me if I had *any* idea what was wrong with Ben, and I said "No," those little pens would zigzag wild lines all over the graph. The truth is, I have this horrible sneaking suspicion that Ben is experiencing something that might best be described as "mochi poisoning." Do you know mochi? Boil brown rice up into a kind of epoxy, and then form this ricey glue into little bricks and sell it as a vegan biscuit, and you'll officially be in the mochi business. It's gummy and bland, and Michael loathes it—but, for some reason, when I choke down a piece, I feel my stomach settle a little. Ben, earlier this morning, gobbled five or six pieces of it in quick succession, and I'm terrified that they are creating an expanding rice anvil in his gut. This is not something I feel I can broach with the ambulance drivers. *Oh, hey, thanks for tearing over here at a million miles an hour because my son ate a weird grain by-product.*

We arrive at the hospital and Michael meets us there, and we are sitting in our little room, listening to Ben's happy tales from inside the "fire truck," when all of a sudden he goes nuts again, grabbing at his stomach and screaming, crying "Please, please, please" as if we might be able to help him. But we are helpless beyond measure. Especially me. Ben nursed until he was two, and this is the first time he's been sick since he quit. I have nothing to offer this small boy; I can only try to rock him while he flails. It's terrible. If I could pay somebody to be his mother for a couple of hours while I put my head between my knees and smoked five hundred cigarettes, I might just do it. Meanwhile, none of the hospital staff seems especially concerned—I guess they just figure he's another toddler pitching a fit, even when we try to explain how totally aberrant this is for him.

The episode passes, Ben falls asleep in my arms, and Michael and I sit quietly together, waiting for someone to figure out what's going on in our son's small body. Sadly, he has even shunned an orange Popsicle. "That was for *him,*" a nurse snaps at me, when she sees me eating it, as if I might be the kind of person who would snatch a treat away from my own sick child.

We wait for hours on end. I try not to notice how rinky-dink the hospital seems to my city-raised self—like a cross between a McDonald's bathroom and the school nurse's office. I try not to worry about the fact that this is where I'll deliver my baby in six months. They wake Ben up to take his temperature (102°—not bad). They wake him up to look in his ears (they're fine). They wake him up to draw his blood (his white-cell count indicates a slight infection). Everything falls away—all the deadlines and errands and dinner plans—and we are just us, in a room, with our sick, sleeping kid who smells like cotton candy from the children's Tylenol. We start to relax a little.

We wait for so long that when the doctor finally comes to talk to us, Ben is sleeping peacefully on the bed, and Michael and I are embarrassed to be caught splitting a turkey sandwich and laughing, like we thought we might just seize this moment to have a little romantic lunch date. The doctor tells us that Ben has probably contracted some strange virus with bad abdominal cramping (scrap the mochi theory!), and we are sent home to care for him while he writhes through another terrible few hours of pain before settling down on the couch under a blanket to watch, at his request, the movies from when he was "small." He laughs at the progression of his younger selves: the little sow-bug baby lying around on a blanket; the maniac toddler yanking all the books off the shelves; the pink-cheeked child staring out the window at last winter's first snowfall. We are so lucky to have evaded loss yet again. We are so lucky to have so much to lose.

Sam and Kahlo have been visiting from Santa Cruz with Sam's partner, Sarah. They've been here almost a month, and, despite all of my pregnancy-induced torpor, it's been grand. These are the kind of folks who know how to turn daily life into a magic show. "Why waste even ten seconds of your life, just schlumping around, when you could be doing something totally outrageous?" seems to be their motto. (If, for example, it's your birthday, you might expect them to break into your house before dawn with weird hats and a basket of oddly shaped muffins, to sing eleven different verses of "Home on the Range.") While they're with us, we light candles with dinner and it feels like a holiday. We stay up late to eat gummy cola bottles and play Pictionary. Someone in the house is always laughing.

We were living with them in Santa Cruz when Ben was born, and that whole year was like a slumber party. Someone was always awake when you were; someone was always making something delicious—or at least *interesting*—to eat (even if Bananas Foster is Sarah's idea of a balanced dinner); board games were exuberantly played; good chocolates were eaten often and with great ceremony; and someone was there to watch the baby when you just had to take yourself out for a little breath of fresh air and a good cry. Plus, when you live with other people, you just can't get into the same fighting jags that you can when it's only you and your partner—it's too embarrassing to let other people see you stomp around the house for days on end about the tone with which a certain question was asked, so you might as well go ahead and get over it. And, to top it all off, *our bathtub was in the backyard*—a pro or a con, depending on your perspective, but I loved soaking under the starry California skies.

I realize that the normal thing is to hole up with your own family, but it really is fun to live in a houseful of friends. Sure, you can't control all the details—like, say, whether the sponge will sit around sopping wet and stinking in the sink all day without getting wrung out and placed neatly to the side, not that I care—but it's worth it. It's *even* worth how strange your parents are likely to think it is, which is saying a lot. Mine used to ask these funny, incredulous questions—"So is Sam your *landlord?*"—which tended to be kind of off.

We moved back East when Ben was nine months old and Sam was pregnant with Kahlo, for the simple reason that another tearful good-bye with my mother, who lives in New York, was going to kill me. Upon his birth, Ben and she had fallen quite desperately in love, and keeping them separated made me feel like the Capulets in *Romeo and Juliet*. So even though leaving Sam and Sarah had a terrible crowbar-y quality to it, we really had no choice. (For the record, my dad also liked baby Ben *very* much—but in a more "Here, take him, he's spitting up on my pants" kind of way.)

Ben still loves Sam like she's another parent—like every cell in his body remembers how much she rocked him, grinning and toothless, that first year. He has a total Mama-hair fetish— "I'm a gonna need some *hay-uh*," he says, and then wraps his whole fist into it and sucks his thumb while his eyes glaze over in ecstasy—and Sam is the only other person to whom he extends this great honor. Lucky Sam!

Now, though, Ben is frankly sick of sharing his toys with the exuberant Kahlo, who, at one and a half, has not yet mastered rational debate. Her way of saying "Please may I borrow that book you are currently reading?" is to snatch it out of his hands and lurch away like a hunchback, screeching something in a Serbian dialect we don't understand. I feel for Ben—he's ordinarily so generous with his things and so heartbreakingly quick to be polite ("Here, Kahlo, would you like to look at *Amos and Boris* instead?"), but those impulses are wearing thin. To my horror, he's resorting to various forms of passive aggression— for better or worse, he won't ever come out and just whack her one—like chasing "games" that (Woops!) end with Kahlo tipping over, or "hugging" sessions that we break up when it becomes clear that Kahlo's eyes are bulging out of her head.

When Ben was an innocent babe in the woods himself, other people's man-eating children used to prey on him in a similar fashion, and it appalled me. "Oh, she's just so full of *curiosity*," they'd say, while I was swabbing a bite mark on Ben's calf, or "She's so *affectionate*." And I would think: "Affectionate? Like Attila the Hun?" And now, as with everything I have ever secretly judged in my life, this has come back to bite me in the arse. Of course, Ben is such a *talker*, even at his most aggressive: "Why am I hugging Kahlo, like this, but then I am pushing her, like this, and now she is falling over?" It's a little bit hilarious. But only a little bit. Mostly, I catch myself feeling embarrassed: "He's not usually like this," I hear myself say so many times a day that it's starting to sound like Ben has a multiple-personality disorder.

In his defense, Ben has had a big week: as if the ambulance weren't enough drama, he had to go and start preschool four days later. Preschool! He goes three mornings a week, and it's just the loveliest little school—full of art supplies and cozy places to read. It seems like just yesterday that Ben was bashing himself euphorically with a rattle. And now he's all grown up, shaking the maracas to lead everyone to circle. He's such a *citizen*.

And Michael and I have to simulate regular, responsible parents. We went to parent-teacher night at his school this week, and we were standing around with our name tags ("Ben's Mom" is, apparently, my actual *name* now) talking to a group of other parents, and everyone seemed nice and familiar, so I said, "Don't you feel like such an impostor? I mean, here we are at parents' night, acting like we're actually somebody's real grown-up *parents!*" Instead of the nodding chorus of "I know's" I was expecting, the other (real) parents all smiled indulgently and backed away from me like I had an arrow sticking up out of my skull.

I forget that not everyone shares my great ironic detachment over becoming a flesh-and-blood adult. At home, we show teenaged babysitters where the good snacks are—the Mint Milanos we have bought to keep them happy and alert—and they nod and smile politely at us. I look at Michael and me, in our sweaters and jeans, and I can see what they think they're seeing: a nice, boring, middle-aged couple sneaking away for a couple hours to watch some nice, boring independent film. In a million years they would never guess that we think we're still kind of young or even, God help us, a little bit cool. And I can't imagine that having *two* kids is really going to remedy this problem. But two kids we will indeed have. Because, at sixteen weeks pregnant now, I can actually feel Birdy moving around in there! Like a pinball machine, but with bubbles for balls. Like a little winged porpoise.

This is the part I love—when sickness goes slowly out of focus and the camera pans away from the pregnancy to zoom in on the baby. The baby! I put Sam's hand to my stomach, and she smiles and shakes her head—she can't feel it yet. I beg her to move here with us, and she smiles and shakes her head. She says, "Okay," and then, "We can't." She makes a puppy sound like "Ooooooh" and repacks their suitcase. It's hard to let so much be so different this time around—to roll with the changes and trust that we will manage on our own. I page through the albums of Ben's babyhood: the California sky like a blue silk parachute in every single picture, Ben's face inevitably obscured by the enormous wet shape of his own toothless smile, Sam smiling back at him like he is just a total miracle. Which he was. And is. Birdy will be the same, even if Sam is not here as our witness. Even if this New England sky is a little less blue.

I know it's totally normal for toddlers to be fearful, but it's just so sad. One day you have this joyful child bouncing through your house like a rubber ball, and the next day he staggers to the breakfast table all haggard with worry, like a promising extra on the set of *A Clockwork Orange*. You can practically see the fears lounging around in his psyche, helping themselves to another bowl of cereal while they plan their latest attack: "Okay, you—yes you, Unshakeable Terror of Drains—you're up today." I can hardly stand it.

We miss the relatively relaxing days of Ben's simple *aversions*—pubic hair, hard-boiled egg yolks, jazz—however passionately expressed. Now the world is suddenly populated by malevolent forces that are truly too scary for words.

"It's not actually the height itself," my father once said about his acrophobia. "It's the *falling and dying* I'm afraid of." And when Ben developed his sudden phobia around drains, it was with similar precision: it wasn't the drains proper that frightened him, it was the *getting sucked in*. Michael and I got backed into endless debates about what could and couldn't fit down the drain.

"Can a speck of dust go down it?" Ben would ask.

"Yes."

"Can a leaf?"

"Maybe a tiny one."

"Can a peacock?"

"No."

"Can an ant?"

"Yes."

Eventually he'd try to trick us. "Can a boy?"

"No, sweetie. A boy could never go down the drain."

"What about a *tiny* one, tiny as a tiny leaf?"

At one point, Ben didn't bathe for two entire months, and we sponged off his sticky toddler self as best we could. He even refused the cool blue of a swimming pool. "What's *that?*" he asked, and pointed to the gurgling gutter running underneath the pool's ledge. Poor guy—kicking his little legs anxiously in a ballooning blue swim diaper, and I tried to pull a fast one. "Uh, that's a, um, *water shelf,* honey," I said vaguely. "You mean, like a *drain?*" He turned his honest brown eyes to my face. "Um, yes, kind of like a drain." Scared kids are not stupid.

When Michael arrived to pick him up from school (School!) last week, Ben burst into tears. Another child had told him that there was a lion in the sandbox, and Ben would not be dissuaded from this fearful idea. Real lions—the kind at the zoo who look like overgrown pussycats but who really would, given half a chance, chew your head off—don't scare Ben at all. He purrs happily to them through the bars of their cages. But *pretend* lions—forget about it. We often read this wonderful book, *Sylvester and the Magic Pebble,* about a hapless donkey who, upon being chased by a ferocious lion, turns himself into a rock and can't return to his donkey self until his mom and dad show up.

Even though the moral of the story is something like *Don't be an ass* or, maybe, *Lucky for you your parents love you so much,* Ben has taken it to be *Illustrations of lions are very, very scary.*

Or "afrightening," as Ben puts it, as in "Was that loud sound of the garbage disposal so *afrightening* to me?" or "Was Mama so *afrightened* when that big black snake came swimming in the pond with us?" (The answer to both of those questions is "Yes.") Besides lions, sudden loud noises, snakes (good work, Mama), dinosaurs, alligators, drains, and cups floating in the bath, the big new fear is noisy machinery, specifically the sound of a lawn mower or the *beep-beep-beep* of a truck backing up. At the merest rumble of a truck, even if it's, like, three zip codes away, Ben leaps into my arms, wild-eyed with fear, and says, "Is that truck not coming into our house?" "No, lovey," I always say, "a truck will never come into the house. I promise you that." Of course, because my mind is such a twisted organ, every time I make any kind of promise, however rock-solid, I picture the bizarre scenario in which Ben feels completely betrayed by me. I imagine the brakeless eighteen-wheeler crashing into the kitchen during snack time, sippy cups and goldfish crackers flying into the air.

Ben scrambled under the covers with me the other morning, at the sound of a loud truck, and I had this dim kind of déjà vu. I said to Michael, "Did Ben used to scurry under the couch, in our Laurel Street house, when a truck went by?" "No, hon," Michael said kindly, "Ben wasn't born yet. That was Tiny Cat. Our *cat.*" Ah, yes. Our beloved cat who died when I was pregnant with Ben—but not, it seems, before imparting a little of his catty soul in the form of a Fear of Trucks. And, come to think of it, Fear of the Vacuum Cleaner, which Tiny used to stare down like it was our family's sworn mortal enemy. Now Ben does the same.

But one thing that frustrates me is the number of fears Ben has developed, ironically enough, from reading books about things you *shouldn't* be afraid of. For instance, *Brave Georgie Goat*, in which a little goat overcomes her fear of the dark. The whole *overcoming* part is totally lost on Ben, of course—you just see him mentally add "the dark" to his list of fears. Kindhearted friends and relatives don't help matters: "Should I turn the light off now, or will the dark be *too scary?*" I could throttle them.

And then there are things you'd think Ben might be afraid of, but they seem not to scare him at all. We were at my parents' house a few weeks ago, and their carpenter friend Brian came over to look at their roof for them. Brian only has one leg, and we were all standing around outside talking, and when Ben came out to join us, I thought, "Uh-oh." Ben walked this big circle all the way around Brian, peeking underneath him surreptitiously, before coming back over to me. "What's happening to Brian?" he whispered, so I said, "If you have a question for him, why don't you ask Brian yourself?" Ben walked over, waited politely for a break in the conversation, then said, "Um, excuse me, Brian, but can you please tell me—where is your other shoe?"

My gracious little guy! Brian told him, in this nice and matter-of-fact way, that he'd had an accident, and even though Michael wondered if Ben would associate loss of limbs with bed-wetting, Ben was totally satisfied by the encounter. "Brian had an accident and now he has one leg and one sock and one shoe." Fearless.

Which is more than I can say for myself these days. I look

back at my old fears, pre-Ben, and I shake my head in wonder. What could I have been thinking? Carnival rides? Panhandling? I mean, really—who cares? It's so simple now: I don't want Ben to die, and I'm afraid that he will. I hold this fear by the cheeks every day of my life, and I look it right in the face, as bravely and tenderly as I can—as if I can ward off harm by embracing it so boldly. I remember sitting around with my new-mamas group back at the beginning, all of us blabbing about this or that pain-in-the-ass thing until, eventually, we'd get to the heart of the matter: after the last cookie crumbs had been licked from the plates and the babies had all drifted off at the boob, someone would finally tell a story, hearsay usually, about a baby who'd been healthy and then oddly tired and then, suddenly, struck down with a fatal illness. About a baby who'd been in a car accident. About a baby, somebody's baby, who had died somehow or other. And we would all clasp our colicky bundles and sob into their blanketed bodies. It was so strange and compulsive, but also utterly cathartic.

I can't believe there will be yet another baby to fret over. Can I survive so much worry? Whenever they interview anyone who lives to be a hundred, the secret is always revealed to be a life without stress. At this rate, I'll be lucky to make it to thirty-five.

The blush is off the rose, school-wise. I remember Ben skipping through the school parking lot, chattering about string cheese and the sand table, humming, "The More We Get Together," and it seems like a lifetime ago from the current dead-man-walking scenarios that get us from the car into his classroom. Michael and I can hardly bear it.

The first two weeks went so well. When we spied on the classroom, we'd see Ben giggling by the terrarium; Ben clapping along at circle time and joyfully blurting out the (wrong) day of the week; Ben sitting himself down to spread jelly on a bagel by his *ownself*. But then, it's as if he suddenly realized that he'd been suckered—just *left* there! With a pack of complete strangers!—and he started to miss us terribly. He's never been a tantrumer—he's not screaming or throwing himself against the classroom door. He's just really, really sad, and that's what he looks like—a sad person who has resigned himself to going about his normal activities: crying quietly at the sand table; eyes streaming at circle; wiping his face with his smock while he stands at the easel. It's completely heartbreaking. Michael and I spent all of last week waiting for Ben to go to bed at night so that we could drop the whole upbeat routine ("Hey! What do you think there'll be for snack at *school* tomorrow?") and hold each other on the couch morosely.

Happily, his mood has suddenly picked up again, thanks to one of his teachers whom we simply adore. She's maybe twenty-two, tops—lots of tanned midriff and reptile-print platform shoes, and also a heart of gold. "I was trying to explain to the interns?" she said to me when we were discussing our poor sad sack. "Ben's just really *sad*. He really misses you guys. He doesn't really want to be cheered up. It's like when your boyfriend breaks up with you? And you're just really sad about it? And your friends are like, 'Come out to dinner with us'? but you're like, 'No, I just want to be *sad*.'" I nodded because, indeed, it seems a lot like that.

Ben is so utterly good-hearted, but I catch myself wishing I were the mother of one of the relaxed kids—the mother who can nod understandingly and make her face into that long, sympathetic shape, and say, "I'm sure he just needs a little time to adjust," while her own kid yells out "Hallelujah!" every five minutes. Intellectually, I don't care what other people think, but my day-to-day feelings seem to be slightly less evolved.

Now I'm delighted by Ben's return to exuberance. "Is this borscht so *heavenly?*" he asked at dinner last night, like some Slavic little Oliver. Later he staggered into the living room with a colander on his head and ordered, in a strange alien voice, *"Take me to your lover."* And this morning, a school morning, he woke up happy and tackled me in bed, groping me from all sides with the attachments on Michael's Swiss army knife. "I'm measuring your nursings," he said, holding the tape measure up to my breasts, "thirty pounds. Birdy measures seven pounds. Now I'm measuring you with this compass. You're frontwards. Now I'm peeking at you with this teeny tiny magnifying glass. Hey, should we get dressed for school?"

"This," I said to Michael, "is the best time of my life. And also the *worst.*" He looked at me from under his eyebrows—"You don't say?"—and, some delay later, I laughed. Speaking in earnest proverbs is new to me since becoming a parent. But now, every day, some or other cliché pops into my head as if it were an original thought. Embarrassingly, I tend to say it out loud before realizing. "I feel like my heart is walking around *outside* my body," I'll say to a friend at the playground, and only when she responds, "Oh, I know—I love that saying" do I realize that this is not a unique articulation. For me at least, parenting may be a slippery slope into intellectual stagnation. I have genuinely considered sending some of my ideas to Hallmark, so tapped am I into the sap-oozing forest of sentimentality. "Tiny hands, tiny feet, a heart bigger than the world." Etc.

It's like a sickness—a lovesickness. I clutch at my chest, *wheezing* with love. Clots of it course through my veins, lodging in my brain at random intervals. It has abraded me, this love, and my skin tingles at the faintest danger that blows in on the breeze. I had no idea it would be like this. Did you read *Medea* in high school? I remember thinking, "Wow, she must have been *really* mad to kill her kids like that!" This thought probably coincided with my bubble-lettering of the words "Duran Duran" on my denim Language Arts binder, and a feeling along the lines of "Bummer!" But as soon as Ben was born, that play moved into a sealed vault in my brain, along with the novel *Beloved* and the movie version of *Sophie's Choice*. I can stand up on tiptoes and peek at them for a second or two at a time, but this usually makes my heart shake in my ears like a tambourine. There is no way to understand the joyful desperation of parenthood until it is already upon you, like a flash flood. Maybe this time, with Birdy, I'll be prepared. Maybe.

I have not been especially healthy for the last few weeks, and this has triggered a little spiral into anxiety. The kind of "little spiral" that pulls houses into the air, swirls cows away into another zip code, and sends Aunty Em screaming into the cellar without Dorothy.

First, there was the Bad Hamburger. We had food delivered to us at work for a meeting—hamburgers, cheeseburgers, and shakes from a diner—and because I was craving the red meat, I ate a burger. Or, I should say, I ate part of it. Because about halfway through, it just seemed too rare for me: the inside too red and soft, and creepily tepid. An undercooked, room-temperature hamburger. Why, you're probably wondering, didn't I just crack a couple raw eggs onto it, add a little sashimi, maybe wash it all down with a nice big glass of mercury? Why indeed.

Granted, my stomach is about as sturdy these days as one of those paper exam gowns you get at the doctor's office. Still, by the time I got home from work I was already sick and darting off to use the toilet every few seconds. So I did what any normal person would do: I typed "rare meat pregnancy" into my friendly Internet search engine and pored over a few hundred of the 43,000 results it generated. To summarize: the worst and most likely thing you would get from rare meat is toxoplasmosis—that same parasitic disease that means that your partner has to change the cat litter for your entire pregnancy. I can't help feeling now like I ate a cat turd on a bun. Every time I think about the hamburger—which is perversely often—I gag.

Naturally, I clicked on all of the most alarming links, to follow the information trail as far into gloom and doom as it would take me. To get what you're really looking for—to achieve Maximum Despair—you have to hop off the reassuring circuit of advice for pregnant women and into the hard-core stuff—the articles written by and for doctors, which they seem to imagine we pregnant laywomen won't stumble onto. This material has been sucked clean of its sugar coating, and it uses lots of words you won't understand, but if your particular cup of tea is worst-case scenarios, you will find them.

"Can of worms" is not quite the right expression for what this search opened up for me. It's like a can of Gila monsters. Or like I unzipped my change purse to grab a quarter, and got sucked inside a black hole. Because eventually, in an article called "Congenital Toxoplasmosis: A Review," I found the very conclusion I'd been stalking: "Acute infections in pregnant women may cause serious health problems when the organism is transmitted to the fetus (congenital toxoplasmosis), including mental retardation, seizures, blindness, and death." Cat turd on a bun. Seizures, blindness, and death. I threw up and put myself to bed for the day.

My friend Megan, who is a talented and gloriously neurotic psychotherapist, once described to me the difference between normal people and people like me. "Not everyone assumes the worst," she told me. I squinted at her and said "Really?" in that way that people have been saying it for centuries, whenever ideas are so foreign that it's not even possible to formulate a precise question in response. "The world is *round? Really?*" "Normal people imagine the most likely outcome and a simple route from A to B: My child is sick; my child will get better soon. But catastrophizers," she said, and smiled at me, "which is what *we* are, start at point A and take every bizarre detour and remote path to arrive at B. B is always death."

This seems so utterly right to me—like people who don't think this way are just naive saps—that it's hard for me to conceive of another style of imagination. But then I remember Michael, who assumes, when Ben's nose starts to run, that he will be well in a few days. Sucker! Because I am smart and strong, *I* imagine that Ben's cold will turn into a systemic infection that will settle in his lungs and become pneumonia, which will be intractable and, ultimately, untreatable, and I'll stare in through the glass window while they do that "All clear!" heart-jumper thing before looking at the clock and shaking their heads sadly. In a few days, when the cold is better, it feels like nothing less than a small miracle.

To return to the anxiety at hand, I called my practice and talked, first, to the advice nurse, who said that I would have *much* worse diarrhea if it were toxoplasmosis, and then to a doctor who said that diarrhea isn't even a symptom, and that toxoplasmosis would more likely present itself as a mild case of the flu. What a reassuring discrepancy! "You guys might want to synchronize your watches on the whole toxoplasmosis thing," I said. Okay, I didn't actually say that, but I did *think* it. I probably just made a lame joke about what a hypochondriac I am and hung up.

But a few weeks later, I was sick for a week with a fever and sore throat. Suffice it to say, I typed my symptoms into the Internet. Repeat the anxiety trajectory above, but this time substitute "CMV"—cytomegalovirus, one of those illnesses you never once heard about during normal life, but which is suddenly at the tip of everybody's diagnostic tongue when you're pregnant.

Again, I called my practice and, again, I waited by the phone for the whole day. I always picture the "Call Catherine Newman" note sitting on somebody's desk for hours—a glazed donut and iced coffee on top of it and then, later, half of an egg salad sandwich. I picture someone brushing the note off to read it, and then rolling her eyes and sticking it back under a mug of chai. And let me tell you: it is not usually worth the wait. "I hear you're concerned about your health again," the midwife said into the phone. "Poor you! You've had *so many* mysterious ailments, haven't you?" She laughed. Now here's the thing: I do, and also *don't,* have a sense of humor about being a worrier. If someone wants to engage my concerns with appropriate gravity, then later, when it becomes unequivocally clear that this or that imagined danger has safely passed, she will have earned the right to rib me a little bit. "Whew!" she will be able to tease, "At least it's not a brain tumor again!" and I will hardy-har graciously. Mocking me over the phone while I'm still worried does not actually fall into this category. "Let's assume it's just a cold, okay?" she said. My cheeks flushed with shame and I hung up the phone obediently. But here's my question: if they find our anxiety so inconvenient and hilarious, then why do they go so far out of their way to make us so anxious? They give you a free copy of that book—*What to Expect When Fifteen Million Deadly Pathogens Are Sabotaging Your Pregnancy,* or whatever it's actually called—and then treat you like a head case.

Am I ranting? I'm ranting. I'm just frustrated and worried, and I want to know that the baby is fine. This last is an impossible thing. I realize that I'm still fighting my desire to be in control of every outcome—the desire I thought I'd given up for good when Ben was born. It's a good thing I'm not bearing children during the sixteenth century, when doctors believed that the mother's thoughts had a powerful hand in shaping the baby. Did you happen to look at a picture of a bear while you were conceiving? Well, that surely explains your child's hairy limbs. Did you dream of serpents? Wish for a bonnet? Yearn for pie? Fear disaster? Every birth defect had an alleged inauguration in the mind of the mother. Clearly, this would not be an ideal gestational environment for me.

It's strange this time, though. I understand that a baby is coming, a baby like Ben whom we will surely adore beyond reason—whatever the particular configuration of its limbs, or its senses, or its abilities. I understand that I will happily fling myself off a cliff for it. But understanding is different from *feeling*: it's more logic than heart; more hypothesis than passion. What's real, and *here*, are my feelings for Ben, the born child. The love of my life.

Soon enough, though, the having of the new baby will become a fully inevitable event. It reminds me of the Big Dipper roller-coaster we used to ride in Santa Cruz on summer Tuesday nights, when all the rides cost fifty cents. First there would be the long waiting in line. Michael and I would trade pink bites of cotton candy and finish our hotdogs as the line moved forward, and my stomach would be a little fluttery but I'd feel mostly excited, game. Then we'd get closer, and I'd watch all the people getting *off* the roller-coaster: I'd study their faces to see if they looked elated or disappointed or even damaged in some fundamental way, and the line would continue to move forward. Inevitably, when we were a person or two away from the very front of the line—once it became clear that we would surely board the next coaster—I would panic and decide that I couldn't go through with it. Usually, Michael would warm my cold feet and coax me onto the ride, but one time I really couldn't, and I snaked my embarrassed way back through the long line of giddy kids.

That's what I feel like now: like I'm excited but nervous, and I'm studying the faces of the people with more than one child, trying to figure out how the ride has been. If I really want to, I could still get off now and find my way back out of this. But it's now or never. Because once that guard rail clangs shut over your lap, you're in for good. And the rest of the pregnancy is like that thrilling, terrifying slow chug up the mountain of track until you teeter on top of the world, clear-sighted for a split second. And then your baby comes, and it's just the flying loop-de-loops after that, screaming your head off and crying with joy, scared witless and peeing your pants the whole time (*literally* peeing your pants the whole time). I'm suddenly conscious of the fact that this is a cliché: that *everybody* says having a baby is like a roller-coaster. But I really mean it: having a baby is like riding on a roller-coaster. I want to get off now, but I know I'll be glad I didn't.

***

If you're pregnant with your first baby and have already undergone an ultrasound, I have a little secret to share with you: the baby will actually be born *in color*. For real! And not only that but also, God willing, you will never again see its internal organs! The ultrasound is just about the strangest introduction to a person I can imagine. As if, before you even met your husband, a salesperson had shown you a series of cross-sections of his brain, the lucky quartet of his heart chambers, a few black-and-white Polaroids of his liver and spleen: *You like?*

And here's my question about the ultrasound: What if it just doesn't move you all that much to see those gray and black blobs pulsing around in there? If Monet had decided to paint a baby in black and white, it might look something like that—an impressionistic landscape of limbs and organs.

"Oh, yeah, I see," you croon, like a sucker, "there's its little

head." Only it turns out you're looking at a view of the abdomen. "Is *that* the head?" Wrong again! Those are the kidneys.
The spine you recognize, like a prehistoric string of pop-it beads,
but are those *arms* sticking out—or legs? It's a terrible guessing
game, and the whole time the grim technician punches in data,
making it clear by her strange sighs and hesitations that your
baby will be the next Caterpillar Man—only she's not at liberty
to tell you outright. Plus, you get sent home with that odd little
strip of snapshots, like you were mugging in a photo booth with
somebody's internal organs. It's a little creepy.

Michael, I'm happy to report, has all the normal responses.
He whispers, "Oh, honey, look!" every few seconds, and I can't
help but be moved by his love and amazement. In all honesty,
there *are* amazing moments: the sole of a foot flashes into view
with all five of its toes like little marbles; a diminutive profile
emerges, and for a second you see the baby's sweet face; the
heart beats wildly, like a flickering sea creature. But I can't help
it—my inclination is to worry and assume the worst. Every
time the tech presses her lips together and makes that little
"Hm" sound, I want to scream, "Get it out of me! Out! We
don't want it anyway!" This is one of my lesser maternal impulses, I realize.

And it makes me completely different from, say, my friend
Emily, with whom I spoke on the phone last night. We chat-
tered away for an hour—about books and food, parents and
kids. It was only when we were hanging up, trying to make a
lunch date, that she said, "Oh, tomorrow's crazy for me. We
have to take Tommy in to get an ultrasound of his head." Ah.
Of course. Tommy's her six-month-old. "What's up?" I said

coolly, like a sonogram of your baby's brain might be no differ-ent from, say, picking up a can of tomato paste on your way home. Emily wasn't fooled. "Oh, I was *afraid* it would worry you," she fretted. "It's just that his head seems to be growing a little bit fast. But I was famous for having a big head as a baby, and he just seems fine to me—so happy and healthy—so I'm not actually anxious about it." I love Emily. I wish I could be more like that—more like the kind of person who assumes the best, and less like the kind of person that you have to comfort because your *own* baby is undergoing a scary medical proce-dure. I am working on it, truly.

But I have a good reason for being like this: our twenty-week ultrasound of Ben turned into an epic fiasco. I could tell right away that something was up by the way the technician kept circling around the baby's stomach like a vulture. "What do you see?" I asked, "What's going on?" "Nothing," she said, and then, "I'm not sure. It's really not for me to say." And finally, "I'll leave it for you and your practitioner to discuss." What she saw, it turned out, was an anomalous something or other in the baby's stomach. "We don't actually know what it is," our mid-wife said later, pointing out the little white stump on the grainy printout. "Cigarette butt" floated into my head, surreally, but I didn't say it out loud.

Our midwife was something of a notorious blurter. "The only thing I can think of," she offered, shrugging, "is that the baby ingested a dead twin." Ah! The baby simply *cannibalized* its sibling. Phew! Now, if you're reading this, and you're an OB or a midwife, here's my advice: Never tell anybody that. Invent a roster of polite and obfuscating lies for the occasion. "That? Oh, it's a mere *mitochondrastic aghast.*" Because the I-ate-my-twin theory is not something a prospective parent should hear. I'd have preferred learning that the stump was a wad of old chewing gum. A tampon. Not that we didn't joke about it for months: "Am I missing something?" we used to say in the baby's voice, about its lost twin. "I feel strangely empty inside. And yet oddly *full*. . . ." Black humor is not the only coping strategy in the world, but it is certainly ours.

Sadly, there came a time when we were actually nostalgic for the eaten-baby theory. We ended up making a half dozen pilgrimages up to Stanford's Children's Hospital to see a renowned perinatologist whom we called "Dr. Fancypants." Fancypants was mystified by the stomach blob. He'd never seen anything like it. The idea of terminating the pregnancy spread around us like a shadow. (I can barely write that. *Our Ben*.) It's not that we needed a perfect baby, or even a perfectly healthy baby—but we didn't want to give birth to someone who was likely to be in a lot of pain. Dr. Fancypants couldn't say for sure that the baby wouldn't be in a lot of pain. We were humbled by the very fact of the children's hospital: all those rooms full of sick kids, all those cars in the parking lot—the parents of the sick kids, arriving with their plush animals, their straining smiles. Every time we pulled up, I had to sit in the car wadding up Kleenex for a half hour before I could pull it together enough to go inside. We were overwhelmed with grief and indecision.

But then, miraculously, over the next couple of weeks the blob got smaller and smaller and, finally, disappeared. Just like that. "We know how to see a lot of things now," Fancypants told us with great candor, "but we don't always understand what we're seeing." The stump had probably been just a normal stage of growth that they'd never happened to glimpse before. We kissed him and cried, and he shuffled us out of his office with terrible embarrassment.

I am still saturated with fear. About every single thing. I'm afraid—for no reason, for any reason at all—that Ben will die. But I know that we live in a state of grace. Every single day we feel the deep luck of Ben—this healthy kid romping through the house like a pony. I can't help worrying, though, that luck must be a finite thing, like a crate of oranges. How many oranges has our family already peeled and eaten? The juice pours down our chins.

Trying for another healthy baby feels like gambling. Like we're at the Conception Casino, dumping all our chips back onto the roulette table. Double or nothing. Well no—not *nothing*. Ben sat in Michael's lap during Birdy's uneventful ultrasound, quiet as a lamb for a long half hour. When it was over, he finally spoke: "Are we done?" he asked pleasantly. "Yes, lovey," I said. "Thanks for being so patient." "It's hard, isn't it?" the grouchy technician snapped at him. "Not being the center of attention anymore." I could have slapped her. We will love Birdy desperately much, I know. But giving up our Ben? Impossible.

The geese are honking by in huge, raggedy vees, and fall is really here to stay. "Do you hear those crazy *honkers?*" Ben asks, and looks skyward for the noisy, flapping birds. Some years I can be a little moony about the end of long summer twilights, or a little anxious about winter's tenacity and darkness, or about our windows, which seem to have been designed by an engineer of sieves. But right now we're all ecstatic about the change in season. For one thing, I'm not sick anymore. Hurray! You think you'll wake up suddenly well one morning—that you'll fall to your knees and cry "Thank you, Lord!" after you brush your teeth for the first time without gagging. I remember assuming, when I was pregnant with Ben, that I would turn the calendar page past that twelfth week and, presto, the nausea would be replaced with an ineffable joie de vivre. Instead, wellness creeps up on you slowly, and you say surprised things like "Hey, look! I'm actually eating *cheese!*" or "Wow, I can see the jar of mayonnaise in the fridge! *And I'm not even barfing!*" And your partner might smile indulgently and say, "That's really great, hon."

The change of season is the perfect punctuation for my exclamatory health. Every one of these cool, clear days is like eating a perfect grapefruit—I'm slapped awake again. Alive. Now I can't get enough of the clarity, the trees wearing their autumn finest, the fresh apple cider, which I guzzle down like I've been crawling across the desert towards it on my hands and knees.

When Michael and I lived in Santa Cruz, the wild beauty of the coast astonished us every day. But even though we loved the ocean, and we loved Sam so much, and our other friends and our California lives, it never, in the ten years we lived there, felt quite like home to me. Wherever you grow up, I think, that's the climate your body keeps blueprints of. It doesn't mean that you won't ever leave it. But it might mean that seasons, in other places, will always feel a little off. "Another day in paradise," Clint, our mail carrier, used to say every morning when he handed me our letters, his face framed by flowering trees, by the bright blue sky, and I would smile and say, "I know! Can you believe it?" But, secretly, I'd squint into that endless sun and think, "Oy vey."

"There wasn't enough *shade* for Catherine," Michael tells people who ask, shaking their heads incredulously, why we moved from heaven-on-earth to this New England place of mosquitoes, humidity, and deep, deep snow—and it's true. A person needs a little shade. A person needs lousy weather to mope around in. A person needs to look *forward* to things, like sunny days and ripe produce. A backyard filled with fruit trees? Avocados and plums and lemons thudding to the ground all night long? Too easy. Clearly I didn't fit in all that well. Being neurotic on the northern coast of California is like, I don't know, showing up at Woodstock when you're Woody Allen.

Perversely, the weather I anticipate most joyfully *here* is the fall—that is, the weather that most closely approximates the year-round sun-drenched clarity of Santa Cruz. Go figure. Summers here are great too—there are swimming holes and warm evenings and sweet corn—but this past pregnant summer, all of the summeriness really made me want to puke.

We buy a share in a local organic farm, which means that once a week, from early June until Thanksgiving, we schlep to the farm to pick up our portion of whatever they've harvested. Usually, of course, this is a good thing. We get to feel very smug, very Organic New England. Everyone at the farm exchanges these little self-satisfied smiles, like, "Hey, check us out, with our organic *farm shares*. Don't come crying to *us* when your supermarket tomatoes give you a big, fat tumor!" But this year, all summer long, Michael and Ben would stagger home with crates of kale and basil, ripe tomatoes, green and yellow zucchini and garlic and cauliflower, and I was miserable. Since I'm the only person in the house who really cooks with any of those things, our refrigerator became a three-month-long experiment in rotting produce.

But now I seem to be returning, tentatively, to the world of the eaters, and it's perfect timing: apple season. Probably you only know about Macoun apples if you live in New England or have an apple-fanatic friend who lives in New England. They are the crisp and fragrant prince of apples. Comparing them to a mealy supermarket red delicious is like comparing the Grand Canyon to a pit in your driveway. Ben will grab himself an apple out of the fridge, take a noisy wet bite, and—because he's like a caricature of a groovy new-millennium kid—ask, "Is this an *organic* Macoun?" and sometimes I have to say, a little sheepishly, "Um, no, hon. We got that one at the supermarket. But I think it's low-spray." "Oh," he says, and returns to crunching. If you're like me, then seeing your child biting into an apple can bring you practically to tears. Such a big, big kid! I could do a whole growth chart, but just with apples. I remember, like it was only yesterday, steaming and mashing them and then scraping them into Ben's bobbing head with a spoon while he spun around in his little flying-saucer baby holder. I remember peeling thin slices of apple and holding my breath, running my mind through the CPR steps, while Ben chewed and swallowed them in his high chair. And now look at him! Just a kid biting into a whole apple. What's next? Turning it into a *bong?*

"Are there any peaches?" he'll ask at some point, and I'll shake my head. And then we have to go through all the seasons again. Summer was the beloved stone fruits. Fall is apples and pears, and a few of his other favorite things, like acorns and bright leaves and his birthday. Winter means decent oranges and snow and Christmas. And spring is when the leaves come back and Birdy will be born and there's a lot of mud and, later, asparagus. If we were in a Gary Larson cartoon about this conversation, you'd see me yakking away, but Ben would be sitting there under a thought bubble, with just the word "Christmas" in it.

All this seasonal talk has, for some reason, got Ben to thinking about nursing again. Since he only weaned himself at the beginning of the summer, it's not like we're talking about deeply buried memories here. But when we were reading a library book about expecting a new baby, there was a drawing of the new baby nursing, and you could practically hear the gears shift in Ben's head. He looked at the picture, and he looked at me, and he said, tentatively, "I think Birdy will like to drink water from a sippy cup." Michael and I laughed. "Sometimes you or Daddy will give Birdy a bottle, but mostly he'll nurse," I said. Ben shook his head. "No, no, no," he said, "I don't think so. Actually, I don't really want to share your nursings after all, so I think Birdy will just stick to water."

Poor Ben. I feel a little sorry that we spent two glorious years nursing, but then his last memories will be of the pallid runoff my body produced after I got pregnant. Where once had been the rich cream of nourishment was now the kind of grubby water that gushes out of your washer during the spin cycle. And while I had once pictured Ben in a coat and tie, confessing to a group of anonymous weaning supporters, "*I* mostly crave it after a stressful day at the office," he kicked the habit quite succinctly. I admit that I won't miss the awkwardness of nursing a galumphing toddler in public. Like last summer, when we visited a friend at his parents' house on the coast, and Ben announced, over a silent, silverware-clinking dinner of corn chowder (picture Annie Hall's family), "Mama, I'm going to need some *nursings!*" "Later, honey," I whispered, but the mother smiled, patted her mouth with a napkin, and said, "What a fun age. Who can ever understand *what* they're saying?" Of course, Ben had to be Ben: "I *said* . . . ," he started to explain, but I shushed him with a blueberry muffin.

But last week Michael brought Ben to visit me at work, and he sat in my lap at my desk and said, suddenly, "Can I have some nursings?" He has not ever once asked to nurse since he stopped. Also, he pronounces it "nassings," which added another little layer of pathos to the conversation. "No, lovey," I said. "We don't nurse anymore. What reminded you of nursing?" He all but rolled his eyes and pointed to my breasts. "Mama, your *nursings* reminded me of nursing." They're smarter than you think, these kids of ours.

B en is three! Three. So many things are for "ages three and up" that I feel like he's really made it. The world is his oyster, an endless smorgasbord of tiny puzzle pieces and complicated, breakable figurines. I also can't help noticing that the lists of the most chokeable foods seem to pertain largely to the "under three" set. And Ben has always been a total choker. "That's a *terrible* thing to say," our friend Molly scolded when I mentioned this in the context of the carrots I was hacking into minuscule slivers. "It's like saying he's a total *drowner.*" But it's true. When Ben was eight months old, he choked on the green stem of a plastic display lemon he was chewing. He'd shoplifted the lemon, sitting in his stroller as we wandered through a thrift store—I didn't even see he had it until he was choking. And then I actually had to flip him over and whack him between the shoulder blades! The stem shot out of his mouth like a pea through a straw, and I was completely wired with adrenaline and relief for months. But now I'm feeling more and more confident that the grim reaper will not show up at our house disguised as a grape or a kernel of popcorn. This is not, I'm guessing, how normal people celebrate their children's birthdays—with a toast to the reduction in choking hazards. Even *I* can see that it's just not that festive.

But we did have a party, despite my great exhaustion at the thought of planning it. I had wanted to invite, like, *one* of Ben's friends to go, I don't know, hang out at the park and eat Goldfish crackers. This would have been an improvement over last year, when we celebrated privately. Invisibly, even. Or over Ben's first birthday party, which looked more like grown-ups sloshing down good beer than like kids playing Pin the Tail on the Donkey. That was really a celebration for *us*. One year! We had made it. Despite the fact that Ben still nursed hourly, woke multiple times throughout the night, wasn't walking yet, and had begun shrieking with rage every time we closed the refrigerator—we had made it! (Even as I write this, Birdy is swimming around, banging against my cervix like a catfish. Will this unborn baby really be *one* one day? Or *three?* It seems impossible).

Anyways, this year it seemed important to try to pull something together, what with Ben being *conscious* and all. And, of course, one thing led to another, and before you could say "Uh-oh," all the grandparents were coming for brunch, plus fifteen or so other people, half of them under three feet tall. Part of my secret dread about kids' birthday parties is that I write for a family magazine, so I feel a great deal of pressure to throw a reasonable facsimile of a normal party. It makes me feel weary and overly responsible—like what a doctor must feel like when someone faints on a plane, only with lower stakes. *Attention, please—does anyone on board know how to make a birthday hat out of this old paper bag?*

I study the pictures of my own childhood—of my gorgeous mother with her hair twisted into a dark, gleaming chignon, presenting various perfectly iced cakes to various fancily-clad configurations of children. There is always a decorative table-cloth and perfectly arranged balloons; the children always seem to sit placidly around the table with their hair ribbons and their patent-leather Mary Janes, their clip-on bow ties and their hands at their sides. One set of pictures I can't stop studying: it's of my brother's third birthday party. "Look," I say to my mother. "Look at you! I wasn't even six weeks old yet!" In the picture, my mother—less than a month after her hospital discharge—is lovely and smiling in her sleek, sleeveless turtleneck, and the table is festooned with cookie people that have been twisted into various gymnastic postures. My mother, who is still sleek and gorgeous, shrugs. "I don't know," she says. "You'll see. It's just what you do." I think ahead to Ben's fourth birthday: Birdy will be almost eight months old. Forget the cookie people; I wonder if I'll even be able to haul myself out of bed by then. "I don't think so," I say, and she rubs the back of my grubby T-shirt.

But we *did* manage a third birthday party for Ben, and it was good. My parents brought smoked fish up from New York (what could be more festive?). Michael's dad played his guitar through many rousing choruses of "The Wheels on the Bus." And my mom made her famous sour-cream coffee cake. When we brought it to Ben, lit up with candles and all of us singing to him, he flushed with such intense, beatific pleasure, you would have thought we were presenting him with the Hope diamond. Or at least a life-size inflatable Piglet doll. I love that he still experiences that kind of deep, pure joy. He looks like a Renaissance painting of an angel—albeit the kind of angel who wears Polartec fleece and still poops on the floor every once in a while.

"What did you wish for?" I asked him later. "A kiss!" he said and kissed me. "Hey, I got my wish!" This is a gimmick stolen from his corny father, and I'm happy enough. At his age, I blew out my candles and wished, with my eyes squeezed shut, that I'd never seen the terrifying Injun Joe cave scene in *Tom Sawyer*. Four birthdays in a row, that was my lone and simple wish. I'll take Michael's sweet nature any day over my own early-onset neurosis.

So last night, Halloween, Ben ate a miniature peppermint patty and a sour gummy something, which, because of the cruel abstinence we practice, is the most candy he's ever eaten in his life. Do we all agree that Halloween is a good thing? Because I'm just not sure. Maybe when Ben is older, and his teeth have already rotted out of his head, and we're just totally jaded, watching him jaw through a tub of Milk Duds while he guffaws on the couch to *Porky's VII*, I'll feel different about it. But right now, the whole candy thing seems a little counterintuitive. This may also be because Ben seems to have a profound sensitivity to chocolate. "Was I so, so hyper after eating that chocolate pudding on the plane?" Ben asked, for weeks after our trip back to California, and we would say, remembering him straining against the straps of his car seat, with a big blue vein pulsing in his forehead, "Honey, 'hyper' is a *polite* word for what you were."

We had been hoping to meet friends at the local costume parade, but we got a late start. I wrangled Ben into black leggings and a turtleneck and then the rest of his cat costume—a masterpiece on my part that involved felt ears sewn onto the hood of a gray vest (believe me, this is an improvement over last year's mouse costume, when the ears were *stapled* on) and safety-pinning a black sock-tail to his pants. Then it came time to do the nose and whiskers, and I, already grumpy from rushing, experienced some weird forest-for-the-trees confusion. Ben wanted to use the face crayons himself, to draw on his own catty features. "I need to do it by my *own!*" he wailed, digging his fingernails into the colored grease. Did I let him? Of course not. Because a person needs a professional-looking cat face at the Florence, Massachusetts, Halloween parade. I really can't explain it—I just know that it seemed really important to me that I draw the cat face myself. Then, of course, I was even grumpier from having been a loser control freak about the world's dumbest thing. (Michael would likely say that "grumpy" is a *polite* word for what I was.)

It took us ten years to drive to Florence, with Michael and me whispering irritated nothings to each other up front the whole way. "What are you guys *talking* about?" Ben kept piping up from the back, and we hissed *"Nothing"* like the kind of parents we swore we'd never be. We missed the parade. But then, I have to admit, our evening took a little turn for the sweet. Ben was so heartbreakingly lovely in his little catty outfit that I thought I might keel right over. Plus, we had the good fortune to run into the very families we had been intending to meet in the first place. These are some of my very best friends from college, and the fact that we all have children now makes me almost woozy with sentiment. I mean, these used to be just regular young women—listening to the *Baghdad Café* soundtrack and baking brownies for their freaky boyfriends—and now they're *mothers!* They even have mothery-looking arms and hair. Everyone was pink-cheeked and excited from the cold, and from the unbelievable beauty of these kids, and we walked around for a while to admire the lit-up jack-o'-lanterns, which smelled like burning brownies. Ben was thrilled every second. "Did I eat that piece of sour candy, and was it so, so *sour?*" He couldn't stop talking about it.

I, myself, felt like I was costumed as a normal person. I'm five months pregnant, and enormous in the nude—much, *much* bigger than I was at this stage with Ben. It's like my body got one whiff of the baby and said, "Oh, this again," before puffing itself out to its biggest size. But with my jacket on, you still can't tell. This is such a funny stage—when you're right on the cusp of looking undeniably pregnant, but people, bless them, are not certain enough to say anything. Inside my jacket, I feel smug with my secret, the way you feel when you fall in love, and you move through the world—stopping for gas, buying your groceries—thinking "None of these people even suspects a thing!" And meanwhile your heart pounds out its passionate cadence; your head swells with the future. It's hard to believe that I could still pass as just a regular, everyday mom, walking with her family. Out on the sidewalk, my eyes filled with tears, and I stood up on tiptoe to kiss Michael's cheek; I bent down to kiss the top of Ben's little cat head.

On the way home, we stopped to see our friends Daniel and Pengyew, who had requested a quick eyeful of the costumed Ben. Pengyew is a fantastic cook—a kind of culinary Olga Korbut—and he and Daniel are each more gracious than everyone else in the universe put together. The two of them are a force to be reckoned with—a deep source of nourishment and inspiration for us. They taught Ben the color "champagne" and were responsible for giving him his first kumquat. "Was that sour kumquat so, so *sour?*"

"If they ask us if we've had dinner yet," I said on the stairs, "we have to lie or you know they'll invite us to stay." But then there we were, the two of them admiring Ben and asking us if we'd eaten, and we could only say stupidly, hungrily, "Um, not yet." So we were led to the table with cloth napkins and fed enormous bowls of steaming soup filled with pork ribs and duck broth, bok choy and tofu and rice. We ate and reminisced about our own early Halloweens. It turns out that we were all hobos at one point in our lives—maybe *everybody* was once a hobo! Except for Pengyew, who grew up in Malaysia and, thus, was never sent out with smudged cheeks and a flannel shirt to masquerade festively as a homeless person. Ben sat in my lap eating sleepily from my soup bowl, his nose streaming from the spices. Later, there would be the candy to wrangle over, and bedtime to negotiate, and the face paint to scrub off, but for that hour we couldn't have been happier, Halloween or no.

———

One of the hardest things about parenting is that you just never know what the outcome will be. It's a total leap of faith. Even with decisions you feel fairly confident about (say, what to make for lunch), you just can't be sure of the consequences they'll have for this person you're raising. Will you like the adult this kid—*your* kid—becomes? We certainly experienced this kind of uncertainty when Ben was a newborn and we were pummeled with so much conflicting advice. If we kept him in the bed with us, would he turn into a secure, self-possessed Gandhi type of person? Or would I end up carrying him to his senior prom in a sling? And nursing him there, in his tux, by the punch bowl? If he didn't wear a little stretchy hat every second, would the cool air penetrate his soft spot and chill his brain and cause him to be forcibly removed from our custody? Was it wrong to fantasize about leaving him out on the porch overnight?

In retrospect, though, that early time seems like a total cakewalk to me. Discipline—this is the big leagues. The stakes feel so high. And *mostly* I trust our impulses, Michael's and mine. But then I have these terrible bouts of insecurity, and I worry—alternately—that we're either overly strict with Ben or overly lax. Sometimes I can't decide which. Will he turn out like Billy Bob Thornton in *Sling Blade*? Or like Brenda Walsh from *Beverly Hills 90210*?

This past weekend we met Sam and Sarah and Kahlo in Boston, where Sarah had a conference to attend, and we spent a glorious few days and nights crashed out in their Marriott suite, grazing for hours at the breakfast buffet and tootling around Harvard Square. But Ben's brotherly aggression toward Kahlo picked right up where it had left off. Within five minutes of our arrival, he hugged her like a long-lost friend, squeezed her like a lemon wedge, then pushed her against the wall, where she slumped to the ground. It was like a grainy *60 Minutes* segment about pimps. We hadn't seen anything like it since they'd left our house six weeks ago, and I was furious. Sam nursed Kahlo, who was screaming, and Ben came over, ashen, to check in with me. "Don't talk to *me*," I said. "Go see if there's anything you can do to help your friend." Ben asked Sam if Kahlo was okay, and then ran back to me, beaming. "I asked her!" he said, smiling like a saint, like he'd bestowed a great gift of charity upon the world. His smugness made me even angrier. "Good," I said, not warmly, "but I'm still furious that you weren't gentle with her."

I just don't always know how to be. I read this over, and I realize that the whole episode sounds like the world's tiniest disciplinary potatoes—no big deal at all. But it's monumental for me, these pangs of resentment I feel toward my small son. We have had a two-year-long honeymoon: a love affair to rival anything Hollywood has ever mustered. I dread its becoming a you-don't-bring-me-flowers-anymore saga of disappointment and nostalgia. And I don't want to ruin this beautiful kid just because I happen not to know a thing about parenting. How on earth is it going to be when we have a new baby of our own? I don't want to be mad at Ben all the time.

Because, boy, was I mad at Ben. And I worried that I'd been too harsh. Ben had been exhausted, after all—"I'm too *lazy* to nap!" he'd yelled from his car seat on the trip out.

Then I worried that I hadn't been harsh enough. At dinner Ben was quiet and sat with his back to me and my stomach felt like it was full of marbles. Then he was happy and sweet with Kahlo the rest of the weekend. I smiled at him a lot and tried to catch his eye, the way you might poke at a new filling with your tongue to test the strength and sensitivity of the repair.

After we got back home—one of those bleary Sunday evenings when everyone is grumpy and you end up having Corn Chex and string cheese for dinner and you would pay a million dollars for it to be only Saturday—we heard Ben speaking, in a terribly fierce voice, to his doll Birdy. "I am so furious with you," he said to her. (The doll Birdy, we found out, also has a baby named Birdy in *her* tummy! As does Ben himself! Just like me! The coincidence is astonishing.) Now I was racked with guilt, watching as the legacy of my unkindness to Ben unfolded. I waited for him to shout "It's only because I love you so much that I have to treat you this badly" or some other horror from an after-school special about child abuse.

"Did you speak so sharply to Birdy?" I asked him. "Yeah," Ben said sadly, and shrugged. A little while later we found him sitting in the rocking chair, nursing her quietly, pressing her head to his chest, her body cradled in his arms. "It's nice to nurse her," he said simply. He seems already to understand the intermingled pain and sweetness of parenting. It has taken me thirty years longer than him, and I have gotten no further.

W

e, it seems, are living with a prince. Yesterday morning, sitting blearily over a cup of tea, I looked at Ben, perched on his throne of a booster seat, and here's what I saw spread on the table in front of him: a piece of toast with cream cheese on it, a dish of raspberries, a bowl of Grape-Nuts with milk and applesauce, and an egg scrambled with mozzarella cheese. Also two different drinks, one in a mug, one in a sippy cup. He was all but swirling wine around in his glass, sniffing at the cork. *"Monsieur approves of the cabernet?"* Michael, meanwhile, stood at the sink, hurriedly peeling him a kiwi fruit. I'm not even kidding. Through a mouthful of egg Ben asked, politely but without looking up from his gorging, "May I please have some chamomile tea?"

How did this happen?

We are so charmed by this regal, funny kid. I guess that's how. But I worry that I'm going to end up in a chambermaid costume, darting around after him with a lint roller and a platter of oysters, and I won't even mind. Or notice. And usually I only like waiting tables if there are significant tips involved. But then there's Ben singing at the table, to the tune of Harry Belafonte's "Day-O," "I wanted some tea and I asked so nicely. *Daylight come and I wanted some tea."* How could I not leap from my seat?

Ben really does have this funny knack for revising song lyrics. When we were threading melon and pineapple chunks onto bamboo skewers for our turn at school snack, Ben sang, to the tune of the "Hokey Pokey," "You do the fruity fruity

81

and you put it on a stick. That's what it's all about." (A room-ful of three-year-olds and a couple dozen skewers—now *there's* a good idea. I'm sure the teachers were really grateful for our imaginative contribution.) Yesterday, Ben hummed part of the Beatles' "You've Got to Hide Your Love Away." Then he cried, with great drama, "Oh, Mama, I hid my love away from you! But I can't get it back out. I'm much too lazy." A total nut.

And a prince. I guess maybe it's a good thing that we're hav-ing another kid, just to unseat his highness the tiniest bit. That's what everyone else says, at least. "Oh, he won't be spoiled!" they tell us, and laugh a sinister snorting laugh. "He'll be lucky if he even gets a meal! Take it from us, having two is *more than twice the work*." Why? Why say these things? Once, when Ben was three weeks old—an absolute low point, as I dimly recall—I threaded his little noodle legs into the Baby Bjorn and hobbled to the health food store to stock up on organic Cheetos. I was also hop-ing that the traffic noise would drown out his terrible, anguished weeping. In line at the store I was doing that frantic swaying two-step, trying to shush Ben without giving him shaken-baby syndrome, or rupturing my C-section scar, or dislodging the Texas-sized sanitary napkin I was straddling, and this woman smiled at me like I was the Madonna herself and said, "Enjoy this. It's such a fun age." Then she slit her eyes and hissed, "It's all downhill from here."

I can't remember if I waited until I was outside on the sidewalk or if I burst into tears right there in the store. Now, if I ever see a woman out with a baby who appears to be un-der three months old, I always make a point of saying "Oh God, this age totally *sucks*, doesn't it? It gets so much better than this." Not everyone appreciates this suggestion—"I'm actually really *enjoying* him," some new moms have ventured tentatively in response—but some seem to. And maybe others do, but only secretly.

But Kathy just had her new baby, and she's like a crisp wind, blowing away everyone else's thick negative energy. "She's such a blessing," Kathy says, and strokes her beautiful Tess's new pink cheeks. "She makes the whole, horrible pregnancy so worth it. But I can't figure out why we needed to be in such a crisis mode after Will was born. It's just not that big a deal." Will is Ben's friend, the same age, who is famous (at least in our house) for rolling up a slice of luncheon meat and demanding "Mama, sing 'Happy Birthday' to my ham tunnel!" Will is doing okay. Kathy, who manages to be both hilarious and wholly kind, tries to preview for us, gently, the unseating of the prince. "Will loves Tess. He's just mad at *us* a lot. But mostly he doesn't even think about it that much. He spends more time wondering about other, random stuff, like why there's no TV show called "Strummin' on the Old Banjo.""

I hope that Ben is similarly distracted when our baby is born. But I'm just not so sure about this whole having-a-new-baby thing. The pregnancy is suddenly flying by. With Ben, I longed for my midwife appointments—I was practically crossing days off on the wall, watching the hands of the clock spin around until each scheduled visit. I loved getting weighed; I loved peeing in a cup; I loved getting my tummy calibrated with an ordinary tape measure, like they were fitting me for a new coat. More than anything, I loved sitting gigantically in the waiting room with all the other pregnant women, leafing smugly through the baby magazines with Michael. I felt like I was part of a secret society. A secret society of potbellied people who get up to use the bathroom a lot.

Now, I'm sorry to say, I find the appointments something of a nuisance. Michael never comes, even though he always offers to. But I'd rather spend our thirty bucks on dinner at the India Palace than on a babysitter for Ben just so Michael can say, "Do you want me to hold that?" when I start taking off my clothes. Which is not to suggest that I'm not thrilled to hear the monthly clompety-clomp of Birdy's heart. I am. But mostly I stare, alarmed, at the three-dimensional model of the female body—at all of the organs coiled tightly into the abdominal cavity like so many red and purple garden hoses. There are the knobby kidneys, there the lobes of the liver. And I can't help noticing this: there is not actually an open space in there. There's no special canyon among your organs, a hole that your body has left for the baby to fill. Your uterus is there, sure, but it's not waiting like a bassinet. In fact it's closed up like a clamshell, packed snugly into the aquarium of your belly with the other reproductive crustaceans. Where does everything go when the baby grows? This may be the question of the year. But I sit around in my paper johnny, burping and wheezing through my pressed lungs; I get up to pee for the fifth time in an hour, my bladder squashed as thin as a dime—and I find something of an answer.

Is this how you did it, Mama?" Ben asked me last night, and I looked at him, hunched over a dollar bill, which he was folding into teeny, tiny squares. "Did what, hon?" I asked. "You know. When that man was playing such beautiful, beautiful music and he smiled and had those teeth, so I was worried he might speak to me? But you held my hand and put that money inside his can? But you folded it all up? Was it like this?" Ben was holding up his folded dollar, and I was dimly recalling how, during our trip to Boston, we had watched a grungy, talented guy play some Lou Reed-ish songs in Harvard Square. I must have put a dollar in his collection can. Now Ben was bent back over the bill, folding and unfolding it like a contestant in an origami competition, perfecting his final crane.

I'm often struck by how little I know about this kid living in my house. What does he think about all day? What does he remember? It's anybody's guess. Michael took Ben to a college hockey game on Friday, and Ben came home flushed with excitement and the cold of the late-fall night. "Did the players skate around with their sticks and score goals?" I asked him. "I don't know," he said, "but there was a huge piece of pizza, who was a guy, and he was skating on the ice. And there was a, uh, a *tromboni* there? For cleaning the ice? And also a blint." "A blint?" I asked Michael—I was picturing a gigantic cottage-cheese-filled crepe skating through the stadium. "You know," Michael smiled, "like the Goodyear *blint*."

Ben's imagination is just churning away, day and night, remembering real events, concocting pretend ones, blurring the distinction between the two. We've been reading *Babar the King*, and there's this part where the Old Lady frightens a brown snake, who bites her, and her arm swells up and she goes to the hospital, but then she's better by the morning. Ben is, understandably, completely preoccupied by this "afrightening" scenario, which is funny, because one of *my* strongest early childhood memories is of a different Babar book, where the ancient king eats a poisonous mushroom, turns a vivid, wrinkly green, and dies—I mean, you could wake me in the middle of the night and hand me a crayon, and I would draw a fairly accurate rendition of it for you, that's how powerful an image it was for me.

Anyways, we spend a lot of time playing "snake bite," which I *hope* is therapeutic for Ben. He comes over to you where you're sitting, maybe trying to read a page or two of the Sunday paper (good luck!), and he says, "Oh! I'm a brown snake and I'm afrightened!" and then he bites your arm and pretends to rush you to the hospital, where your arm swells up, but, luckily, you are likely to make a full recovery by morning. Thanks to our friend Judy, he also has a doctor's kit now, which adds mightily to the drama. If you're in real bad shape, you might need a "prick" from the "shotter," and you are sure to get your temperature taken with the "thermonitor." Ben might also peer at your face and booty with the stethoscope. Failing all else, Doctor Stumpy is called in to consult. Doctor Stumpy is a long-armed, legless stuffed monkey with sewn-shut eyes that, nevertheless, peer very intently into your face if you're suffering from snake-bite fever. Believe me, we've seen less attentive doctors than Stumpy at some of the clinics we've frequented over the years. Usually Stumpy thinks you'll be fine by morning.

But when Michael went to pick Ben up from school last week, one of his teachers rushed over and said, "Jeez, I heard about your weekend. That's so intense! Is Catherine feeling better now? Do they know what kind of snake it was?" I wonder what else Ben's teachers "know" about us.

Mostly, though, our lives revolve around these wild devouring games. "You're pizza!" Ben will shout, and then devour you with loud chomping sounds. "I'm a scary beasty that came out of your watermelon! And I'm eating you!" Chomp chomp. Mum's the word, but I find these games *kind of boring*. I'm more of a felt project kind of person. Or watercolors. I love doing arts and crafts with Ben. I like cooking with him (though, in truth, I can weary of his imprecise stirring technique). I love reading to him. But this straight-up, repetitive make-believe kind of playing? *A little bit tedious*. I get home from work, I lie on the couch pregnantly with a fake beer and a bowl of green olives, and Ben pretends to devour me. "Give me a minute to relax," I say, like somebody's remote dad from a fifties TV show. "Come sit with me." Chomp chomp chomp. We're counting on Birdy to pick up some of the slack around here.

Because forget about energetic parenting—it's all I can do to get my sorry self from the couch to the bedroom. In the last few months, I've fallen asleep putting Ben to bed just about every single night. "Do you want to get ready for bed first so you don't have to get up and brush your teeth later?" Michael asks me every night before we settle in for stories. And every night I say, "Oh, no. I have a million deadlines. I absolutely have to get up and write." And then every night I fall asleep with Ben and have to haul myself up at one in the morning to stagger into the bathroom. It's pathetic—not even the falling asleep so much, but the nightly denial. And the fact that I'm usually still wearing an underwire bra and my elastic-panel fancy pants, which smell like mothballs from their passage through the Salvation Army. Suffice it to say, these are not the comfiest snoozes of my life.

It also means that I spend zero (0) time alone with Michael. I know that we should go out together, catch up a little, but— this is a confession—we are *total wimps* about babysitters. It's too expensive to pay a sitter *and* do something fun. We can't afford it. "Honey, heat for the month of December or a night out—which do you pick?" We could pay the sitter only if we spent the time, I don't know, sitting in the car in the driveway.

But it's more than the money. We're just kind of nervous about leaving Ben. Okay, *I'm* nervous about leaving him. And not "kind of." Before she graduated, we had this great college student babysitter who was—get this—an EMT! Forget about Play-Doh skills and whether or not the sitters like kids. Emergency medical training? *That's* my idea of a good babysitter. (Although I did worry that she might be a little trigger-happy if anything ever happened—like Ben might cough once and, boom, end up with a ballpoint pen in his trachea.) But she's gone—and I think we actually only hired her twice anyways.

I worry, simply, that something will happen to Ben—and I'll have to think, "This, because Michael and I wanted to go argue in a hot tub for an hour?" When he was one, we left him for an evening with our friend Sue (who was, I should point out, *very kind* to offer to sit for him), and it didn't go that well. Well, that's not true. The *babysitting* went fine, but our return home didn't go that well. Just as we were pulling into the parking lot outside our building, an ambulance went screaming past us. An ambulance! So we raced up the stairs and pounded on the door in a fright, and Sue opened it and said, all in one breath, "Hi! Did you have a good time? Ben bumped his head pretty hard and fell asleep." She then had to spend the next twenty minutes convincing me that she hadn't meant to make it sound like he'd gotten a concussion and fallen into a coma, only that those had seemed to be the most salient facts of their evening together. I woke Ben as soon as she had gone—you know, just to look at his pupils.

But last week, on Thanksgiving, Michael's parents watched Ben for us so that we could go to the movies. This may even have topped gravy as the thrill of the season. I worried a little, but then relaxed my way through our tub of popcorn, and Ben was, of course, fine. So I am giving thanks for Ben's grandparents. And for Michael and for Ben. And for this Birdy baby that flaps around like it should be heading south right about now. Instead, it's stuck here until spring.

winter

I learned to croon to you,
to cry and moan, and all this time
you were getting your first looks at the earth, it was
you, and I did not know you, I was not
there to greet you, I didn't exist
until you smiled at me, and in your
brilliant loam-colored iris I saw,
tiny as an embryo,
your mother smile.

Sharon Olds
"The New Stranger"

Winter has arrived in a paroxysm of its own ill nature. I'm reminded of the old Rudolph claymation special, Mr. Coldmiser grumping out his frosty anthem. Our floor is so cold that your feet practically stick to it—like a tongue to a train track. The sun sets by lunchtime. Plus, Michael was sick all weekend, and he's one of those people who *never* gets sick but then suddenly gets, like, dengue fever and is down for the count with chills and a terrible, hacking cough. It was sadly ironic, too, because I actually forced him to get a flu shot at the supermarket just a few days ago—which is where he thinks he picked up the virus, waiting there in line with all the other suckers. Poor guy. Not that I've been an especially patient caretaker of him. I'm not sure why this is, although the all-night snoring episodes—like a chainsaw slicing through a barrel of Jell-O, but *forever*—might offer some clues.

So, last night, there was the snoring. And then Ben, who got *his* flu shot yesterday, peed the bed and woke up soaked and miserable with this horrible, dead club of a leg. He cried through his chewable Tylenol, and then choked, and cried some more and fell asleep in my arms on the couch, with Birdy under him, squeezing my bladder like an oompah accordion player. I was reminded of this photo caption in Lennart Nilsson's book *A Child Is Born:* "A mother-to-be, heavily pregnant and tired, whose tasks are not yet done. Big sister-to-be also needs attention." The picture's just what you might think: a gigantically pregnant woman, her whole face is sagging off with exhaustion, holding a cranky toddler whose mouth is shaped like the word "NOW!" or maybe "NO!" (Okay, she's probably Swedish, so I don't actually know what she's saying.) In the background you can see the woman's husband asleep in bed with this obscenely blissed-out expression on his face, like he's dreaming of sugarplums or hockey tickets. When I was pregnant with Ben, I loved this book for its incredible, high-tech photos of babies in utero; I loved learning all about "vernix" and "lanugo"; I loved seeing all those tiny underwater limbs and faces. But now—*this* is the picture that I'm obsessed with.

It's funny, about the pregnancy books. Ask any pregnant woman, and she'll tell you about the one image or quote that she can't stop looking at. Usually, it's of something that scares the bejesus out of her. For my friend Megan, it was this picture of a woman delivering a baby on her hands and knees, with some kind of bad thing—imagine a banana peel splitting open—happening in the space between her vagina and her butt hole. For me, it was this quote in a groovy labor and birth book I'd borrowed in Santa Cruz. I still know it by heart: "When the baby started to descend, it felt like a grapefruit was trying to pass through my rectum." *A grapefruit through my rectum!* It *still* makes me shudder—and I should talk, seeing as how I have a hemorrhoid the size of a tangerine hanging out of my own personal rectum even as I write this. (I spelled "hemorrhoid" wrong on my first try and the spellchecker program asked, chirpily, "Do you mean *'hammerhead'?*" Um, yes. I guess I do.)

During the first pregnancy, I was also a different mess of

anxieties from having had the earlier miscarriage. So there I'd be, trying to look up some benign thing in one of the books—and I *expect* you know which book I'm talking about—and on the way to "Kegel exercises" I'd stumble onto some passage about how it could seem like you were really pregnant, only what was gestating was something more like a bunch of grapes than a baby. I'm sorry, but you shouldn't be able to just come across that information without looking really hard for it. A friend calls that book *What to Expect When You're Expecting a Robot*.

I mean, must they be so alarmist? "You didn't paint your toenails before you knew you were pregnant, did you? Don't worry—if you're lucky, at least one hemisphere of your baby's brain should still develop normally." It's as if you're *already* a bad mother—doomed from the get-go. And that whole "best bite" pregnancy diet? Please. "Is *that* the very best bite for the baby?" Michael likes to tease when I'm hunched like a criminal over a bag of gummy bears. "Be sure to indulge yourself at least once a week," the book advises. "A fruited yogurt makes a nice treat." A fruited yogurt! As if. A pound of cookie dough washed down with a quart of half-and-half—now *that* makes a nice treat.

In one book there's even one of those exclamation-point warning boxes on a page about bathing. And if you think it's just the usual reminder about keeping the temperature down, you're wrong. No. It says, "Be careful not to slip getting in and out of the bathtub!" Oh! Like I never would have thought of that on my own. If it were a book about how to be the *village id-iot*, that would be one thing. But geez. I guess they think it's only the gestating baby that would occasion basic caution—like you're usually in there doing some solo slapstick Marx Brothers routine, sliding around on the tiles and whacking your head into the faucet.

Even the one book that I like—because it's mostly just funny and real—is written by a woman who is so damned *rich* that I end up feeling like I can't relate to her at all. With every problem she writes about—even all of the regular stuff, like bloating and barfing—I think, meanly and with great jealousy, "Why don't you just write somebody a big, fat check. I'm sure they'll take care of it for you."

But it's those mother-hating books that really get me. The ones with the condescending tone that alternately scares and enrages everybody. "You have really biffed it now," they scold, page after page. Plus, there are always the requisite illustrations of the most promising sexual positions—not for the faint of heart or anyone in their first trimester. Who *are* these women, so big and buoyant and into it? In *my* pregnancy book, there'll be a picture of a ten-foot pole included in this section. In my pregnancy book there will be practical advice—like how to throw up quietly in public, and how to maximize the nutritional value of Fritos, and how not to punch anybody in the face, even when you feel like you've been injected with some crazy rage hormone. And how to sleep with two babies—one three, and one not yet born—lying on top of you on the couch. If that book already exists, please let me know.

So I flunked my latest round of blood tests: iron (low) and sugar (high). Anemia and gestational diabetes. Woop-dee-doo. I just can't seem to summon my usual energy for freaking out. When I was pregnant with Ben, I probably would have been hysterical; I would have been trolling all over the Internet, latching onto faint suggestions that gestational diabetes causes fetal brain tumors—or is caused by maternal brain tumors. (Don't run off in a panic to check: I made that up purely for emphasis.) "Whatever" seems to be my general feeling about this—maybe because this is my second pregnancy.

Or maybe because our friend Judy is starting her third round of treatment for breast cancer. She first had it ten years ago, and then again a year after that, and now we were just getting into a kind of celebratory mood about the ten-year mark when a spot on her annual mammogram turned a little murky. I drove over to sit with her last week, and I kind of unraveled. "I'm not *at all* worried that you're going to die," I blurted out, unbidden, and then burst into tears. "Good," Judy said, and smiled at me. "That's really reassuring." She laughed, and then I did, snot everywhere. "I'm sorry to be one those people you have to take care of when you're sick," I said, and she said, "That's okay. Oh, I mean, *you're not,*" and hugged me. Come Christmastime, she will have a bilateral mastectomy, and then start chemotherapy. Right now, the possibility that, due to some misfiring in my islets of Langerhans, I might have to limit my eggnog consumption—well, it kind of pales by comparison.

Lots of you, I'm sure, have moved onto round two of the diabetes screening. To begin with, you have to fast from midnight until after the test. It's one of those funny things, because it's not like you probably tend to do a whole lot of eating after midnight. But as soon as somebody tells you that you can't, you're suddenly *starving* at one in the morning—you'd mug somebody for a bowl of Grape-Nuts. By dawn, your body is fully cannibalizing itself. You drape yourself around the kitchen, weak with hunger, until it's time to drive your starving self to the lab, where everyone coughing on you in the waiting room is—you can only imagine—there to be tested for German measles and some homicidally tenacious form of the flu. Then you guzzle down that freakishly sweet orange soda, which is universally understood to be gross, but which I secretly sort of like. Then you sit around while they draw your blood hourly for three hours.

Three hours! It had sounded vaguely luxurious over the phone—like a big old chunk of quality time. I brought tons of work with me, forgetting, of course, that I'd be completely demented from not eating for so long. And completely demented I was. I couldn't even settle down with a *novel*—let alone my laptop computer. Please. Instead I spent three hours flipping through women's magazines in this frantic, squirrelly way—*10 Great Chicken Casseroles! 5 Frosty Colors for Winter! The One Best Way to Excite Your Man!* (I trust it involves doing your best impression of the Hindenburg)—and reading nothing. Mostly, I felt like I was on an airplane—stuck in my seat and craning my head around a lot, although, alas, there was nobody coming by with pretzels. You start to look *forward* to them drawing your blood, just to mix it up a little.

And the longer I waited, the more I noticed how many old people there were, arriving for their various routine and less-than-routine tests. I started to feel as rosy and conspicuous as a ripe peach, sitting there so huge and blessed and healthy. Everyone smiled at me a lot, and I smiled back, and I felt happy and heartbroken at the same time. I wanted to tell them that I *know,*

I really do, that this is as good as a life gets. Even deranged on a bad orange-soda trip, with a to-do list longer than the phone book, I feel like the luckiest person in the world. It was snowing, too—these heavy, beautiful flakes falling thickly outside the window—and I was remembering the night before, when I'd felt so weepy and wistful putting Ben to bed (*everything* makes me cry these days). "You're my love," I'd whispered, stroking his hair. I thought he was asleep. "You're *my* love," he whispered back, and smiled at me in the dark.

So, needless to say, I was a little tearful and deranged when they finally released me, but then I got to eat lunch in the hospital cafeteria, which is my absolute favorite. It's dirt cheap and staffed by thousand-year-old volunteers. They're always totally scandalized that I want mustard on my ninety-five-cent sandwich.

"Cheese on wheat, Dotty. No ham. And she wants *mustard* on that!"

"Mustard?"

"*That's* what she says." Everyone at the counter—this is not a youthful crowd—turns to stare at you. You might as well be buying flavored condoms.

Later, my practice called me at work to tell me that not only was I *not* diabetic, but I was, in fact, mildly hypoglycemic. Not *enough* blood sugar. Was I feeling okay? they wanted to know, since my blood sugar had been very "erratic." You're kidding? After fasting for fifteen hours, chugging a bottle of carbonated corn syrup, and then having all the blood drained slowly out of your veins? Hard to believe your blood sugar wouldn't be nice and even. "Eat a lot," they told me. Um, yeah, okay. Done.

What a couple of days we've had! Ben woke up on Christmas morning and sat up in bed, practically shivering with excitement. "Do you remember what today is?" Michael asked him. Ben looked out the window and raised his eyebrows. "A day when it's snowing?" he asked. "Yes," we said. "It is. But do you remember what else today is?" "Um . . . the day when Grandma and Grandpa are still here?" It's like living with an oddly joyful amnesiac. After all of the holiday hubbub—the wrapping of gifts, the hanging of stockings, the endless discussions of Santa and his methodology—we could have skipped the entire day, and Ben wouldn't have even noticed. But then we would have missed out on the Great Unwrapping Ecstasy. He was just so entirely happy, so utterly gracious. "Can you believe this?" he said about every little thing he pulled out of his stocking. *Glue! A lip balm! Stickers!* "How did Santa *know?*" On Christmas night, he lay in bed, reminiscing already. "I just can't stop liking all my presents," he said. "I can't stop liking my new glue and my Mr. Potato Man."

I loved it. I know I wouldn't be anybody's first choice to play Mary in a nativity scene, but Ben's pure joy just made everything about the day feel holy for me—you know, in a secular kind of way. When Ben and my mother made gingerbread people together, I couldn't take my eyes off them. My poor mom tried to teach Ben the normal ins and outs of decorating— the raisin eyes and cranberry mouths of the general cookie population—but Ben would not conform. "Ah," he'd mutter, smooshing two cranberries down into the dough, "she needs two big nursings so she can nurse her babies." "Two big *what?*" my mom said. "*Nursings,* Mom," I told her, and pointed to her chest. She laughed.

In truth, Ben's been in the holiday spirit for ages. First, there was the snowy procuring of the tree—a real beauty, which we draped in our motley assortment of ornaments: a miniature cheese grater, a coffee can lid with a picture of the band Kiss glued inside it (don't ask), as well as some lovely glassy things from my mom and the flea market. Ben hung most of them himself, so the bulk of the tree is sort of scantily clad in ornaments, and then there's this thick band of them about a foot off the ground. Ben can stand in front of the tree and admire it, hopping from one foot to the other (this could be either delight or needing to pee), for ages. "Are these cookies for eating?" he asks over and over about the cinnamon-and-white-glue ornaments we made last year, and when we say "No," he teases us. "I'm just taking a *tiny nibble,*" he says. "You won't even notice."

There has also been a fair amount of random holiday commentary. A couple weeks ago, Ben was naked after one of his rare baths, grimacing at himself in the full-length mirror and rubbing copious amounts of lotion onto his bottom. "I'm a mean guy!" he snarled at his reflection. "Because my booty is itchy!" "Maybe that's why the Grinch was so mean," Michael offered—we had just watched the old classic together on our VCR—but Ben said, "No, I don't think so," and screwed up his face. "The Grinch was mean because his *penis* was three sizes too small!" According to Dr. Seuss, the size problem was, of course, with the Grinch's *heart,* but you can't help wondering if Ben might be onto something. . . .

That great old movie led to some other wondering around

101

here, besides the size issue. Ben became very curious—and I think, frankly, that this is a fine question—about how we knew for sure that the whole Santa/gift thing would only move in one direction, chimney-wise. "Do you think Santa might come down the chimney and into my play area, and put some of my toys in her sack and take them back *up* the chimney?" Ben kept wondering. "No, lovey," we'd say, "Santa just brings toys for kids and after he puts them in your stocking he leaves. He just *gives* toys." "Because she's a sweetie-heart?" Ben wanted to know, and we said, "Yup." Ben's convinced that Santa's a woman. "Does she have a white beard?" he asked me, worrying, a week before Christmas, and I nodded. "Then I'm just going to *blow* her a kiss instead of kissing her prickly, prickly face. Is that okay?" We reassured him that he'd be sleeping through any potentially awkward kissing-type scenarios. But, sheesh—you'd think we knew a lot of heavily bearded, sack-bearing women with their hearts set on a kiss from Ben.

Also, I should mention here—and I know it's controversial—that I am not in favor of pretending that your child is meeting the *real* Santa at, say, JC Penney or a neighborhood caroling party, or, heaven forbid, at the Yankee Candle Company in July. "That," we say, "is a person *dressed up* to look like Santa." I just think it's too depressing, even for kids, that the world's most important person would actually be sitting right there in your very own lousy shopping mall. One might naturally assume that Santa would be quite busy at this time of year, bustling over a big heap of gifts at the North Pole, not lounging around and sweating with a Dunkin' Donuts bag balled up under his chair. It would be like if you were at a diner, and some gray old guy was sitting at the counter hunched over a plate of pork chops, and you nudged your kid and said, "Look, honey, isn't that *God?*"

Anyways, thanks to our interfaith style of holiday dabbling, we'd also gotten to squeeze in a week of Hanukkah, quick on the heels of Thanksgiving. We lit the menorah every night with Ben staring silently, his eyes shining over the candle flames. And suddenly, on the last night, with matzo ball soup and latkes steaming on the table before us, Ben stopped us halfway through the candle prayer. "Cattie wants to sing that song," he said shyly, and then ran to get his stuffed black panther. He held Cattie up to the table, ducked his head a little, and sang the last part of the prayer with us. Sure, maybe Cattie's not the most devout Jew in the world. But Ben's high, sweet voice? I'm sure you feel this, whatever you celebrate—what a magical thing it is to have such a new and beautiful person in your life.

Every day, however Ben acts that day, I'm convinced he's *always* like that, and will be forever. It's like a recurring memory warp. "When did he get so annoying?" I'll ask Michael, while Ben sprints crazy eights around the kitchen, clutching his crotch but refusing to pee, and bursting into tears if you insist that he try. "I'm not sure, hon," Michael will say to me. "Yesterday you got all teary about how lucky we are. Remember? Yesterday you said you thought he'd been in such a great place lately."

Oh. Usually I'm positive that Ben always has been and always will be the most irritating—or, on a different day, wonderful—person on the planet. It's like when he was a newborn, and he'd have *one* good night, and we'd think, "Now he's really *sleeping!*" only to be dismayed by his hourly waking the next night. Or when he's sick, but we kind of forget he's sick and feel, instead, like he's suffered an unfortunate, and permanent, personality transplant—maybe from Felix Unger. But then he wakes up one morning, all healthy and grinning, and we remember again.

But mostly, these days, I'm mad at the person who coined the phrase "Terrible Twos." I think it's just a sadistic trick, to make you think, "Phew, that's over!" and then—bam—your kid turns three and the real terror begins. Granted, Ben was kind of an easy two. I mean, there was the requisite whining about juice cups and the exhausting Mussolini impersonations, but he was still mostly a round, pink-cheeked baby with a headful of curls and a ready smile.

And in some ways he's *still* that, only taller. He really is an exceptionally enthusiastic and easily delighted person. But in other ways, he's like a teenager, quick to negotiate and brood and fall into fits of hysteria. For instance, he won't wear his mittens some days, so I ask him to walk with his hands in his pockets, but then he *runs* with his hands in his pockets, down the icy path. I picture him falling onto his face and knocking all his teeth out and wearing a neck brace for the rest of his life—I mean I *really* can picture this, and it stiffens my whole body—so I say, "Please don't run with your hands in your pockets. It's not safe." You can guess the rest: *But you said to put my hands in my pockets; But I won't fall; See, I didn't fall,* etc. At some point I'll lose my patience and force the mittens onto his hands, and he'll go completely insane—you'd think the mittens were scalding him or that they were filled with scorpions. I can really understand his frustration. I mean, if Michael were suddenly like, "Here, you have to wear these itchy wool tights that you hate," and started pulling them up over my legs, I would be more than a little upset.

And it's also so clear to me that so much depends on *my own* mood in any given moment. I know this is not a shocking revelation, but I'm often really struck by it. If I'm happy and relaxed, I have all the patience in the world to help Ben figure out how to do things the way he wants to. I can sit on the bed contentedly for half an hour while he struggles into his pajama bottoms like he's wrestling with a crocodile: first both feet go into the same leg, then suddenly, the pajamas are backwards with one leg inside out and the waist band twisted into a scroll. Then Ben's foot is stuck, flexed, in the ankle of the pants. No worries. But on a night when I'm stressed out, I feel like I'll lose my mind watching him for so long, and I'll offer to help and he'll be devastated and sulky through story time. "Why did you help me but I wanted to do it by my own self, but you said, 'Ben, it's really bedtime now,' and you helped me? Why?"

Those are the nights when you lie in bed as they fall asleep, glad that there will be another morning soon and you can start over, work harder to be the patient self you want to be. Some nights, that half-asleep cuddling is like a last little gift. I feel like Ben's my baby all over again. Sometimes I can tell that he feels it too. The other night, after a particularly tiresome series of post-dinner altercations (picture the unwinding of an entire roll of crepe paper streamer, but without the festivity), Ben said, "First I'm going to turn off the light and then I'm going to lie down and then I'm going to say, 'Will you rock me in your lap, Mama?' and then you're going to say, 'Sure,' and then you're going to rock me in your lap and sing me 'Golden Slumbers' and then I'm going to go to sleep. But wait for me to say it, okay?" "Okay," I said. Ben turned off the light and lay down, and I waited and waited, poised to rock him. I willed the baby out of the way so that my lap would feel familiar and expansive. The minutes ticked by until I realized that he was already snoring softly. "He's such a complete love," I wept to Michael a little later, and he just gave me a funny smile and went back to rewinding the crepe paper streamer.

What happens to this singularity of focus when the new baby comes? As it is, I'm so exhausted from so much feeling, so much negotiating, so much explaining of every single thing. For Ben, everything is an epistemological can of worms: Why? Why? Why? he wants to know. About books, especially. Thank God Birdy's coming. Soon, we can return to the mind-numbing world of board books, where every page offers a simple noun, maybe a primary color or two: *Red triangle. Baby's hat.* Not that I was especially grateful back when we were reading those gems to Ben—in fact, we had to stow *One Baby Clapping* in an attic-bound storage bin (along with *Touch and Feel Farm* and the riveting truck odyssey, *See Them Go!*) before I went completely insane from the tedium of it all. I couldn't wait to move on to Dr. Seuss.

But now we seem to have entered a new literary phase, in which each book trails along with it a host of mind-blowing concepts that we're expected to explain to Ben's satisfaction.

I'm thinking about writing a picture book called, I don't know, *Maisy's Big Flap Book of Existential Philosophy*.

For instance, in William Steig's book *Amos and Boris*, Amos, the mouse, rolls off his ship and, stranded at sea, wonders what it would be like to drown. "What's 'drown'?" Ben suddenly asked one night, and a million terrible thoughts unspooled immediately from my crazy mind. I remembered that twenty-page section on drowning in the book *A Perfect Storm*, which describes, in shattering detail, how long you can keep yourself from inhaling under water, and then how it might feel as your lungs fill up with the sea. Nah. I thought about the *Titanic*—those countless good people rolling off the tilted deck and into the dark water, like potatoes into a stew pot. Nah. How do you balance the requirements of honesty with the risk of a lifelong terror of liquid? Because believe me—we're bathing infrequently enough as it is.

"It's like swimming," I finally said, "only, um, the water makes you too tired." Michael overheard this and raised his eyebrows at me. "Nice one," he teased. "Clear and honest."

My friend Barbara laughed when I told her about my equally lame explanation of "war." "Ah," she said, "you went with 'The mean guys who can't share.' We went with *'Greedy* guys who don't know how to *use their words.'* Similar approaches."

But "drown" and "war" are easy compared with our current obsession: Death. "This is Tiny," Ben likes to say, pulling a stool over to the mantel so he can reach the framed picture of our beloved old cat. "He died when Mama was pregnant with me. Ooooh, I miss him so much," he says, and he makes a long, sad face, like he's receiving condolences at a funeral. "Where is he?" "We don't really know," Michael or I will say nervously. "Different people believe different things. He might be sleeping in a quiet, dark place, or maybe flying around somewhere with other catties. We just know he's not here with us anymore— although a little bit of his spirit might be inside you." This is true, and makes me somewhat superstitious about pregnancy and rebirth. I swear, if Ben could lie around in the sun all day just getting his tummy scratched, he would.

So, the Tiny Lamentations are manageable overall. But then, a few weeks ago, Death showed up in a new form and rocked Ben's world. Michael's brother Keith was visiting us from Denver, and because he has the common decency not to have a family of his own yet, Ben got his undivided attention. This meant the toddler version of Twenty Questions (Do you like olives? Do you *not* like watermelon? Is my daddy your sister?), which then segued into an inquiry about the constituents of Keith's family—all the brothers and the sister and parents and grandparents. At some point Keith mentioned his mother's dad, Ray. "Oh," Ben said, "is she dead?" Now, naturally—on account of the female pronoun and all—Keith assumed that Ben meant his *mother*, not his grandfather, even though Ben meant to be asking about Ray. "Yes," Keith nodded, "my mom died a few years ago."

Ben's face became a still life of terror. It was like a door had cracked open from the sunny, flower-filled meadow where his brain had been living, onto a howling, demon-filled hurricane just outside. *Mothers die.* His eyes turned into black saucers and he stood perfectly still. The fear was so huge and palpable— like another person hulking there in the room with us. I knelt down by him. "Is that hard to think about?" I asked, but Ben didn't want to talk. This is what he did instead, and I swear this is true: he walked over to the Christmas tree, where we have three clay gingerbread people hanging, one for each of us, with the words "Mama," "Daddy," and "Ben" painted on them. He gathered the three ornaments from their different hanging places, held them in his fist for a minute, and then hung them all, together, on the same branch. Keith and I didn't say a word. I wanted to tell Ben that it wasn't his job to come up with a magical way to keep us all safe. But I reconsidered. His way of understanding the world just might make it feel a little safer for all of us.

If our furnace were coin-operated, someone would have to stand there, day and night, feeding a stream of silver dollars into it. I hear its steady hum all the time these days—the sound of our bank account draining away. It's been about a thousand degrees below zero for weeks around here and we are all frankly bored. Despite the arctic turn of events, I happen to be broiling to death with this gigantic, hot baby living inside my very own body. But I know it's tough on all these poor house-bound kids. And parents.

My own parents live in New York, and my dad always likes to dismiss people's concerns about the city: the crime's not so bad anymore, the people are friendly, you can eat a truly great meal for under ten bucks. "But you know what really *is* terrible?" he likes to say. "The *noise*. The car alarms and sirens and buses. It's the noise that gets to you." Well, that's how I feel about cabin fever—about Ben's in particular. I don't so much mind the indoors-ness of it—the days filled slowly with endless stories and puzzles and art projects. It's the *noise* of Ben—the way he's so hyper and stir-crazy and *loud*.

Whatever energy he used to expend sweating it out on the playground—running and climbing and just generally bouncing all around like a coked-up chimpanzee—now seems to get converted into decibels. There must be a law of physics that explains the wintertime noisiness of preschoolers. Trying to make a phone call? Why, there's Ben with his tambourine, coming to sit with you on the couch! Talking briefly with your dinner guests? Ben is likely to go strutting by, doing, it seems, his best impression of a teenager making the heavy-metal air-guitar sound "Nyah NYAH DAH, dah DAH ree-OW." Even simple communication has taken a turn for the deafening. "HEY, MAMA?!" he yells when he wants to ask you something, even though he's sitting right in your lap. (Although, come to think of it, I still do this to my own mother. Only I call her "MA," which she hates—she always says it back to me, "Maaaaah," like we're sheep.)

It probably doesn't help winter matters that we actually live in a *cabin*—a pretty one, with reasonably high ceilings and lots of windows, but a cabin nonetheless. A cabin pressed in from all sides by towering pines. Don't tell anyone, but I wouldn't mind if some tree vandals came and sawed a bunch of them down while we were sleeping. *Are* there tree vandals? We could act really astonished and outraged about it when the earnest environmental journalist interviewed us. Alternately, I'm thinking about capturing a beaver and letting it loose in the yard. Is it so wrong to want a little *light?* "Look out, *you*," Michael whispers to each tree as we walk by, teasing me. "You're next."

The cavelike quality of our house actually seems to inspire Ben, who's totally game and willing to make the most of the winter. "Come on, Mama," he shouts from under a blanket. "Be a bear with me in my bear hive. Come and *hibernacle* with me." I get the confusion between "cave" and "hive," although I have no idea how "hibernate" ended up morphing with "tabernacle." Go figure. But since the hibernating games mostly involve lying around on the couch and snacking, I really can't complain.

But I'm grateful this winter that we're all relatively happy and sane. And that none of us (knock wood) has had the barfing flu! These are tender mercies indeed. Plus, I can't quite wish for spring yet, because spring coming means Birdy's birth. And I'm not ready. I still want just Ben—my only Ben—without this other person coming along to glump everything up. At my last appointment, the OB had tried to schedule the C-section. "How's February twenty-seventh?" she asked, and I blinked at her. "No, no," I said, "*March*. I'm not supposed to have the baby until March." She laughed and reminded me that February is a short month. "But February is *next* month!" I tried to explain, panic-stricken. "Next month is too soon! Next month is *now*. March is in two months. March isn't until the spring." I'm guessing that, in a practice where they see a hormonal mélange of pregnant women, menopausal women, and women struggling to conceive, I'm not their very craziest patient.

Or maybe I am. Right about now, a million other gigantically pregnant women are nesting properly, I'm sure—sorting and folding all those tiny onesies, checking Web sites to make sure their changing table hasn't been recalled, sweeping dust bunnies out from under all the beds. Me? Day and night I'm sewing miniature felt animals. Because a friend gave me these intricate German patterns, and now I'm completely obsessed. They're actually very cute: a fat little seal, a polar bear, a floppy-eared elephant. But with the holidays behind us, my excuse for making them has entirely diminished. You'd think I'd be in a delirium of writing, trying to bank a little more cash for my maternity leave, or, at least, soaking up these final weeks with Ben. Instead, I'm enthralled to some seductive felt siren song. I'd stay up all night sewing if Michael would let me.

"What do you think *Kopfeinsatz* means?" I ask him.

"I don't know, hon."

"Do you think I'm supposed to sew the *Unterteile* to the *Oberteile*?"

"I really don't know," he says. "I think you should come to bed."

In truth, this is not entirely different from the end of my first pregnancy. At forty weeks, staggering through the house like a derailed parade float, I stubbed my toe on a chair and broke it. So, instead of spending those final two weeks (after which they finally induced me) walking on the beach with Michael, or writing moonily in my journal, or making minestrone soup to freeze, I sat on the couch with my foot in a splint and did a million-piece jigsaw puzzle depicting Princess Diana's face composed entirely of flowers from her funeral. Don't get me wrong—it's not like I did a bunch of other stuff, and *also* worked on the puzzle. I *just* did the puzzle. I didn't talk to anyone or even answer the phone.

Now, in fairness to me, this was not wholly unreasonable avoidance on my part. Past your due date, you get a lot of calls from a lot of well-meaning people—like, say, your own parents—who are just making sure that you haven't *had* the baby and then accidentally forgotten to mention it to them. They make up these sadly transparent excuses for calling: "Just wondering if you saw that article in the paper on sea vegetables and iodine. Call us the second you get home!"

By the very end, it had gotten even worse. People were leaving us messages inquiring into the status of my *cervix!* And the status of my cervix was not good. "Still long and hard," my midwife said every week, shaking her head. I felt like the star of some bizarre obstetric sideshow: *Step right up, folks! She's forty-one weeks pregnant, with a cervix harder than diamonds!* And this despite the fact that I tried all the groovy labor inducers—downing shots of evening primrose oil, guzzling dark, bitter tinctures, and practicing a grisly parody of foreplay called "nipple stimulation." I cried when people asked after my cervix on our answering machine, and Michael was baffled. "But imagine," I said, "if all our friends and family called to ask how your *penis* was doing! *Still hanging there between your legs? Any notable changes?*"

It hasn't come to that, yet. So far, it's just the felt animals. But, really—this is not a glamorous time. The beginning of the last trimester is so much fun, when your belly's getting so big and round, and everyone smiles at you at the supermarket, and your skin looks a little bit pretty. But after that, it's more about losing your train of thought halfway through every sentence, and peeing your pants when you sneeze. And constipation. I've had to warn Ben about what will happen to him if he eats my horrible bran cereal, and now he screws up his face before trying a bite of anything I'm eating: "Is this a *pooping* kind of food, Mama?" he asks, and I usually nod.

And don't you love it when your OB asks if you're getting enough exercise? What, in the dead of winter, with a three-year-old, and three jobs, and a tremendous annex attached to the front of my body? Why on earth wouldn't I be getting enough exercise? (Actually, I always answer "Yes," on the assumption that getting up to pee every five minutes constitutes "enough exercise.") "Hey, Mama," Ben asked me last week, "do you want to do your Crunch Mama yoga video with me?" "That's a great idea," I said. "I'll get the mat." "Wait. I have a good idea!" he smiled. "Let's just watch it in bed, snuggled up under the covers. Maybe you could make popcorn." Now *that's* my kind of exercise.

Well, that and worrying. I trust worrying counts as exercise, because it sure seems to have a cardiovascular component to it. I visited Judy in the hospital after her surgery, and I am now filled with both a carpe diem zest for life and also, paradoxically, a near-paralyzing dread. Oy. "Trooper" does not begin to capture Judy in her fabulous high-spiritedness: propped up on pillows and cracking jokes, asking after Ben's latest tricks, and totally indulgent of my crafty nervous habits. (I had brought a red felt lion to the hospital, and I spent my entire visit there tangled in embroidery thread. A total loser.)

At some point, though, she was swept over with a drug-induced migraine—knocked flat with pain and nausea. I sat close to the bed and summoned the feeling I have that stands in for prayer: a thick kind of hope that sits behind my eyes. I pictured the summer: Judy laughing under a baseball cap, me with a new swaddled baby. This is not so ambitious, as visions go, but for now it will have to be enough.

A few mornings ago, Michael and I were having a little argument at the breakfast table, and I burst into tears. Here's the pattern these days: I launch a bitchy, bizarrely exaggerated accusation—"You never even pay any *attention* to me"—Michael gently suggests that I find a better mode of communicating my dissatisfaction, and then I burst into tears and need to be comforted. So there I was, all weepy at the table, and Ben paused over his eggs and looked at me. His eyes widened in complete amazement. "Why's your face all wet, Mama?" he asked. "Why are those tears drip-dripping out of your eyes?"

"I'm crying, sweetie," I told him. "I'm fine—just a little bit sad. I have hurt feelings." (Technically, in our house, this style of desolation is called "hurting your *own* feelings.")

Ben climbed down from his stool and came to stand by me. "You know what this reminds me of?" he asked after a minute. *"Sylvester and the Magic Pebble."*

I knew the page of the book he was talking about. After their beloved Sylvester turns himself into a rock and disappears, the donkey's mom and dad are, naturally, beside themselves with grief: there's a picture of Sylvester's mother, standing by the window with tears running down her face, that has always fascinated Ben. "I think it's like the book," Ben said. "So, Daddy, are you doing your best to comfort her, like Sylvester's dad did?"

Ben's compassion really took the wind out of my aggrieved little sails. Michael laughed and rubbed my back. "I'll do my best," he said, and Ben said, "Okay, then I'll get her a Kleenex." My dear boys. There's nothing that can make you feel pettier than the bighearted wisdom of a three-year-old.

What, exactly, were Michael and I arguing about, you ask. There's a very short answer to that question, which is that I'm not sleeping well and seem to be getting progressively more exhausted. "I'm so tired," I say, about a thousand times a day, and really—why? Is there anything more boring a person could say? *Everybody's* tired. It's about as scintillating a topic of conversation as *breathing:* "Whoowhee! Here it comes—*in!* And now this other part—*out!* In again. And then the *out* part." But I'm in that pregnancy moment where my hips fall asleep in bed, so I have to haul my gigantic groaning person from side to side every ten minutes, rearranging my ridiculous body pillow (fondly nicknamed "Big Pinky" by Ben) with every shift.

But there's also a longer answer to that question. Every night I say to Michael, "Will you please get up with Ben in the morning and let me sleep in a little?" (Note: this is a dramatic re-creation of the scene, and may therefore contain polite language that was actually omitted from the original.) And every night Michael looks at me soulfully and says, "Of course, my love." Perhaps you can guess this next part. . . . Come morning, Ben scrambles his warm pajama-clad self into bed next to me and nests in my hair, tugging on it and wrapping it around his fists. He whispers all sorts of morning commentary right into my ear, and I kind of love it. "Did you have a pleasant dream, Mama?" "Do you see those orange clouds, Mama?" "Should we get up and draw a picture of a flamingo?" At some point, Michael—who doubtless has the best intentions—will say a groggy something to him, like, "Hey, do you want to go downstairs with me and let Mama get a little more sleep?" And Ben always says, "No, that's okay." And that's that. Michael rolls over and goes back to sleep, like, *You can't say I didn't try*.

I am reminded of the early nights after Ben's birth. Not the truly early nights, which were just a surreal circus of nursing and diaper changing. (Michael is famous for having woken in the middle of a feeding to ask me the demented question "Is this still the last time, or are you already nursing him *again?*") Michael was a hero in those early days: he lurched out of bed hourly to change Ben's diaper (who knew they pooped so *voluminously?*) and do a burping rotation. He fetched me big glasses of ice water, even in the middle of the night. He was cheerful and competent and kind. But then things slowed down a little— which looked, really, like Ben still nursing every hour, only not pooping so much—and Michael seemed to relax. Way too many mornings, Michael would wake up, stretch, smile at me, and say, "I'm sorry, was it just me, or did Ben have a *great* night last night?" "Um, no, it was just you," I'd say. "I nursed him every hour, same as always." The next morning it would be the same: "Wow," he'd say, "now *that* was a great night, right? Ben's a great sleeper." "Honey," I'd say, "*you* had a great night. *You're* a great sleeper. I nursed Ben every hour. I now have no choice but to leave you."

So I'm tired now, and I assume I'll be unspeakably tired after the baby is born. This worries me. But as exhausting as Ben is in all his threeness, I also find myself buoyed by his enthusiasm. If I had Ben's passion and energy, I could translate *War and Peace* into Sanskrit, and still have time before dinner to become ambassador to Greece. Instead, I seem to have just the right amount of energy to lie on the couch with the *One Step*

Ahead catalogue—do we need a "shampoo visor"?—and yell into the kitchen for Michael to thaw the minestrone.

Ben's zealous learning all started when he was just a bitty thing, first deciding to roll over. Mind you, I have absolutely no idea now when this was—how old he was at the time. Two months? Ten months? (I keep swearing I won't forget these things, but then I forget them. And of course my baby journal is no help, since I was too busy documenting the minutiae of his antics—"He's lying on his back now, doing the 'th' sound and grinning at his own fingers"—to record anything of actual significance.)

Anyways, Ben had these competing passions back then: on the one hand, he loathed being on his belly; on the other, he'd been bitten by the rolling-over bug and his new motto seemed to have become "Roll over or die." He'd spend all night practicing, and then sobbing in his crib because he'd gotten stuck on his stomach and needed to be rescued. "Maybe you should quit rolling over for a while," we'd encourage him, like the go-getters we are. "You're doing just fine on your back." But there was no stopping him.

This is still true, about all kinds of things. I somehow thought that if we weren't those Baby Einstein–type parents—you know, flashing cards to teach him the dates and dignitaries of all the Chinese dynasties—he would just be a kind of relaxed guy, taking the world in slowly. This does not seem to be the case. Last fall, for instance, he was suddenly entirely preoccupied with teaching himself about distance and optical interpretation. It started one evening after we'd driven home from dinner. On the walk up to our house, we saw our neighbor's black-and-white cat sitting on our stoop. "Hey," Ben said, "is that Paul's dog, Spot?" We laughed. "Let's see when we get closer," I said, and when we did, Ben was amazed. "Hey, it's just a little cat. How come I thought it was Spot?" We explained that it was hard to tell how big things were when they were far away, and, with that, Ben became a dedicated student of perspective. "Is that tree far away, or is it just really tiny, tinier than my hand?" Distance? Or a forest of bonsai? If he could have written, Ben would have become a modern-age toddler Leonardo da Vinci, filling notebooks with his observations. *January 14. Breakthrough! Trees usually* bigger *than the human hand*.

Currently, it's the alphabet that has him in its grip. He sits in his car seat, yelling letters out euphorically. "S!" he cries when we pass the supermarket, "K! T!" And you can tell he's just thinking about them all the time. He'll be quiet for ages and then blurt out, "Hey, Mama, 'T' is for 'China.'" "Wrong, wrong, and triple wrong," I tell him. No, just kidding. But it can be hard to decide between condescension ("That's right, honey! 'T' *is* for China! Good for you!") and what feels like the thwarting of his zeal. "Ah" is the middle ground we tend to strike, as in "Ah. It *sounds* like China starts with 'T,' doesn't it? It actually starts with 'C-H.'" "How strange," Ben answers.

Last week he was studying an alphabet poster and came to "Y," where there was an illustration of some animals dining al fresco on a large, fancy boat. "'Y' is for . . . *yicnic?*" Ben offered. "Ah," I said. "Good guess. I think it might be *yacht*." When you're reading to him now, you have to hold Ben's finger and point to each word as you go. He studies the letters like scripture.

There is also—and this may be developmentally related—a sudden interest in representational drawing. A few weeks ago, Ben announced that he was going to make a picture of his

Uncle Keith. He picked up a pink crayon and drew two parallel lines up the entire length of the page. "There's his long, long legs," he said, and then paused. "There's no more space. This is my whole drawing of Uncle Keith." A prodigy, no? But now the floodgates are open. He seems most often to draw something and then study it before determining what it actually is. It's like he's creating his own personal Rorschach ink blots. Last week he drew a curly purple line, squinted at it, and determined that it was a cat's tail. Then he drew a long, black tower shape with eyes, which turned out to be, of all things, Miss Clavel from the Madeleine books. A smaller blue tower shape, also with eyes, was examined and declared to be "a penguin."

His other main obsession—and, in truth, this has been going on since he could first talk—is with music, which we listen to a lot of. He needs to know the name of every song and every singer that comes on—in the house, the car, the supermarket, his own mind. "Hey, Mama," he yelled from his car seat yesterday, "who'sthissingingandwhat'sitcalled?" (This is such a common utterance that it gets spoken as one word.) "I don't know," I said. "We'll have to ask Daddy when we get home." Ben sighed, the little pedant. "It's Bob Marley, Mama. I think it's called 'Guava Jelly.'" Oh. Later that evening, we were all in the car together and a Cole Porter song came on. After we told him "S'wonderful" and that it was Ella Fitzgerald, Ben was silent for a while. "Like at the zoo?" he finally ventured, and Michael shot me a questioning look. "Like *what?*" I asked. "Like at the zoo. Like *Elephants Gerald?*" Three-year-olds could be stand-up comedians if they wanted. Or, of course, they could be president. God knows they have the ambition for it. And the intelligence.

B en's least favorite thing—and, come to think of it, it may be mine, too—is being misunderstood. It drives him to the very outer limits of frustration and dumps him right out there. The other night we were wrestling on the bed and he wriggled triumphantly out of my arms. "You're getting so strong!" I said to him. "I know," he said, "because I'm fwee!" "You are," I nodded. "When you were only two, you could hardly ever get away from me. And now you're three!" Ben's face fell. "No," he said. "Not fwee. *Fwee.*" I smiled at him in a stalling kind of way. "FWEE!" he said. "Fwee." "Oh," I said, finally, *"free?"* "Yes!" He was totally relieved. "Fwee. I got away from you."

Mostly, we understand him just fine. Despite the fact that he sat up, I don't know, a full four months later than the other babies in his baby group (I remember them all perched there on the grass like smug little Buddhas, while Ben lay around on his back staring happily at his toes and the sky), and despite the fact that he can't throw a ball to save his life (he kind of cocks his arm dramatically and then lets the ball drop behind him), Ben has been quite a big talker. ("I wonder where he gets it," people can't help teasing. *Ha ha.*) But sometimes, you watch him try to say things that aren't coming out right, and he struggles so much—even *he* hears them sound wrong—but he can't figure out how to fix them. I really feel for him.

In the bath a few weeks ago, Ben got water in his eyes and started to cry. "Help!" he said. "Get me a toothpick to wipe my eye!"

"A *toothpick?*"

"No no no. Not a toothpick. An *ear* pick." Michael and I opened wide eyes at each other and tried not to laugh. "No no no. Wait. A *Q-tip!*" His triumph was brief.

"I don't really think you can wipe your eye with a Q-tip," I said.

"Okay," he sighed. "Then please just get me a washcloth."

And last week, Ben was showing me how Michael had fixed the hinge on our cookbook holder (never a dull moment around here!). "There," he pointed. "He fixed it with a, uh, a quewf? No no no. A piece of a *quewf.*" "What?" I said. "A *quewf.* No, wait wait, a *quewf.*" Every time he said it, he grimaced and shook his head. It was clearly not the word he wanted to be saying, but somewhere between the shape of the word in his mind and the sound of the word coming out of his mouth, some synapses seemed to be misfiring. "A quewf," he said, one last time, and shrugged. I looked at the hinge more closely—I could see a little piece of bamboo dowel poked into it. "A *skewer?*" I offered, and Ben said, "Yes! A *skewf!* A skewer."

Then last night he came to the dinner table with his little toy monkey (this is Monkey, not to be confused with the famous legless Dr. Stumpy). Monkey peered over the edge of the table at Ben's macaroni and cheese. "Monkey's Freud to be sitting in my lap!" Ben said happily. "Freud?" I asked. I'm so strange myself these days that I immediately pictured Monkey with a gray beard and glasses: *So tell me, Ben, about these dreams you've been having . . . are there always alligators in the toilet?* "Freud," Ben said. "No. *Freld.* Frulled. *Thrilled!* Monkey's *thrilled* to be sitting in my lap!" Phew.

But the misunderstanding can cut both ways. Or, at least,

Ben seems to suffer from bouts of a willful inability to hear. We were eating clementines the other day (or "Oh-my-darling clementines," as Ben calls them) and we hit an oddly seedy one. "Does this piece have a seed?" Ben asked, holding a segment out for me to inspect.

"Look." I showed him. "Hold it up to the light. See that little dark shadow? That's a seed in there."

"What?" Ben said and blinked.

"That dark part. That means there's a seed."

"What?" He stared at me blankly.

"I'm not going to say it again, Ben. I already explained it."

"What? I mean, *why?*"

"Because I don't want to keep saying the same thing over and over."

"Why?"

Because it makes me want to poke my own eyes out with a quewf.

This cotton-ear syndrome alternates with phases of incredible bionic hearing. Michael and I can no longer gossip, anywhere in the house, about anybody we know (this is, I realize, probably a good thing). "Who are you guys *talking* about?" Ben will yell from the living room while Michael and I are hunched together whispering at the kitchen table. "*Who* is so, so disappointed?" I can't even unwrap a hard candy surreptitiously in a different part of the house. "What are you doing, Mama?" Ben yells. "What's that sound and that fruity, fruity smell? Can I have one?" He's the Six Million Dollar Boy.

"I f Birdy's a girl," Ben is fond of saying, "then I'll be a big sister. But if she's a boy, I'll be her brother." Right now he's pretty sure that Birdy'll be a girl, and—knowing him and his massively intuitive small self—he's probably right. He thinks about the baby all the time these days. He touches my big belly and then, when Birdy kicks him, pulls his hand away like he's been scorched. Sometimes he even runs to the sink to *wash* it.

But mostly he's preoccupied with logistical stuff—like where Birdy's going to sleep, which is a fine question. Ben currently sleeps in our bedroom, in a little bed. Well, technically, it *was* a little bed, until Ben insisted that it be tall like our bed, so Michael built wooden stilts for it. Now the beds are the same height, and pushed together to create a gigantic Bed Island that barely leaves space enough to get up and get out of the room. But, this sleeping arrangement seems to be working for everyone, so I don't give it a whole lot of thought. Sometimes I suspect that *everybody* sleeps with their kids, and the only difference is the level of denial you're in. I'm of the school of thought that, if Ben's going to end up in our bed anyway, let's not devote an entire room of the house to his *not* sleeping in it. Maybe if we had a bigger house I'd feel different.

Ben has also been wondering about how the baby got into my "wooomh" in the first place. This line of curiosity I find slightly *awkward*. "Well," I say, "one morning while you were busy downstairs building a garage for your tractor, Daddy and I gave each other a big, big hug and . . ." No, I'm kidding of course. We're going with the old reliable agricultural metaphors—the whole planted-seed thing. "Remember how we watched those bean seeds sprout in a jar?" I ask him. "And how they grew into plants?" Ben nods, puzzled. He probably thinks that Birdy will be a spindly, neglected vine that twines itself up into the kitchen light fixture only to be, mysteriously, gone one morning when he wakes up.

But I'm grateful for the focus on facts and practicalities. Of course I want Ben to be excited about the baby, and he does seem to be—he holds up the tiny onesies and hats and can't *believe* they ever fit him, until I dig out the photo album and show him pictures. Ocular proof. "Look," I say. "See? There you are in the Paris hat. Here's you in the spaceman suit," and Ben nods in amazement. But it's totally up to him to feel how he feels—we don't want to act like the baby's an unambivalently good (or bad) thing for him. Penelope Leach puts it best—in her wonderful, crisp way—in *Your Baby and Child:* "Just for fun," she says, "imagine your husband coming home to tell you that he was proposing to take on a second wife as well as you and imagine him using the various phrases that are frequently used to break the news of a coming baby to a child:

"I like you so much I just can't wait to have another gorgeous wife.

"It'll be our wife. It'll belong to both of us and we'll both look after her together.

"I shall really need my reliable old wife to help me look after this new young one."

The polygamy metaphor seems so apt, since I feel exactly like we're cheating on Ben. We're still so completely in love with him—I wake in the morning with my heart pounding over it— that it feels bizarre to add a new baby to the mix so soon. It's like sneaking off during your honeymoon to sleep with the bellhop.

The three of us attended a sibling class at our local hospital—
one of those nouveau-mandatory components of having a second baby. I liked the emphasis on facts (babies sleep and nurse;
they don't eat solid food; they poop and cry and have oozing
belly button stumps) without all that psychic delving that you
don't want other people doing to your kids. I'm not, for instance,
crazy about those picture books that are like: *There will never
again be space for you on your mom's lap and you might as well kiss your
three squares good-bye, since everyone will likely be too busy painting all
your things pink to feed you.* I know it's a good thing to let kids ex-
press their negative feelings, I just don't want Ben to be hatching his escape plan before the baby even comes.

I liked how the kids were in the class. I liked them for
laughing so unabashedly over the idea of the babies pooping. I
liked this one four-year-old who interrupted a vague "your
mommy's big tummy" presentation with a precise question
about how the baby would know "when to break the amniotic
sac." I liked Ben, who, after holding his diapered baby doll for
about two seconds in his lap, stood up and unceremoniously
dumped it back into the bin. It was even giving *me* the creeps,
what with its wrinkled plastic skin and all.

At the end of class, when we went up to tour the birth center, Ben, the multitasker, said, "Hey, Mama—since we're already here, why don't you just go ahead and have the baby
now?" And then, just as we were leaving, we walked past a door
that was cracked open about a foot, and I got just a glimpse inside. I wasn't even sure what I was looking at for a second. "My
God," I said to Michael, "did you *see* that?" His eyes were shiny
and he nodded and took my hand. It was a woman—a pink expanse of skin and breasts—reaching out for her just-born baby.

A baby still slick and unswaddled. Michael had seen the same thing in that tiny wink of space. The very start of a new life. We trembled at the enormous beauty of it. No new wife, no bellhop after all, but a *baby* coming into the world. Wow.

If giving birth to a baby is somewhere in your possible future—but not yet a part of your past—why don't you just go ahead and skip this chapter. I promise you won't miss much. Ben's birth was a total piece of cake—it was so relaxing and straightforward, it was actually *boring*. Have a nice day!

I know you're still reading. But don't say I didn't warn you, because I, for one, hated to hear everyone's horror stories when I was pregnant. Sadists seemed to crawl out of the woodwork to share them with me. Once, at a friend's birthday party when I was eight and a half months pregnant, a strangely animated man—a person I didn't even *know*—thought to regale me with a profoundly gruesome C-section story. I seem to have repressed the details, but suffice it to say a serrated grapefruit spoon played a major role. It's all relative—compared to *that*, Ben's birth really was a piece of cake.

We've been reminiscing like mad about it now that Birdy's is impending. And also because we recently watched the video from Ben's birth. This is not your typical birth video. Come to think of it, there's probably no such thing as a typical birth video. But for us, the model is Ayanna's, the first daughter of our friends Andrew and Megan, at whose birth Michael and I were euphorically present. Andrew is Michael's best friend since high school, and our families are *extremely* close (with "extremely" italicized like that, it kind of seems like there's something a little *off* about the whole relationship, which there isn't, I swear). Anyways, Ayanna was born back when we all still lived in California—before we moved to Massachusetts and, later, convinced Andrew and Megan to move to Providence so that we wouldn't have to miss them too excruciatingly, and so we wouldn't miss the arrival of Carly, their second daughter. This was back when we were still young—you know, five years ago, before we all aged so precipitously after the babies came. We all refer to Ayanna as "our first baby."

Michael videotaped the whole birth splendidly, and it's the funniest, most moving few hours of film in the world. (Except for the embarrassing part where I seem to be moaning in sympathy with Megan, only I'm actually *louder* than her. Or the embarrassing part where I tell a nervously endless, pointless story about a trip to the florist gone awry—right after which Megan gets her epidural. Coincidence?) We all laugh a lot; the anesthesiologist rushes in at some point to—inexplicably—order a pizza from Megan's phone; Megan's epidural seems to take only on one side; Ayanna's head crowns like a purple cabbage; her glorious, gorgeous face appears; everyone bursts into tears; Megan eats a turkey sandwich while delivering the placenta. All of this is captured on film. We watch it every year on Ayanna's birthday, and it still makes us all cry.

Ben's birth video involves only a five-minute segment of labor, and some footage from after the birth. It's as much like Ayanna's birth video as *The Shining* is like an episode of *Mr. Rogers*. It could be called "Maybe You Should Consider an Epidural After All," and the drug companies could show it and they'd triple their sales. The labor part, if I can say this myself, is totally pathetic. It's about fifteen or twenty hours into it (Ben was born after twenty-four hours), and it shows me, pre-epidural, trying to get from my hospital bed to the bathroom, where someone has kindly filled the tub for me. You watch me hobble about three feet—like there are enormous boulders chained to my knees—and then I stop and am seized by a long and horrible series of contractions. It looks like I'm battling an invisible swarm of demons: I cry and moan and swat my arms around a little. Then I turn around and stagger back to bed. I never make it to the tub. That's the gist of it. There are notable details: how Michael asks me so gently to relax my shoulders, and you can see that I do; how, after the contraction ebbs a little, I turn my face to the camera and say, "Kill me"; how Sam is snacking guiltily on a Snickers bar and laughs when Megan points the camera at her.

Plus, there's the sound that I'm making. It's like one of those thirty-person choruses of Tibetan monks, all doing that eerie, low chanting in their throats. "Did you practice that before the birth?" a friend of ours once asked, and Michael and I laughed. It really had nothing to do with me, that sound, despite the fact that it appeared to be generated from somewhere inside my body. Labor does strange things to a person. *Back* labor does even stranger things. But that's all I'm going to say about back labor.

The thing I remember most vividly is the way a contraction would start, and I would get this image in my mind of something Michael and I had seen just the week before, when we'd been walking along the ocean at night: the moonlight had glittered white on the tips of all the little wavelets, and when a bigger swell started to form, you saw all the white rush together into an illuminated cresting wave of moonlight, and then it would crash, and the whole ocean would look black for a moment. That's what the contractions were like—like a gathering up of diffused pain into a giant, cresting wave of it. But it's not even that metaphor that I remember so vividly—although I do. It's the fact that during every single contraction I thought, "When I catch my breath again, I'll tell Michael what this is like." And then I never caught my breath—I never told him. Even now, that just makes me shudder.

So, needless to say, there was not a lot more filming of the labor. In fact, the video picks up again hours later—after the abrupted placenta, the precipitous drop of Ben's heart rate ("Oh my God!" our midwife cried. "Oh my God!"), and the emergency C-section. After the moment when I thought, "We're going to leave here without a baby in our arms."—an outcome that had seemed at once likely and impossible. On film, things are looking up. In fact, there's a full-blown party under way. Michael's still in his OR scrubs—so handsome and lit-up with joy that you almost have to look away—holding the little blanketed bundle that is our Ben; Megan and Andrew and Ayanna, who's two by then, are there, also Sam and Sarah, our midwife, and a handful of nurses. Everyone is tired and ecstatic, talking a hundred miles an hour about the birth, drinking champagne, and snacking copiously. At various points, people are laughing so hard that you can't hear what anybody's saying.

But wait, look closely—what's that in the background, behind the party? That unmoving thing wrapped tightly in bandages? Is it a corpse? A mummy? No, it's Catherine! Alone in her little postoperative bed, barfing quietly into a bowl. This is my favorite part of the video—it's so tragic, but also so completely hilarious. Is anyone keeping me company? No—nobody can bear to be away from the baby. Is the hospital staff attending to me? No—they're hanging out where the party is. I am, literally, all by myself, wrapped in bandages and throwing up. I have no memories of this, I promise you—I was so out of it for so long. I remember only that the nurses would swing by periodically to ask if I could wiggle my toes yet. I couldn't. They'd always look completely alarmed, but would say, "Oh, that's fine, fine. Perfectly normal." I spent most of the first night imagining what it would be like to be newly a mother *and* newly paralyzed, all at the same time.

But then, much later—everyone had gone home, and Michael was asleep on a cot beside me—I woke up and the anesthesia had finally worn off. It was dark and quiet, and someone brought Ben to me so that I could nurse him. Sure, later there would be the various postoperative humiliations, the copious sweating, the hunchbacked attempts at walking, the horrible sticking of the baby's heel like a first punishment. But when I looked into that serene little face, the world stopped and started, and I became, in an instant and forever, a mother.

There's something so incredibly humbling about a baby shower. Perhaps there are lots of women out there who unwrap gift after gift, nibbling home-baked lemon bars and feeling cradled in the tremendous blessing of community and friendship, and they think, "*Yeah,* I deserve this! In fact, this is the *least* they could do!" I don't seem to be one of them. At my baby shower last weekend, I wavered between the sublime pleasure of tremendous friendship and lavish attention, the kind words and hilarity of friends, and abject horror at the amount of effort that had gone into the lovely event: a table buckling under the weight of homemade treats, gifts so lovingly created or chosen that they made your heart ache. And me, having brought only my regular complaining self and hemorrhoids. Perhaps everyone had mistakenly thought that it was a shower for somebody else. There is picture after picture of me opening gifts, a gigantic smile practically cracking my face in half. I look a little like a glad zombie.

When I lay in bed that night, dreamily recounting the details to Michael, I was half asleep. "Where was *Ben* during our California baby shower?" I asked. "I can't picture him there." "Uh, Cath?" Michael said, and I laughed. Oh, right—the whole not-born-yet thing. It's so hard to imagine a time before he was in our lives. It seems so strange.

And now it's that after-the-baby-shower moment—the moment you can't imagine early in the pregnancy—when all that's left between you and the birth is a week or two of work (by "work" I mean, of course, zinging around the Internet doing Google searches like "C-section complications") and, maybe, packing a little satchel to take to the hospital. I'll be more conservative this time—fewer aromatherapy oils, no maxipads (they actually have supplies right there at the hospital!), more candy, and maybe a nice, bright shade of lip gloss. When Ben was born, Michael, in a clueless fit of optimism, had brought his *guitar* to the hospital—you know, in case we felt like *singing* during the birth: *Hang on, let me just finish this last twenty hours of uninterrupted back labor, and then maybe we can squeeze in a few rounds of Kumbaya.*

It seems so businesslike to be having a scheduled C-section. March third. I wrote it right into my day planner: "Meeting about September craft piece," "Dentist," "Birdy's birth." At least we don't know Birdy's sex, so we'll have something to tell people besides "The baby, whose sex and name you already know, was born on the date we told you it would be born on." For weeks before Ben's birth, I would think—and now this seems almost tragically wrong—"Maybe today will be the day!" I'd lie in bed, imagining the story we'd tell the child one day: "Well, we had eaten a delicious chickpea and potato curry for dinner and argued over a load of laundry, and we were just lying down to sleep when my water broke. . . ." Or "I had just devoured an entire cantaloupe and put in the last piece of Princess Di's tiara when I felt a strange cramping!" Instead we tell Ben that he hung on for dear life—that he would be there still, enormously three in my belly, if they hadn't gone in after him. "I would," he agrees.

With Birdy, we know. Technically, I suppose, the baby could come early—but I find this frankly hard to imagine. I also find it frankly hard to imagine why my OB practice, at every appointment, gives me the "Vaginal Birth Consent Form" to sign. Every time I have to say, "Uh, I'm having a C-section, which was actually *your* idea. You guys know I'm having a C-section, right? I mean, someone will be expecting me and everything?" It's kind of unsettling. One OB, in particular, always asks me if I want to try hypnotherapy as a labor strategy. "There are great local classes on it," she always says, absently, and then I remind her that I won't be going through labor. "Maybe the hypnotherapy would help you be less *afraid* of labor, so you could try it," she says with a blank smile, so I say,

"You're not *allowing* me to have a vaginal birth." She shrugs and says, "Suit yourself." It is all I can do not to cry with frustration.

I confess that I'm so happy this time not to be consumed with the minutiae of the birth, like whether or not to get drugs. With your first baby, you think this is actually an important decision. Only later do you realize that a) You understand nothing about labor until it is happening to you, and b) The birth is just the first tiny town—barely a black dot—on the enormous, complicated road map that is the rest of your life as a parent. Mistaking the birth for the main event is like thinking that the floral arrangements at your wedding will somehow determine the quality of your marriage. You don't realize that the hard part—the *real* part—comes later.

I was talking with a friend recently about childbirth, about the drug debates. "Why are the women who don't want drugs during childbirth the same people who used to do a *lot* of drugs at parties?" she said, and shook her head in wonder. "I mean, it's a *party!* It's fun! If it's not fun, go home! I'm not judging anyone here, but a long day of inevitable, excruciating physical pain—this seems like the more appropriate time to numb yourself out a little, no?" Of course I think it's great to have the kind of birth you want. And women should never be pressured one way or another about these decisions—I, for one, had intended to give birth to Ben with no drugs. But the second time around, you understand that the birth is not a final destination. The *babe's* the thing.

Although, oddly, I am still picturing Ben at the center of this next birth. I don't imagine that I'll give birth to him again (I wish!), but he's who I see when I think about the hospital: I see Ben rushing through the door to kiss me; I see myself in the crank-up bed with Ben lying in the crook of my arm. The baby is just a blurred, blanketed spot in the picture—off to the side somewhere. We got Ben a Play-Doh Fuzzy Pumper to give him when he first visits us in the hospital. If I can't exactly imagine Birdy, I can at least picture Ben squeezing out long coils and ropes of colored clay. And that's exciting enough.

S omebody took Ben in the night and left behind a miser-able wretch this morning. At first he seemed okay. He crawled under the covers next to me and asked me in whispers about my sleep, my dreams. (It's crushing to realize that no-body again—in his whole life—will love your child's morning breath the way you do. Or, really, *at all*.) But then he noticed the clementine boxes that we had—Egads, no!—painted in bright colors the night before and set out on top of the dresser. We're planning to fill them with all the tiny paraphernalia that seem to replicate themselves overnight around a new baby: nursing pads and diapers, hats and socks.

Ben scowled. "I don't like those boxes up there," he said, pointing with his two thumbs the way he does. Then he noticed the three gorgeous little watercolors of birds that our friend Ann had painted for Birdy. ("First I painted them big, to fill the frames," she told us. "But they just looked so *menacing*, with their expressionless faces. I made them really tiny so they wouldn't scare the baby.") We'd hung the paintings by the rock-ing chair. "Or those," Ben added, and pointed accusing thumbs at them.

"Really?" I asked, brimming with Pollyanna good cheer. "You don't? Daddy and I *really* like them. They're so pretty and colorful."

"I'm taking them down," he grumped, and hopped up to drag a chair over to the paintings.

"No, hon," I said, "I'm sorry if you don't like them. I'm sorry if there's too much new stuff going on in here. But we're going to leave them where they are."

And with that, Ben burst into a raggedy fit of sobbing and fell, inconsolable, onto the bed. Michael and I raised questioning eyebrows at each other. We thought: Poor guy, what with all this new baby stuff. But I was looking closely at Ben—just starting to notice his pale little face, his puffy little eyes, just remembering how he'd snored all night long, and then—presto—he took a big breath in and coughed out one of those terrible barky seal coughs. *Aha!*

I can't explain why it seems to be taking us years to establish the connection between the sudden onset of weeping despair and *illness,* but we never get it right away. And we shouldn't have been surprised. We'd just been to our local Family Dance—a bohemian afternoon of do-si-doing, where one of our midwives laughed to see me so big and close to my due date and dancing around like a jubilant watermelon on legs—and I can't remember the last time we went to the dance and didn't get sick afterward.

Clearly, it's not a good way to stay healthy: it's the dead of winter and you're holding hands with strangers, dancing with them and their germy kids, and you might as well be peeling a wad of old chewing gum off the floor of the pneumonia ward, popping it in your mouth with a shrug. Every little while I would surreptitiously rub Ben's hands with antibacterial gel, which makes me feel like a huge jerk—germ phobia is, I'm thinking, *so* not in the spirit of Family Dance.

But believe me, my current anxiety about contamination is a pale shadow of its former robust presence. There's an origin story: when Ben was two months old he had a lousy bronchial infection. Sam had flown up to Vancouver and then returned home to us with a terrible, hacking cough. "Oh, don't worry," she'd said, and reached to take the baby from me—they'd missed each other horribly. "I'm not contagious anymore." Now, it's not like I mistook Sam, in that moment, for an infectious disease specialist. But, for some reason, I imagined she knew what she was talking about. Why are we lay people so quick to offer our own theories about contagion? These theories usually involve a bedrock certainty that the person uttering them—or somebody in their immediate family—could not possibly communicate an illness. "Oh, yeah, she was up all night, vomiting into a dishpan. Do you guys want to come over and play? I'm *sure* she's not contagious anymore."

Suffice it to say that Ben woke up coughing. I mean really coughing and coughing. Coughing until he would gag and barf, with his smiling little baby head bobbing around cheerfully the whole time. In my mind, I relived, over and over, the moment when I had handed him to Sam, like some terrible slo-mo scene from a soap opera: "I'm not contagious, contagious, contagious. . . ." I was paralyzed with fear. I called my brother, who actually *is* an infectious disease specialist—both he and his wife work for the Centers for Disease Control in Atlanta. I asked him tearfully if it was possible for a baby to choke to death from coughing. "I've never *heard* of that happening," he answered carefully, and I spent days trying to interpret this. "Is he trying not to scare me with the truth—that thousands of kids a day, all around the world, choke to death on their own phlegm?" I asked Michael. "Or is he just trying not to treat me like a paranoid freak?" Michael didn't know. I accidentally memorized the three pages on coughing in our baby book, including the black-bordered sidebar with some scary icon—A bomb? A baby with X's for eyes?—called something like "Dangerous Coughing." I read them so many times that the book still falls open there automatically.

At our pediatrician's office, we were no longer permitted to wait in the little pristine newborn waiting room. This was a terrible rite of passage. We were sent to the big germ-infested Lord of the Flies waiting room where everyone's sick kid darts over to cough into your baby's car seat and stick their fingers in his mouth. In truth, I had a little crush on our pediatrician (nothing, in my whole life, has ever made me feel more like a housewife than getting dressed up to take my kid to the doctor), and he treated us with great compassion. "I see," he'd say, looking at Ben's chart, "that you called twice yesterday evening and then twice again in the night. Let's take a look." Ben would smile and cough and bob his head around, and the doctor would shake his head. "It's viral," he'd say. "We can't treat it. Let's hope it clears up before going too deep into his lungs." I'd race home to steam the baby in our bathroom and reread the three pages on coughing.

Eventually Ben got better, but I suffered something like a low-grade post-coughing stress disorder. I was petrified that Ben would get sick again. I became so afraid of germs that I had to fight my urge to treat every friend and houseguest like they had escaped from our local leper colony. I called my brother again, in tears, and he sighed. "You can't live like that," he said to me, not unkindly. "I mean, for all you know, germs are coming in on the *mail*." This advice backfired. For days, I eyed our mail slot warily and prodded its offerings with a pair of long tongs.

I'm better now, I swear. I'm working on that really hard-to-grasp lesson, and it's one I hope I remember through Birdy's first rounds of illness: kids get sick and then, amazingly, God willing, they get better. But still all day today, and tonight too, after we put Ben's croupy little seal self to bed, I hummed the lines that the folksinger Greg Brown wrote for one of his daughters (I heard Michael humming them too). *Yes, and I know—it's just a cold or it's just the flu, but I say a little prayer, I say a little prayer for you.* "I hope you get better, get better soon, please do."

It's the last week before Birdy's birth. I'd imagined writing something kind of flowery and romantic about these exciting, expectant days: about the bittersweet tenderness I feel around Ben; about this unknown baby we're bound to be nuts over. But—drum roll please—Ben has the barfing flu. I had just said—aloud to Michael, like a person *begging* for it—that, wow, the flu season's almost over, and haven't we been so lucky to get away with just a few colds, and wasn't it *terrible* that so many of our friends had had the barfing flu sweep through their homes like a tornado, puking up all the towels and leaving half-drunk cups of ginger ale in its wake?

What am I, *crazy?* If I were in a Greek play, I'd be the figure of Hubris—that terrible I'm-invincible kind of pride—and you'd shake your head from the very start, and think, "The gods are gonna smite that one for sure." Consider me smote.

The night started normally enough. Ben's had a cold, so he and I have developed a sweet bedtime ritual, involving my wiping his face with a warm cotton ball, putting lotion under his nose, and then rubbing Tiger Balm into his chest. He's like a pussycat—he totally loves it. He calls it "decorating." "I still have a cold!" he yells from bed. "Time to decorate me!" Anyways, he fell asleep normal as can be and woke up a few hours later, a veritable geyser of barf. Michael was at my office, doing a little late-night grant writing. I was alone with Ben. With more vomit than you could shake a stick at.

Isn't it amazing the way you can show up for your kids? I mean, let me tell you, my impulse around barfing people is usually to run in the other direction screaming (I don't say this proudly). But there was Ben, throwing up all over me and himself and everybody's bed, and I was grossed out, sure, but mostly just sad for him that he was so scared and miserable. At some point, after I had cleaned Ben up, wrapped him in a towel, and put him back to sleep on the couch, I returned to the bedroom to face The Horror—vomit everywhere, like someone had sprayed it into the room with a hose—and that goody-goody saying floated into my head in this really deadpan way: "If life gives you lemons, make lemonade!" It actually made me laugh out loud.

Ben seemed totally fine by morning ("Did I barf and barf all over the place?" he asked, his eyes wide with the drama of it all). But now, Michael and I are trying not to panic about the fact *we're* likely to get this thing, oh, the day before Birdy's scheduled C-section. Oy vey. I'm putting off calling my OB practice to ask about it, because I just know they're going to scare me and also make me feel somehow like I've done this really reckless thing, having a three-year-old get sick right before the birth. Ack.

When I went in for my last checkup, the OB I know least well there examined me, and then rattled off a list of surgical risks from a form I was supposed to sign. The form said, in essence, "I, the undersigned, understand that I am likely to die during the surgery, and I feel fine about it." X_____. Let me just say that this was not a shining moment of grace and reassurance. The OB reminded me, in fact, of one of those teenage waitresses who looks out the window, chewing gum, while she lists the salad dressing choices. "Ranch. Parmesan peppercorn. Blood clots. Hemorrhage. Infection. Acute infection. Creamy garlic." Consider my confidence un-boosted.

There was also the sad fact of my peeing my urine specimen into a cup that—I'm not even kidding—had a *hole* in it! The pee dribbled out onto my jeans and then ran onto the floor, and I had to sit around the waiting room, reading *People* magazine until another specimen had accumulated (luckily, this took all of one minute). Michael laughed when I told him about it. "Maybe they get their specimen cups from a gag medical supply outlet," he offered.

Later, when Michael, Ben, and I stopped by the drugstore to pick up a few things, we ran into an older colleague of mine from work. She peeked right into my basket, and I consciously straightened my back a little so that I would look tall and proud. Here's what she saw: mattress-sized sanitary pads ("Are

those diapers for *Birdy?*" Ben asked, puzzled), glycerin suppositories, stool softeners, Preparation H, and Brach's Peacock Egg
jelly beans. She was heading for check-out with just a small
bottle of Tylenol, and it suddenly seemed to me like an icon of
normalcy. Tylenol! I was a little jealous.

But *still* I'm excited about this Birdy flying so quickly towards us now. I'm prepared for the night sweats, the outrageous
pooping, the constant yelling out for large glasses of ice water.
But I'm sure I'll be blown away, all over again, by the enormity
of a new life joining ours. I am thinking lucky thoughts.

Tomorrow morning we will have a new baby. In just
about twelve hours, actually. Disturbingly, the whole thing
still seems somewhat hypothetical to me. "If we have another
kid . . ." I catch myself saying to Michael, and he looks at me—
at the Mount Vesuvius of my midsection—and laughs. We're
spending the night at our friends Bill and Jennifer's house,
partly because they live a stone's throw from the hospital and
partly because their daughter, Sophia, is one of Ben's best
friends. They'll look after Ben in the morning after we leave.
Also, it's just nice to be with friends—with their warmth and
distracting upbeatness, instead of darting around nervously at
home, making last-minute notes on my will. I'll say this quickly,
but not linger over it: I'm a little afraid that I'll die on the operating table.

Anyways.

Ben has never woken up without us before, so we tried
practicing tonight, and it went about as well as your average

hydrogen-filled blimp. Which is to say: not so well. The drill was this: wake up in bed, alone, and then trot into Bill and Jennifer's room and climb into bed with them. It was a sound plan, except for the fact of their sweet German shepherd, Lucca, who took her role to be that of a barking cheerleader. Ben would pretend to wake up, then he'd toddle into the bedroom, with us coaching him, "That's right. Now up and into the bed," but then Lucca's huge barking head would be peering down over the side of the mattress and Ben would go rigid with terror. "Come on," we were yelling into the din of animal sound, "up into bed, just like at home!" Yes, just like at home, in our den of howling wolves. Eventually Ben fell against me and burst into raggedy tears. I tried not to take it as a bad sign—you know, about the whole baby thing. The new plan is that we'll wake Jennifer at the ungodly hour of our departure, and she will climb into bed with him. I will send the Vatican a little telegram about why it is that Jews should be canonized, along with a picture of Jennifer and, maybe, some nice brisket. In the meantime, we're grateful beyond words to have such wonderful friends.

But, my God, how do you manage this kind of thing if you have *two* kids? If. There I go again. We have a Lennart Nilsson kids' book called *How Was I Born?* about expecting a new baby, and the narrator is this amazing Swedish preschooler. She's so gracious and forthright—worrying that the baby is lonely in her mom's tummy, plucking apples from her own backyard tree and crunching right into them—that you actually want to move to Sweden so your kids can grow up with her. Her wide-open heart seems to close only once, and only the tiniest bit, and it's when her mother is leaving for the hospital. " 'Let's forget about the baby,' " the little girl says to her mother. " 'Two children are enough.' But Mom said we couldn't forget about the baby, because now it didn't have room in her tummy anymore. It wanted to be born now, no matter what." I feel a little bit like the girl: let's just forget about the baby. One child is enough. You'd think the fact that we even know when it's happening—and that, clearly, there's no more room in my tummy—would help hammer home the "no matter what" part. But no.

It's just oddly unsettling to be having a scheduled birth. There's something so efficient and detached about it, like you've made your final payment on a layaway bedroom set, and now it's just a matter of driving to the furniture store to pick it up. I hope that Birdy's ready to be born.

I had to go to the hospital this afternoon, to get blood work done in case I need a transfusion during the surgery, and I'd double-checked with my practice a million times about the blood work. "So the lab is really open on Sunday?" I kept asking. "That seems so strange to me." They'd been irritated. "Yes, of course it's open or we wouldn't *send* you there, now, would we?" Do I even need to tell the punch line to this story? When I staggered into the hospital like a gigantic down parka come to life, the lab was dark and hung with a CLOSED sign. I panicked. But then I saw that there was a little phone receiver there, and a plaque that read "Pick up receiver for help." It was totally *Alice in Wonderland*. I picked up the receiver and said, tentatively, "Help." The voice on the other end said, "What?" and then "The lab is *closed*. It's *Sunday*." I burst into tears, of course, and then explained in great choking, wet sobs how I really, really needed to have this baby *tomorrow*, how I thought that if I didn't have it soon, I would lose my nerve and never have it at all. They sent a lab tech over from the ER to deal with me. (A phlebotomist. There's no way around that word, is there? The way it sounds like "phlegm" and "bottom." Maybe, though, you never noticed that.)

Of course, once I'd started, I couldn't stop crying. "I'm sorry," I kept saying—crying and laughing, snot everywhere. "Thank you." The lab guy took my blood with emphatic surliness, but then looked at my chart and laughed. Real, unbridled glee. "Woops!" he said, and picked up the phone. "Yeah," he said into it, "the numbers on her chart are reversed. I don't think they'll be finding her blood too quickly with *the wrong identification number!*" Ha ha ha. Ah, life and death! Who can even keep them straight?! Like, *Oh, wait, you ordered the McFish and this is a Sausage Eggwich!* Ho ho ho.

A child has just died during surgery because of this exact mix-up. It was all over the news two weeks ago. When I got home, I called Megan in a panic, and she made me laugh. "During the surgery, mention your blood type as often as you can. But casually, like, 'You know what I love about being A-positive? It just has such an upbeat feeling! A-*positive!* The big fat A-plus-aroo! Some people have *other* blood types. But not me! It's just A-positive or nothing!'" I love Megan.

Bad signs are just in the attitude of the beholder, I'm sure. I try not to be too superstitious. But I can't help worrying that we'll get to the hospital in the morning and they'll shake their heads, "What? Who *are* you? Nope, nothing on our schedule." In truth, I can't help worrying about way worse things than that. The week before Ben was born, we hit a deer on the highway in California. A fawn. It happened so quickly we weren't even sure at first: a tawny peripheral blur, then a big, dull thud that rocked the car. "Was that a *deer?*" I asked. "A *fawn?*" "I don't think I hit it," Michael said, absurdly, and I said, "Maybe not," and craned my head back to see the mother deer, at the side of the highway, scanning the eight whizzing lanes of traffic for her baby. I was devastated. I worried that it was a bad omen or that we'd be punished in some way for our carelessness. And when Ben was born healthy, I thought of that mother deer and cried and sent a little thanks her way, in case she'd given up her own baby so that ours could be born. Who knows?

Now that baby's an enormous three-year-old, and he's about to be a big brother. And I'm going to be a mama to somebody brand-new. If I prayed, I would pray now, of course. Instead I send my hope up into the stars like an invisible paper airplane. Like a carrier pigeon with a note tied to its leg. And the note just says, "Please." And "Thank you."

O**ur Birdy is here**! A fuzzy-headed little baby girl named Abigail Shirley Millner Newman. Born on March third at eight and a quarter pounds. She has stubby eyelashes and a fat bottom lip and is, all in all, a keeper. Let me say first off that I was prepared to like her *okay*, you know, to tolerate her and put on an excited face for Michael and everything. But—and you'll think "Of course" and shake your head at me—I'm crazy about her! Who knew?

She is a gloriously healthy, obscenely gorgeous baby. She looks only *the tiniest bit* like Walter Matthau.

The birth was great. We arrived at the hospital before

dawn, under the coldest, starriest black sky you can imagine. I was nervous, but we were greeted by a warm and reassuring delivery nurse, Pat. Probably due to a combination of nerves and exhaustion on my part, along with Pat's slight strangeness, I kept not understanding what she was saying. After I'd gotten undressed and peed, for instance, Pat held up a metal bowl. "Hoist up your johnny," she said. "I'm just going to have you crap a little." She left the room, and I looked at the bowl. "So I'm just supposed to poop in there?" I whispered to Michael. "What?" he said. "I'm supposed to 'crap a little'?" I asked him, and he laughed. "No, hon. She's going to *prep* you a little. Look." He tipped the bowl to show me the razors and antiseptic inside. "Lucky for you that I'm here. Lucky for *Pat.*"

So, okay, that was me. But then, while she was shaving me, Pat said, inexplicably, "Ah, under these bright lights they all stand up like soldiers!" I tried not to catch Michael's eye. "What did you hear her say?" I asked him when we were alone again, and he repeated the line word for word. "But what do you think she meant? My *pubic hairs?*" We giggled and then we were too nervous to pull ourselves together, and we laughed and laughed until we cried, like the kind of kids who get kicked out of class after learning that the French word for shower is *douche.* Us, with our new baby on its way into the world. Total losers.

The anesthesiologist arrived and sobered me right up by jamming a huge needle into my spine. But then he was called away to do an epidural, and we were stuck waiting in the OR— prepped and ready to go—for over an hour. I felt like the hostess of a dinner party that had gone horribly awry—all the doctors and nurses standing around making bored small talk ("Did you see that new Meryl Streep movie?" "No, not yet. Did you?" "No. But I want to."), without so much as a dish of cashews or a glass of Chianti as the minutes ticked by.

To kill time, I guess, they put the catheter in—and then they put it in again. The first time it had gone into the *wrong hole!* "You have two little openings down there," the nurse apologized. "I put the catheter in the one that wasn't your ure-thra." Uh, right. We lay people call that the *vagina.* I felt like I was being prepped by a fifteen-year-old boy—like next they were going to be fumbling around, trying to unhook my bra. It had all the makings of a good dirty joke, but I burst into tears instead.

Finally, though, the party got rolling, what with the scalpels flashing around and "You're going to feel a lot of tugging" (in-deed!) and Michael, the king of all comforters, squeezing my hand. I fell a little bit in love with the anesthesiologist, who kept leaning over me—so close that his beard tickled my face—to announce, "It's going just great!" This really took the edge off my anxiety. The anxiety that came to a rousing crescendo after the surgeon had poked me to ask, "Can you still feel this?" and I had said, "Yes." "Yeah, well, that's okay," she said. "We're just going to go ahead and get started." "Maybe then don't ask," I had whispered to Michael, before starting to cry again.

But I did not cry so much that they had to postpone the surgery (this had been my fear). After what felt like only a few vague and mysterious minutes of clanking instruments, surgical muttering, and a dull, creepily remote kind of pain, there was the sweet and sudden sound of a baby—a baby yelling about all the dry air and gravity. Birdy! I cried and cried and asked the pediatrician about a thousand times if she was okay. "She's perfect!" she said, happily and then with increasing irritation. "Really, she's fine." "They think I'll freak out if they tell me," I whispered to Michael, "and they're right—I will. But will you try to find out which things are wrong with her?" Michael just patted my hand—his mental patient of a partner—then reached up for our bundled, beautiful baby.

The cleaving of one body into two whole lives—this is the greatest wonder of the world. Even if you've done it before, you look at the baby, slippery and howling, and your heart drops in awe. Then it flaps around in your chest like a trapped bird. "Is she really a girl?" I asked. "Is she really okay?" I think I worried that they'd cut me open and find only a pile of crumbling old photographs, maybe a jelly jar or two of pennies. But a baby! This baby, here.

After they'd sewn me up, performed the final and unsettling "instrument count" to make sure my abdominal cavity hadn't filched one of their scalpels, and shown me a little slice of heaven in the form of a Demerol shot to the quadriceps, I got to nurse her. Sure, later I'd be lying about having passed gas just to secure a measly packet of saltines. Later there would be the bottomless tar pit of meconium. There would be lots of crying—mine and Birdy's both. There would be the moment when Michael went to rewind the first roll of film, realized that the camera was empty, and, in a grandly understated gesture, slapped his own forehead. But I wasn't prepared for that first moment of nursing her—this grunty little baby animal, with a face so much like her brother's, but so entirely her own, too. Love at first sight, but with a big jolt of nostalgia thrown in for good measure.

A few years ago, there was a poem in *The New Yorker*, "We Walked Out of the Hospital" by Jessica Greenbaum, and I remember thinking that it so beautifully captured what she described as the "time of timelessness" of bringing home a newborn: "My husband bought fifteen containers of Middle Eastern food / then we holed up—the house / a flea market of disorganization, the phone / ringing even in dreams." I can see, already, that it's not going to be like that with Birdy—there's not going to be that wonderful and terrible and *total* immersion in a strange new world. There will be no time of timelessness.

I can see this because even in the post-op room, nursing Birdy for the first time in our lives, Demerol and Pitocin staging their little showdown in my uterus, I was thinking about Ben. I had become a mother of two—a person divided—just like that. Michael called Bill and Jennifer to hear that Ben was cheerful but seemed droopy, a little under the weather. "Crap," I said to Michael, the blood pressure cuff beeping, nurses bustling around the bed, Birdy staring up at me with her new, new face. "I hope he's okay."

Two older nurses gave me a sponge bath—warm washcloths and talcum powder, so tender and intimate I almost cried—while I called our pediatrician and scheduled an afternoon appointment for Ben. Michael left then to pick him up and bring him by the hospital, on the way to the doctor's. Even through the blur of drugs, I could discern that maybe this wasn't such a good idea—the introduction of the sick child to the newborn—but common sense kept slipping in and out of focus. Besides, the older child *has to* visit right away: it's in all the "Your New Baby" picture books. And I was missing Ben so much—his familiar little self—that I couldn't imagine waiting.

I heard him before I saw him—heard his squeaky, excited voice ("Is this such a long, long hallway?") and his clomping snow boots—and I scrambled to get the baby into her little crib, the way you might, say, hide a bong in the closet, and shoo the smoke out with your hand. *Baby? There's no baby.*

And there he was, my little Ben, big, suddenly, as an oak tree. We were shy with each other—both of us smiling too much and not really making eye contact, neither of us looking at the baby. "Is this right?" I was wondering, like the interaction was a multiple-choice geology final. "Is this how it's supposed to go?" I concentrated on clearing my head so that I wouldn't sound like somebody's slurring drunk relative at a party. "Whooza big, big boy? Eh? *Eh!*" I'm not sure if Ben noticed. "Hey," he said, "what's that drip, drip, dripping into your arm, Mama? What's in that yellow bag coming out of your leg?" Ben sat down with Michael to draw pictures—"This yellow crayon is for the bag of pee, okay, Mama?"—and he told me a long story about Lucca stealing his hot dog, while I surreptitiously nursed the baby.

I think, looking back, that we may have erred on the side of ignoring Birdy. I suspect we were unconsciously following the guidance of *The New Natural Cat Care* book on the bringing home of a new kitten: act like you don't even notice the kitten, and, if this becomes impossible, act like it's somebody *else's* kitten, whom you are kind enough to watch, dispassionately, until they return. Bringing a new tabby home was our only point of reference for this whole thing. I guess we didn't want Ben, you know, hissing at the baby, clawing her eyes out while he scrambled to get at her 9 Lives giblet dinner. Instead, at some point, he wandered over to me, looked at Birdy, and said, simply, "Isn't she adorable?" "She is," I said, and he smiled and went back to his drawing. Thank God we have these kids around. *Somebody* has to act normal.

But when he clambered up to kiss me good-bye, I saw, as if for the first time, how ghostly pale Ben was. His breath smelled terrible. And so I was not so surprised when Michael called me from home with the grim report that Ben had strep throat. He had barfed twice at the doctor's office: once during the throat swab (poor Ben!) and once right into the hood of Michael's jacket (poor Michael!). Now he was asleep, antibiotics already gathering in his bloodstream to plan their microscopic ambushes. The doctor thought it was unlikely that the baby would get a strep infection, and I tried not to panic.

I stretched my toes, took another sip of cranberry juice, and looked at Birdy's sleeping pink face, her whole body nestled into the crook of my elbow. "I feel so guilty," I said to Michael on the phone. "I feel like I'm on a spa vacation—like I've run off with this gorgeous littlekins to laze around at a resort—while you're just at home getting barfed on and squirting pink medicine down Ben's throat and mopping up barf." Michael laughed. "I rented a movie," he said. "Ben's asleep. We're fine. We miss you, but everything is totally fine." This may be the Vicodin talking here, but perhaps everything really is fine.

Mostly I'm consumed with my newly polished maternal impulses, of course. But I admit that a less profound thought or two creeps in periodically. Like about how I still look eight months pregnant. I think that I remembered looking, maybe, four months pregnant after Ben's birth. But now it's definitely more like eight. Or nine. People visit us, and I see their curious eyes dart over my belly before coming to rest on the baby. I was so aware of this with Ben—of the nervous glancing at my enormous postpartum bulge—that I actually go to great and excessive lengths to *avoid* looking at anyone's middle when I visit them in the hospital. It's probably way more awkward and conspicuous that way—how I get a visual lock on their eyes, their face, the baby—than if I would just go ahead and peek to see how pregnant they still look.

Part of the hugeness of my belly is, well, how shall I put this? Gas. It's treacherous, this post-op combo of gas and constipation. I feel like a corked bottle of champagne. But not in the celebratory sense.

The hospital, in a fit of sick humor, has mandated a scatological catch-22: you're starving to death, but you can't eat anything until you "pass wind." But then the wind *can't* pass because you're so constipated; it's like somebody has poured cement into your bunghole while you were sleeping. But you can't poop because you've been instructed, on account of all your stitches, "not to bear down" when you pass a bowel movement. Let me tell you: I am more likely to join the IceCapades in the next week than I am to poop without bearing down. Luckily,

Michael has smuggled me in some glycerin suppositories, and I seem to be on some kind of a waiting list for a stool softener here. ("Is there a *shortage?*" I asked the nurse politely, since I hadn't gotten the one I requested first thing this morning, and she said only, inexplicably, "We'll see.") Hopefully things will get moving again soon.

I remember when I was in the hospital with Ben—this fancy Santa Cruz birth center that was like a hotel, with 24-hour room service—and I called down to the chef to order up a grilled cheese sandwich. "Catherine?" he said. "Catherine Newman in Room 115? No can do on the sandwich. It says here that you haven't passed gas yet." I am not a modest person, but right then and there, whatever hostage of pride I had left, hiding in a corner of my psyche, darted out and into the gunfire.

Already I have begged for—and gotten—an illicit packet of saltines, which tasted so delicious that I shook out the last salty crumbs onto my tongue. Meanwhile, I'm on the hospital's "liquid diet," which means a thrice-daily smorgasbord of Jell-O, Tang, and—mysteriously—black coffee. Black coffee! Could there *be* a less nutritious thing to feed a new mother? They might as well give you a Dr. Pepper Slurpee and a pack of Lucky Strikes. Not that I don't *drink* the coffee, mind you. But: to be offered a tray of multicolored liquids when you're very hungry? It's almost worse than nothing—like I had crawled for weeks towards an oasis, dying of thirst, and somebody handed me some biscotti.

As soon as I can eat for real, I'm lugging my bloated excuse for a body to the fridge down the hall, where there's a bag with my name on it. Our friend Molly has visited, and she brought me the most perfect treats in the world: a box of sushi, three fragrant, ripe pears, and some fancy kind of tropical juice that's thick as a shake. Judy and Liz have come and gone, leaving bags of sour fruity candy and a box of dark and boozy truffles in their wake. My friend Alix brought a smoothie on her way to work. And Emily has promised to sneak by later tonight with an entire sleeve of saltines. Gas fascists be damned.

There are flowers everywhere, too—tulips and grape hyacinths and a huge bouquet of freesias and roses. I feel like I'm floating down a river of friendship with this blessed, beautiful little girl right here with me, along for the ride in the crook of my elbow. In the world outside it is snowing and snowing, and friends arrive with pink cheeks, their eyelashes wet with melting flakes. They're like ambassadors from the normal world.

I love this part: the baby so peaceful in somebody's arms, friends coming by to sit and talk with us, to praise her soft little self, folded up in her blanket like a bean burrito. It's even nicer this time, too, because I can nurse her without thinking too much about it. It doesn't take eleven different hands to get her onto the boob, like it did with Ben, when I'd be nodding and trying to converse casually, but really the whole time I'd be sticking my finger into his mouth and popping him off the nipple so that I could try again to latch him on properly. I'd be cramming my breast between his lips the way you might shove a meatball hero into the mouth of a college student, if you were in a fraternity and hazing him.

Now I feel so relaxed about nursing, and—a guilty admission—it's a bonus pleasure to sit around gabbing, without the ruckus of Ben! I'm *finishing* more conversations than I have in years, which is a welcome break from that distracted thing you do with other parents when the kids are around—where, by the end of an evening, you could pick up all the half-finished conversations like an armful of loose wires: *Where were these supposed to attach?*

And then everybody leaves, and, aside from the nurses coming by to ask after our bowels—"The baby had another meconium poop. Nothing on my end yet."—it's just me and Birdy. Here are my current favorite things: her baby-seashell fingernails, her swollen bottom lip, and the dark swirl of hair on the crown of her head, just like her brother's. I also like the way she yawns: the way her dainty little rosebud mouth morphs into a gaping wet cave, with an emphatic little *khrunn* sound. Really, I like everything about her.

I feel guilty about staying in the hospital for so long. It's so easy here. I have nothing to do but nurse this nice baby and practice my sweaty impressions of a constipated Quasimodo lurching to the bathroom.

The nurses want me to walk, and so I try to walk. Partly it's because I believe that walking will, as they say, "get everything moving" again, but partly I just want to be a good kid—the easy, hard-working patient who does the right things and doesn't complain or make trouble. I seek praise the way our cat used to chase the sun, single-mindedly following the dwindling bright patches around our hardwood floors. I mean, I even flush with pride when the dental hygienist tells me I'm doing a good job keeping my mouth open ("Am I?" I always fish, coyly), so you can imagine how delighted I am when the nurses call me a trooper for taking so little pain medication. "I just really don't want to become a drug addict," I tell them, truthfully.

But I also have bravado in excess of my actual strength or pain tolerance, and so one of our walking exercises ends with me wobbling around like a Weeble before fainting into the nurse's lap and knocking her to the bathroom floor. "Use your quadriceps!" she'd admonished, but I was seized with a crazy case of what can only be described as the Shaky Legs. Apparently that Demerol shot hit a blood vessel, and now on my thigh there's a spreading eggplant-colored bruise that's the size of an eggplant. I can't bear any weight on that leg. Plus there's the terrible bloating that makes me feel like my body will burst apart at the seams if I straighten my spine. "Tell me I'm still your best patient," I said to the nurse, lying on top of her in the bathroom, and she smiled and patted me. "You're still my best patient."

These are the daytime nurses, mind you. At night—and I use the term "night" loosely here, since all the light and the bustling around and getting shaken awake make you feel like maybe you're a wino who's fallen asleep at the bus depot— the nurses hate me. They would very much like me to drop Birdy off at the nursery for an eight-hour approximation of nighttime, and I very much won't. I've become completely belligerent about it, but in this maddeningly passive way. "I'll ring you when she's done nursing," I say, after they try to ratchet her out of my arms. But when they return for her unbidden, some number of hours later, lo and behold: she's nursing again! I do my best impersonation of the Madonna shrugging. "I guess I'll just let you know when she's done nursing." Which, luckily, is *never*.

What's their angle here? Is it a liability for the hospital to let her sleep with me? Do I seem too dopey to care for her? Do they just want to tickle her feet all night and stare into her lovely face? I'm not sure. I can't imagine they're motivated by a concern for *my* well-being, since they don't seem shy to wake me at three AM to have me, say, check off my breakfast choices from the liquid menu. ("Check three!" the menu teases, before listing only: "Orange drink. Gelatin. Coffee.") They also harbor an especial fondness for weighing Birdy in the deep of the night. "Is there any way we could weigh her in the morning?" I ask, and they say, "No, there's no way," before stripping off her diaper and whisking her away. Sometimes she leaves bareheaded, and returns with her knit hat back on. It always feels like an accusation.

But last night, after one of these perverse weighing episodes, they brought Birdy back, checked her little ankle bracelet, and then went to check mine—the routine Security Matching Game. But where once had been a loop of identifying plastic was now just a pale expanse of wrist. The bracelet was missing. I had my arms out for the baby, but the nurse holding her took a step backward. "Where's your bracelet?"

"I guess it fell off," I said. Birdy started to cry. "Do you mind giving me the baby while we figure this out?"

"Well, I *can't* give you the baby," she said, and took another step back.

Birdy was really crying, and something happened to me that was like being injected with the estrogen of a mother alligator. Whatever it was, it coursed through my blood and made me feel like a vein was going to pop out of my neck, like my heart was molten lava, erupting from my rib cage. "I promise I did not fake a C-section and sneak in here so that I could make off with somebody's poopy old newborn," I said quietly. And then I said, less quietly, "You just give me that baby while you figure out the bracelet thing." I must have looked like a Maurice Sendak wild thing, roaring my terrible roar and rolling my terrible eyes. The nurse gave me the baby. The bracelet was later discovered on the floor in a pile of blankets. I swear it wasn't my fault that I became so fierce. That mama-bear thing? It's not something you do. It's something you *channel*.

And now I'm alone again, the little lamb asleep on the meadow of my expansive bosom. I'm bored, but in this entirely contented way, flipping over and over through the same copy of *Organic Style* magazine—the recipe for Salmon Burgers with Caper Butter, the shoe-organizing tips. (*Organic* shoes? I'm not sure.) I don't actually read anything; I just look at the pictures. There's a TV in the room and, old addict that I am, I'd imagined watching it for days on end here. But when I turned it on, there was a jumpy commercial for some boozy kind of drink distilled, maybe, from ice?—everybody boinging around on a glacier in small, white fur skirts, a loud "da da *dee*, da da *dum*" pounding from somewhere—and it seemed like an unforgivably crude thing to have in the same room with this teeny peach of a baby. I had to turn it off.

Soon, Birdy will peep out her small waking sound, and I will nurse her again. Michael will call so that I can bid good night to him and the much-recovered Ben, whose framed picture will beam at me from my bedside. I will hobble into the bathroom to wash my face and put on a clean T-shirt. My advice? Wear your own clothes in the hospital. Why add the shame of the johnny to your catalogue of postpartum indignities? Believe me, it's enough that you'll be wearing that peculiar fishnet thong (if your hospital is black-humored enough to offer you one) with a maxipad the size of a crib mattress. Maybe someone will fund a study to prove that your naked bottom dangling below a hospital gown actually impedes the recovery process.

I miss my boys so terribly, but suddenly I'm not in any real hurry to get home. This is it right here—my honeymoon with Birdy, one wink of time with her before the outside world presses in on us insistently. I gobble up the baby smell of Birdy's neck, her hair. Already she's so dear to me, this little girl. I hadn't really imagined I'd feel this much, this quickly. But here it is, the love as real as a smooth stone in my palm. As a typhoon.

The writer Amy Bloom has an excellent short story called "Love Is Not a Pie," and even though the story never really explains the title, I imagine it means that even after everyone gobbles down their share of love, there's still a whole pie there, not just a smear of coconut custard in the bottom of an empty dish. I secretly worried that love, for me, would be *exactly* like a pie—as in "Sorry, Birdy, Michael and Ben devoured the last of the lemon meringue before you even got here." But, it turns out, there's plenty of pie for everybody!

Which is a relief, because our Ben has returned, frayed around the edges but on the mend. His pale moon-face floated around my hospital room like the Ghost of Illness Past, and he played a little morosely with his new Play-Doh pumper. But it's just so good to see him. Good and indescribably painful. He climbed into bed with me to twirl some of my hair up into his fist, and it was sweet and sad to feel his little body near me again. What is this loss? Something that was whole has been split, and instead of feeling like more, it just feels a little unraveled right now. I can't describe it.

Luckily, Ben was too preoccupied by the gustatory pleasures of the hospital to notice any of my druggy weepishness. First he devoured a buttered roll from the dinner tray that arrived at 4:15. (Real food!) Then I walked him down to the maternity ward refrigerator, where they keep small containers of pudding for desperate moms and lucky kids. (In truth, "walked" is a *polite* word for what I managed, but it did involve moving my legs in some kind of ambulatory parody.) Ben was offered, and he politely accepted, a piece of candy from my growing stash. And then he climbed back into bed for a little more cuddle time—just enough for me to wonder how he had become The Boy Made of Elbows, with enough bony points to dig simultaneously into my incision, each of my engorged breasts, and the baby's soft skull. I said, "Be careful of the baby's head, okay?" and felt like a rite of passage had been enacted in that moment. Now Ben's the galumphing big kid. Birdy's the fragile egg in a velvet box. And I'm like a cross between the Madonna and Kurt Cobain.

And a fountain built from boulders. The milk seems to have come in, and my breasts are so enormous and rock hard that nursing is like the proverbial wringing of water from a stone. It happened to me with Ben, too, but still I'm amazed. You go to sleep with breasts that might be a little large, but that still seem to be made from human tissue, and you wake up with these aching sacks of wet gravel affixed to your chest. My breasts stick out past the side of my body like arm rests, and my arms rest on them.

When I nurse Birdy, her dark head looks tiny, like a Ping-Pong ball held up next to a bowling ball for scale. She looks like a person trying to bite into the side of a whole watermelon. But she perseveres, brave baby. I'm grateful for her pluck.

Even though I've been through this before, I can't imagine how it will end—the terrible engorgement. The skin of my breasts is stretched into a disturbing pattern of red-and-white stripes, like human seersucker. I know that I'm so lucky with milk, but I can't help despairing over this fullness. "Full to bursting" is an expression that seems, suddenly, quite frightening. "Nurse the baby a lot, to relieve the pressure," one nurse here has advised. "But be careful, since this will signal your body to produce even *more* milk." A lactational paradox.

At some point my breasts got so achy that I asked after ice packs. "Ice?" the nurse repeated, like I had inquired into borrowing a vibrator for the afternoon. "We don't really have *ice* for the patients." "Really?" I asked. "No ice on the maternity floor?" "Well," she said, and I swear her eyes glinted a little, "you could get some ice cubes from the freezer and fill a couple of exam gloves with them." So Michael sat with a pair of latex gloves and filled them to the wrist with cubes before tying them off. I spent the day holding the icy hands over my breasts, like the star of a pornographic horror movie about the abominable snowman. "What about the women who've had vaginal births?" I say to Michael. "Do they really have to sit around with a frozen rubber finger up their vagina?"

Later, the nice woman who cleans the rooms came in, found

the gloves thawing in the shower drain, and laughed. "Honey?" she said. "Don't you just want some regular *bags?*" And she was back a moment later with a perfectly normal pair of ice packs. Since then, every other nurse I've asked has said, "*Of course* we have ice packs. It's a *hospital.*" Maybe that first person wasn't even a real nurse. Maybe she was just the resident practical joker. Or a disguised Alan Funt, here to do a postnatal series of *Candid Camera* episodes.

Later it's peaceful again—the boys have gone—and the nurse I like best comes in quietly to do some last-minute fussing over us. "Look at her," she whispers, smiling at Birdy's new pink face, and my eyes fill with tears. "Thank you," I say, and she pats my blankets around me.

I try to imagine what it will be like to return home tomorrow. I crave our bed, the comforting bodies of Michael and Ben. I am homesick. But I'll miss this little loop of my life, here with Birdy outside of real time and space. I will bring her home, and then we will really be doing it—we will really become a family of four. Where there was wondering there will be life. There is life already. Let me say this—if love *is* a pie, it's a really big, really delicious one.

Did *I* say that love was like a big, delicious pie? Oh *please.* I don't know what kind of pie *you* like, but chances are good that it doesn't make you sit around crying into your Häagen-Dazs and soaking through the front of all your T-shirts and yelling at everybody at unpredictable intervals. That's the kind of pie we seem to be eating around here.

I kind of forgot that I'd just be sitting in the same spot all day, nursing the baby. In this house, it's an aqua-green rocking chair pulled up by our bedroom window so I can look out at the trees—like I've checked into a combination country inn / mental institution. Ben joins us occasionally, to play listlessly with his stuffed animals on the rug, and while he's in the room I try to keep myself from bursting into spontaneous tears.

The baby books identify a trio of postpartum possibilities: the blues—just your run-of-the-mill crying, compulsive snacking, and bone-tiredness; then postpartum depression, which sounds a little thicker and harder to shake, and probably looks more like *sobbing* than plain old crying, with—I'm just imagining here—a few fantasies thrown in of leaving the baby out in the backyard overnight. I'm currently on the merely weepy and irritable end of things, although I did go to the supermarket—all by my ownself, as Ben would say—and as soon as I got in the car and turned the radio on, a command floated into my head as if from outside of it: "Drive! Keep driving! DRIVE AWAY!!!" Instead I bought three bags of gingersnaps and returned home in a panic. All of which is to say that I don't fall into the *third* category we read about, the one beyond mere depression: postpartum *psychosis!* Yikes! Who knew? Now I like to shoot Michael a wild and unraveling look just so he will say, "Uh-oh, honey! Postpartum psychosis?"

Okay, in truth we're doing pretty well. So much better—my God, *so* much—than after Ben was born. My clearest memory from the weeks after Ben's birth is of our first day home from the hospital, me standing, naked and crying, while Sam cooed comforting words and duct-taped a plastic grocery bag over my incision—all so that I could take a one-minute-long shower before leaping out to nurse again.

Ben had picked that day—the coming-home day—to begin dabbling in what would later become long and quite masterful crying solos. I think of that every time we visit first-time parents in the hospital: the new baby is always so rosy and beautifully swaddled and asleep in the crook of somebody's arm, like a miniature saint, and the parents always shrug smugly and say, "I guess we just got really lucky! He's *so* calm and easy." "That's great!" I always say. "How terrific!" And I smile a smile that I hope doesn't look too grimace-y. "Just you wait," I always think, "until you get home and the baby wakes up enough to impersonate a car alarm crossed with Marlon Brando in *Apocalypse Now.*"

It's that first day home from the hospital I really remember. And waking up a million times a night to check to make sure Ben was breathing—and being so profoundly exhausted that I would think: "If he's *not* breathing, do I have to make a whole bunch of phone calls *now?* Or could I maybe go back to sleep and make them in the morning?" *That's* how deranged I was—so painfully in love with the baby, but so drained by the new responsibility of it all. Maybe just the *teeniest* bit psychotic.

Now I can't quite figure out why we were so panic-stricken every single second when Ben was newly born. I sit in the rocking chair, nursing Birdy—I watch her latch on and shake her head from side to side, like a lion breaking the neck of a gazelle—and I can feel her babyhood like a wind blowing so quickly through the house. Maybe that's the biggest difference: after Ben was born, every day seemed to last about four months, and I felt like I would be nursing him at five-minute intervals for the rest of eternity. I was terrified that it would never end. Now, with Birdy, I'm terrified about how *quickly* it will end.

Which is not to say that we relish every second, as we should. Yellow baby poop spraying over the changing table and into your bare, cupped hand is still really gross. But maybe that's the big difference—I know now that my whole life doesn't boil down to spraying yellow poop. This is just a moment. We understand how fleeting it is, this gorgeous, milky baby time. And it's actually *easier* to fall in love with the second baby: you already know how to.

This, of course, does not describe Ben's experience. He elaborately avoids eye contact with me all day, but then suddenly leans in close to ask a million questions, usually hydraulic in nature. For instance, every time I eat anything especially delicious, Ben gives me a wary look. "Is Birdy going to nurse that syrup right out of your nursings?" he asks over a dripping plate of pancakes. "More or less," I tell him. "And then the pancakes will just squeeze on down and turn into your poop? And your poop will just squeeze out into the toilet?" "I should be so lucky." I laugh, and Ben scrunches up his nose. The baby is damper than he had imagined she would be; in fact, the whole thing is just a little bit grosser than what he'd bargained for.

The other day, when Ben was voicing his vehement contempt for all "scary animals," I thought I'd try a new tactic to cultivate his acceptance. "You know," I said, "even scary animals love their babies."

"Really?" he asked. "Even lions?"

"Yup. Lions love their cubs."

"Even tigers?"

"Uh-huh."

"Even alligators and slithery, slithery snakes?"

I pictured the nature shows I'd seen, all those millions of alligator babies hatching out into the bayou with no reptile parent in sight. But—my goodness—the mother alligator had at least *laid* all those eggs! "Yes, alligators too," I fudged.

Ben thought about this for a while. "What about lily pads?" he finally asked. "Do *they* love their babies?"

"I don't know," I answered him. "Most people think that plants don't have feelings."

"I think they do," Ben concluded. "Lily pads do love their sweet little babies." Perhaps this will be his path toward understanding the new intrusion: if even lily pads love their babies, maybe it will make some small sense that we love Birdy. Maybe.

spring

You do not have to be good.
You do not have to walk on your knees
for a hundred miles through the desert, repenting.
You only have to let the soft animal of your body
    love what it loves.
Tell me about despair, yours, and I will tell you mine.
Meanwhile the world goes on.

Mary Oliver
"Wild Geese"

'm torn: I can't believe how well we're doing, on the one hand, and, on the other, how appallingly. Certainly our general level of coping is just so much higher than it was when Ben was a newborn. I remember when people would visit us then—when our parents or friends would come stay at the house—and I'd make up the guest bed for them. I'd pull the sheets tight and shake the clean comforter out over them, thinking of our own bedding, which was more like a chemistry experiment in bodily outpourings—every orifice accounted for—than like something an actual human should have been touching without appropriate protective gear. Then, because I was so, so tired, I'd lie down for just a second on the nice, clean bed. And then I'd think about offering our guests a million dollars to sleep in *our* bed with the baby so that I could stay right where I was for the rest of the night.

Don't get me wrong—our sheets are more revolting than ever. But I'm so accustomed to not sleeping that I don't even feel that tired this time. I write that, and then laugh: it's not exactly true, of course, but claiming it gives me a little flush of energy. The immediate postpartum period is never what you think it will be. You spend the first two weeks thrilled that you're feeling better than you thought you would—a sensation of well-being that is either enhanced or entirely produced by the various lovely pills they send you home with. Then you spend the next two weeks feeling worse than you expected to. The adrenaline tapers off, your hormones caper wild circles through your brain, you wean yourself from painkillers, and you grow accustomed enough to the miraculous face of your baby to notice other stuff—like the sudden annoyingness of any older children who might happen to be skulking around.

And pain. Because, among other things, the C-section incision seems to be healing a little erratically. This time around, I turned out to be allergic to the kind of sutures they used. My OB removed them only after the incision had started to look like something Ben himself might draw by moving a red marker back and forth across the page. "This should still be below your bikini line," she reassured me as she grimaced over the festering mess of my abdomen. "Thank God," I said, "because after my clinically depressed three-year-old, my anxiety about the baby dying, and our friend starting chemo, a new bikini was going to be next on my list of worries." The OB gave me a strange look, but then laughed.

Judy started chemotherapy the week Birdy was born, and she comes over to keep me company in the morning, dozing in our bed while the baby and I nurse in the rocker. If some Extreme Sports TV show did a segment called "Medical Recovery!" maybe we could star in it. "Now Judy's eyes are closing! Now Catherine's! No, wait—Catherine's are open again, she's taking a sip of water. . . ." I find this companionship very comforting.

So that's the one hand. But this time around we have this beautiful kid already in our lives—this Ben whom we love so much—and he's undergoing a sudden and precipitous fall from grace. This is the other hand. In truth, it's almost too painful to write about. For long stretches he'll be totally fine, totally himself, humming a happy little tune while he fills the sink with water, humming a happy little tune while the water spills over onto the bathroom floor. But then he'll lapse into this devastating kind of moroseness, where he'll squash Play-Doh or crayon a happy, colorful picture, only he'll be resting his cheek on his fist, doing his lackluster impersonation of the kid in *Kramer vs. Kramer*. It kills us.

Birdy is like this great, unspoken betrayal—he doesn't actually talk about her. Sure, I'll be burping her, and Ben will look completely horrified when a quart of partially digested milk goes splatting onto the floor behind me, but he doesn't say much.

The worst part is that I seem to be picking this exact moment—not coincidentally, I realize—to become impatient and intolerant. It's probably hormones, but it is truly terrible. I have reduced Ben to tears more times—and about more entirely stupid, insignificant things—than I can actually bear to say. Imagine a fight about how much soap he uses to wash his hands. Or about bread and butter, Ben's current and only source of nourishment. Since we got home—and because we have duped everyone into caring for us—our friends and family have treated us to an unimaginable wealth of home cooking. It's been completely outrageous: fennel soup with orange and olives, corn chowder, chicken in a richly dark Mexican mole, spinach lasagna, lemon cake. Every delicious thing in the world has made its way onto our dinner table.

But Ben has picked this moment—not coincidentally, I realize—to become a picky eater. Watermelon used to be the only thing he wouldn't eat ("Because of the juice," he always says, "and also the black, black seeds. And the *grind*—that yucky part on the outside."), but now you can add just about everything else to the list. Except bread and butter.

Since Ben's so fragile, this seems like a *really* good time to snap at him. Yes indeedy. "We're not even going to *have* bread anymore until you start eating more dinner food." (I just read that over and realize that the utterance itself doesn't really capture the Mommy Dearest spirit in which it was said. Trust me.) What's my problem? I go to bed so racked with guilt that it's all I can do not to wake Ben up to tell him how much I love him. It's good that I don't—I'd probably just end up yelling at him. "Jesus, Ben, it's the middle of the night! Why are you awake? Oh, right. I woke you. Sorry."

The saddest thing is that I still can't pick him up. "Carry me up to bed," Ben says every night, and even though this is the exact kind of reconnection that we need, I have to say, "Oh, honey, I can't carry you upstairs yet." He settles reluctantly for holding my hand while I haul myself along the banister—like a hunchback using a ski lift.

Last week I nobly encouraged Michael to return to his Wednesday dinnertime yoga class, and let me say this simply: it was a huge mistake. Because as soon as he left, I just felt wholly overwhelmed. The nights are still not a good time for me. Birdy cried and cried while I was helping Ben get ready for bed, and her wailing affects each of us differently: while my own heart pounds out its Morse code of panic, Ben becomes hypnotically calm. So preternaturally calm that, it seems, he can move his limbs only at the rate of an inch a minute. "Brush your teeth, okay?" I said to him, tugging up my shirt while the baby screamed herself into a puddle. A minute later I looked up from nursing, and he was still standing there, staring into space. "Jesus, Ben," I said, *"go and brush your teeth!"* He scuttled away like a shooed cat—claws scrabbling over the wood floor—and I thought, "Uh-oh."

Sure enough, when I found him in the bathroom, he was fumbling with the toothpaste and sobbing—his mouth pulled down into a long, open shape of misery, snot and tears everywhere. "Oh, sweetie," I said. "I'm sorry I spoke so sharply to you." The way he fell against me—thudded into my lap—you'd think that sorrow and gravity were the same force. Ben was still awake when Michael returned home, and he whispered, "Tell Daddy what happened with the tooth brushing." Ben pulled the covers up over his head while I relayed the story to Michael, and when Michael said, "Ooh, honey, that sounds like a sad time for you," Ben's head popped out, his eyes wet again. "It was," he agreed. "It is."

Ben's abject grief is so hard for us to take that his tiny bouts of aggression are almost a relief. One day he runs in with the red hexagon from his wooden puzzle. "Stop!" he yells. "This shape means 'Stop nursing the baby!'" Another day he's sitting, holding a broom on top of his head. "Uh-oh!" he says. "My dander is up!" Then he puts the broom down. "Now my dander is down. I'm done being angry. What does 'dander' mean?"

Still, Ben is so fundamentally kind, I think, that niceness sort of leaks out of him, even towards the baby. One night I'm lying down between Ben and Birdy, trying to get them both to sleep. Birdy is starting to gritch around, doing what Megan calls her baby dinosaur routine, and I'm trying to think about what I should do next. Suddenly Ben's little hand reaches over me in the darkness to pat her back. He strokes her small, feathered head, and she quiets right down. My heart does a little somersault, and then I quiet down too.

———

Birdy might have cystic fibrosis. I feel like my limbs are hinged together with rubber bands. Or like I'm made of one solid piece of something hard. I have so much fear in me that I drop away from my regular feelings about regular things, into a universe with a different kind of gravitational system. I am barely tethered to the world. At night, Michael lies with his whole weight on top of me so that I will stay here with him. He hands me Birdy to nurse, and I can only squint at her out of the corners of my eyes. It's too painful to look right at her—like she's a sudden bright and beautiful light. .

Cystic fibrosis. A chronic, progressive disease of the mucus glands. The average life span of a person with cystic fibrosis is thirty years. I wish so desperately for my kids to outlive me that wishing, ever, for anything else now seems utterly obscene. There is nothing more to want. I can be comforted only by odd thoughts. "You know," I say suddenly to Michael, over dinner, "it's pretty unlikely, isn't it? That Birdy will die of cystic fibrosis before the whole world is destroyed by a nuclear war?" From the look on his face, I'm guessing that Michael is not reassured by this idea.

It all started the day before yesterday when I answered the phone and heard our beloved pediatrician's voice. "Catherine? It's Dr. Roche." Maybe there are people who could delude themselves, for an instant, and imagine that their child's doctor was calling out of the blue to, say, borrow a punch bowl, but I'm not one of them. I *knew* it was going to be bad. It turns out that Massachusetts has a pilot screening program—apparently I signed consent forms in the hospital about this—that tests newborns for a bunch of genetic disorders. Birdy had failed the first round of tests—where they look at something about your pancreas—and then the second round, where they look at the genes themselves.

"But, wait," I said. My hands were shaking and I was trying to think clearly. "Michael's a carrier—they tested us when I was pregnant—but I'm not. So she can't actually have it, right?" Dr. Roche was terribly relieved by this news. She hadn't known about our own screening tests. "Oh, that's great," she said. "Yes, she probably doesn't have it—she's probably a carrier, like Michael. But I'm going to have her tested anyway, just to be sure."

I was relieved too—until I called my brother, who offered his mix of gracious concern and alarm. He has kids himself—a three-year-old and a new baby, just like us—so he really understands parental worry. But then, he has so much knowledge, about both likely and unlikely scenarios, that it can be a little scary to talk to him. Because he works for the CDC, he's very well connected, doctor-wise: he talked to a CF-specialist friend of his and called me back worried. It turned out that the screening test I'd taken picks up most—but not all—of the disease's mutations; I could still be a carrier, and Birdy could still be sick. Apparently, the specialist friend was concerned about why Birdy would fail the pancreas part of the test if she were only a carrier. "He's a great guy," my brother said about his friend. "He'll be a terrific resource for you guys as you move forward with this." *As we move forward with this?* My God. I feel like climbing into bed and staying there until there is some kind of certainty. Birdy will have something called a "sweat test," but it's not scheduled until the beginning of next week. I'm not sure how we're going to get through this weekend.

To top things off, the baby suddenly *seems* sick—she's phlegmy and wheezing. I cry and cry, and Ben, whom we've been pestering to wash his hands for the last three weeks, says, "Did I give Birdy my cold, Mama? Is that why you're crying?" I can't stand it. "Oh, sweetie, no. Of course not. Birdy's just a little sick. It's nobody's fault." Every time she coughs or fusses, Michael and I exchange surreptitious peeks at each other, to determine how worried we are. When I catch his eye, he smiles at me gently and I burst into tears.

Judy and Liz come over, just to sit with me, and I take so much comfort in their friendship that I feel, suddenly, lucky again. "Uh-oh," Liz says, and takes the baby from me. "Look at her. She's *wasting away!*" We all laugh—Birdy really couldn't be any fatter without bursting open her own skin. Then she cries a little, and Judy nods. "The notorious *cystic fibrosis* cry," she says gravely, and I laugh. This—gallows humor—is the only type of comfort I can bear. I feel like I'm catching my breath for the first time in two days. Fear is so *lonely*—and now I feel less alone. We gush, too, over the baby ("I'm sorry," Liz says at some point. "She's just too fat and pretty to be sick."), and over Judy's newly bald head, which looks fabulous—Liz has shaved it to keep a beat ahead of the chemo. It is the purest expression of friendship, these traded reassurances. In this way, we are replenished.

I try to access some of my amateur Zen spirit. These are

real days of our only lives, I think—why waste them on fear? But then fear takes me over again—like voracious jaws I am thrust into at intervals—and I wring my hands and pace circles around our house. I think a lot about a new friend who has a daughter with cystic fibrosis. I remember him saying how much he tries to live every second with her. It's amazing how your own pain can so starkly illuminate the pain of others. The thought that his daughter is sick is suddenly more than I can bear.

In this way—moving between life and fear—I will pass the days until the sweat test. Well, that and *licking* everybody. Apparently, people with cystic fibrosis have "salty sweat," and this is information I don't know what to do with. "Doesn't *everyone* have salty sweat?" I ask Michael. "I mean, isn't that kind of the *nature* of sweat?" He shrugs. Birdy's sweat does taste salty, and, I'm suddenly noticing, she seems to sweat a lot. I touch the tip of my tongue to her damp scalp: salty. Then I lick the sleeping Ben to compare. He seems salty too, but maybe a little *less* salty than the baby? I can't tell. "Honey, quit tasting the kids," Michael chastises gently. But I can't. I even lick Michael, on the sly, while I'm hugging him. "I felt that," he teases. "I know you're licking me." Moving between life and fear.

I *know* that if Birdy is sick, we'll learn so much from her about love and courage. I know we will have a rich, wonderful time with this daughter of ours—that we are lucky to know her now, to have spent even these three weeks with her. But still I want so desperately for her to live a long and healthy life. We'll see what Tuesday brings.

Birdy doesn't have cystic fibrosis. The nurse just called—I was waiting with my hand on the receiver—and said, simply, "It's the best possible news." We are so lucky. A well baby! We want for nothing.

Really, nothing else seems to matter now—our lives are pared down to what's vital. Which is, of course, life itself. Talk about perspective! "Yeah, a little too much perspective," Liz says, laughing, when I call, and I'm not sure if she means to be quoting that line from *Spinal Tap*—where Nigel crouches over Elvis's gravestone, shaking his head philosophically: "Too *much* fucking perspective."

The sweat test itself was an odd and primitive affair. They hook the baby's tiny arm up to something that looks unequivocally like a car battery, zap it, and then wrap it up in gauze and send you both out to wait while she sweats enough for them to measure the salt. It's terrible to sit in the waiting room with your electrified little sweating baby, because you're wishing so desperately for your kid to be healthy, but then there is a *bunch* of sweaty babies waiting, all of them getting the same test, and the odds are against everyone being okay. One in five of the babies who get this far in the screening process will have the disease. I kept formulating these complicated wishes—like praying, I guess—with little clauses and disclaimers attached to them. "Please let Birdy be healthy," I wished. "But not at the cost of one of these other kids being sick. But please let her not be the one. But let us *all* be lucky." It's hard to look the other parents in the eye.

Our friend Jennifer—whose beautiful daughter, Sophia,

has both severe hearing loss *and* a rare, unrelated condition that keeps her from gaining weight—hears odds like "one in five" and assumes the worst. "Actually, forget 'one in five,'" she says and laughs. "I hear 'one in a million' and I nod. 'Yup. That'll be us.'" Now I wanted it to be *not* us, but also *not* anyone else, even though I know that's not how odds work. When our test was over, I smiled at the last mother left in the waiting room— "Good luck!"—and she smiled back: "Good luck to you!" Our eyes filled with tears, and we both looked away.

I can't help wondering about her now. No matter what, I hope she's holding that little baby close, breathing in the baby smell of his scalp, maybe putting an ear to his ribs to listen to the little hoofbeats of his heart. Maybe she's putting him to her breast, brim-full with joy while she watches him swallow, watches his eyes flutter and then close, and she's thinking: *Yes.* Or: *Just this.* I hope so.

I really think that something is wrong with me, and I can't tell if it's still just postpartum sludge or if it's something deeper. I cannot stop worrying. It's a bad habit of the mind— like my psyche is a compulsive nail-biter.

But it's like this: we get a break, say, by finding out that our newborn does not have a fatal genetic disease, and for a day or so I am relieved. In the big picture, in fact, I am permanently relieved. But on some other level, almost right away, another concern moves in to fill the space that gets left open. My mind is like a warehouse of worries, and even as the forklift is beeping out with a huge crate marked "Cystic Fibrosis," the guy is waving in a new truckload. Real scares and made-up scares are blurring together.

My newest worry is that Birdy has some kind of seizure disorder. I am telling you the truth: this is my worry. If you're like me, you start out thinking that maybe you'll just keep a normal little journal of your daughter's first year. But then it mutates into a disturbing logbook of psychosis and pathology, and you realize that you might not show it to her after all. I envy the scrapbooks of normal mothers, all those jolly snapshots and ticket stubs: *Here's your first smile! This is when we took you to your first circus!* I seem to record only the mounting evidence of my own mental deterioration: *Look, Birdy! Here's the pamphlet from the newborn genetic screening! This is when I stayed online all night trying to figure out if you were retarded!*

I really need a break from myself. A little vacation on the soothing shores of somebody else's mind. Instead I log onto the Internet and look up Birdy's symptoms. When she's falling asleep, her eyes fix on the nearest light source, then they shudder a little under half-mast lids, then they roll all the way back into her head before shutting. Also, there's the shallow panting, like a demon spirit's, that accompanies the whole creepy-eyes routine. Michael claims not to know what I'm talking about. He also claims not to notice that she avoids eye contact (she does), but when I got down the photo albums of Ben at this age—in a green onesie, smiling up at Michael or holding up his jingle-worm while he stares right at the camera—he did have to admit that Ben might have seemed a little more engaged. "But so what?" he said, which is so far from my style of thinking that he might as well be speaking Dutch.

Every baby is different. I know this intellectually. Birdy

seems like a baby who should have been born a few weeks later: she's been curled up into herself still, sleepy and unprepared to be a person of the world. And that's fine with me. What I don't like is when I become convinced, from my online disaster marathons, that she suffers from "absence seizures": a kind of clinical space-out that means your brain is misfiring. When I bring this up at one of her appointments—and I mention it somewhat casually, like, "Oh, and I almost forgot, I think she might have brain damage!"—the grandfatherly pediatrician corrects my pronunciation: "*absaunce* seizure," like it's some kind of French gravy. And then he laughs at me (which I find reassuring) and dismisses my concern unequivocally (which I also find reassuring). He reminds me that newborns have underdeveloped nervous systems, and that shuddery falling-asleep stuff—however disquieting—is still well within the realm of what's normal for Birdy's age. He has probably treated eight million babies by this point in his career, and I am utterly convinced by his bravado. I return home relaxed and lighthearted.

But then, it's like an addiction, the worry. I try to shrug it away, but it creeps back and gnaws at me until, finally, I get up in the middle of the night and spend a few hours plugging in "mercury" and "autism," hunched so guiltily over the computer you'd think I was downloading pornography. I become convinced that, thanks to the flu shot I got when I was pregnant, the tuna fish I ate, and the six dozen or so enormous fillings in my teeth, Birdy is suffering from mercury poisoning. At least half of the stuff I read seems to have been written by bona fide crackpots—people who have all their teeth pulled, for instance, "just to be on the safe side," or who claim to determine the metric units of mercury in their blood purely by intuition—but still

I'm petrified. I return to a stomach-knotting despair that is so deep and strange and shameful that I cannot talk about it, not even with Michael. Michael, who teases me because every time he walks into the bedroom, he catches me saying "Birdy! Birdy! Look at Mama!" while I peer into her face and try to force her to meet my eyes. She looks out the window instead. She's probably thinking, "Jesus Christ, get a life already."

At Birdy's two-month appointment, our regular pediatrician is on maternity leave, and I, compulsively, mention my fear again—this time to the new doctor. I hope that she'll laugh at me the way her avuncular colleague did, but instead her brows pull a furrow into her forehead and she starts taking notes. "Mmm-hmm. Just when she's falling asleep? Hm. Fixed and *then* rolling?" When I ask about waiting on Birdy's vaccinations— something I'm sure she'll pooh-pooh instantly—she nods thoughtfully. "That's probably a good idea," she says, "just so we don't add in another variable at this point, while we're waiting for the neurological issue to resolve itself." *The neurological issue?* Maybe she's doing a little reverse psychology, because I back-pedal almost immediately. "You think so?" I ask. "It's probably just regular newborn stuff." "Probably," she hesitates, "but let's wait just to be sure."

The postpartum period is like *The Perfect Storm*: all the wild forces of new-babyhood collide to make you ragingly, epically nuts. I know that I'll look back on this period and understand the equation perfectly. I understand it even now: hormones + mewling subhuman + strange, sore body + moping older child − sleep = utter lunacy. I am an utter lunatic. An utter lunatic who takes oddly little comfort in the knowledge that this is just a bad cocktail of brain chemistry and timing. The idea that I may once again be sipping from the happy gin-and-tonics of parenthood—it just doesn't take the edge off right now.

And I know for a fact that there's an edge. Ben came into the living room tonight, where I was nursing Birdy and beginning to unravel a little bit earlier than usual, and he took one look at me and scampered out. I heard him in the kitchen, where Michael was washing the dinner dishes. "Uh-oh, Daddy," he said. "I think you better go in and talk to Mama. She's crying again." I can't tell if I'm relieved or depressed that my crying seemed about as remarkable to him as a baked potato. I have a vague feeling, though, that the chain of concern is supposed to go in the other direction. Poor Ben.

Last week we were at Ben's friend Sophia's house, and Birdy started crying. "Why is Abigail crying?" Sophia asked (all of Ben's friends call her by her given name—a formality that I find completely endearing).

"Maybe she's tired," I told her. "Do you ever cry when you're tired?" Soph smiled and nodded, and Ben nodded too. "You too, right, Ben? Do you sometimes fall apart when you're tired?"

"I do!" he said, then added, "And you do too, Mama."

I laughed. "It's true! I do!" Then I asked a trick question—"What about Daddy?"—but Ben didn't fall for it.

"Oh, no," he said, "Daddy can't fall apart. He has to comfort all of us." Poor Michael. He is one of the greatest unsung superheroes I know. Postpartum Man! Brave enough to buy maxipads at the supermarket! Forgiving enough to be yelled at over domestic trivia! Kind enough to soothe crazy women with a single hug! Maybe I'll sew him a little cape. Or at least try to remember to say "Thank you."

———

People have good intentions, I know, but I think you should leave little kids alone when they have new babies at home. Squat down to greet the older sibling, and the compulsion to mention the baby in a high-pitched, excited voice will surely strike you, but you can just go ahead and recognize the urge, and then let it pass. Because Ben will happily engage you in a conversation about any of your own personal bodily functions—"Poop or pee?" he might ask you when you return from the bathroom. Or he might refer elegantly, like my English mother, to the "shoulders" of the carrot you are eating. He will happily give you a long tour of his latest artworks. But try to talk to him about Birdy, and he will likely look at you blankly. "Is there something new at your house?" people goad him, with great animation, and he taps his chin before answering, "Lincoln logs?" He genuinely has no idea what they're talking about—an oblivion that borders on the pathological, but, then, who can blame him?

Ben's newest coping mechanism is to pretend that Birdy is an orphan baby who has been left for us, in all our gracious *noblesse oblige*, to care for. He might turn suddenly in his car seat and feign a great surprise to see her sitting right next to him. "Hyuh!" he gasps. "Who is this baby that we've never seen before? Why, it's Beedy! The *strange* baby!" Beedy is Birdy's alter ego. Birdy—well, we're kind of stuck with her, what with her being our actual baby and all. But Beedy? *Easy come, easy go* seems to be how the game works. We might care for her briefly and then return her to the darkness whence she came, or we might keep her on a little longer—but only if we feel like it. "Poor Beedy," Ben says, and shakes his head sadly. "It's time for the strange baby to hit the road."

This, let me confess, is far from the hard part—Ben's imaginative strategies. What's hardest is simple: it's all of us being at a loss about how to do this, how to become a family of four. One especially trying night, I look at us, as if from outside, and I see a newborn baby screaming alone on the bed while her mother squats in front of a little boy standing in just his "Delaware County Fair" T-shirt. The mother squeezes his bottom to keep in a glycerin suppository. This little boy has not pooped in days, and his belly sticks out like a beach ball. The mother herself looks like a person in whom caffeine is fighting a losing battle with exhaustion. Her mind is as clear as the cabinet under your kitchen sink—the one with all the scouring powder and old sponges. Or at least that's how I *feel*. Birdy is crying and Ben is crying, and there is snot everywhere, and I'm still squeezing Ben's butt cheeks, and he starts to laugh. "Everybody's falling apart!" he says, cheerfully, and I laugh too.

But later that same night I yell at him because Birdy is crying again and I think that he's drawing with markers right on our blue table. "Jesus, Ben," I snap, "you know better than that!" When he holds up the blue paper he's actually coloring, tears shining on his cheeks, I want to get in the car and drive myself away.

Visit Florence, and a dozen strangers there will tell you how the Duomo—the enormously domed cathedral that defines that city's glory—was built. Here's what you'll learn: when they built the cathedral, the architects left a hole that was actually bigger than any dome they yet had the technology to build.

They simply *trusted* that somebody would figure out how to engineer the dome before the building was finished, and, sure enough, Brunelleschi came along and invented Renaissance architecture and built the Florentines their monumental Duomo. This is the kind of faith I need now. Here we are: we have taken on this fourth person, with the assumption that we will become a family, but she is here, now, and we don't know quite how to do it yet. And we're hoping to figure it out before, you know, the first really big rains come pouring through that enormous hole.

I may be coming back into the light. *May* be. I feel a little clearer in the head, a little lighter in the heart. I think that Birdy's probably healthy and fine. I imagine that Ben may return, from his sojourn into the pits, back to the bowl-of-cherries life he left behind. Or at least that's what I think today. Because, really, it's just a matter of which dots you happen to connect in any given moment. Drawn one way, you might see a smiling family of four moving capably through their days with an easy new baby and a beautiful, golden-hearted boy. But focus on it from a different angle, and you'll see a swamp of alligators nipping at our heels. You'll see a baby who cries every evening and spits up at ten-minute intervals while her older brother broods. Each of these stories is the absolute truth.

I took both kids to the supermarket today. I know that this is the most mundane of activities—a mom out shopping with her brood—but it felt, to me, like an Olympic event for which I had not properly trained. Like I'd been out doing wind sprints, and now somebody was handing me a shot put—or a dozen car seats—and wishing me luck. On the one hand, it went fine. If you'd run into us, you would have seen a woman with moderately clean hair and some white barf on her jacket, holding a baby in the Bjorn while her son shouted instructions from their shopping cart. "No, no, Mama. That big red apple. No, not that dark, pinky one. *That* one that looks like a ball made out of apple." You would have seen me do my little swaying two-step, then kissing the top of Birdy's sleeping head while I performed a deep knee bend to reach the organic hotdogs that our entire family eats in shrugging but shameful abundance.

But inside? Inside, it was like a horror movie: the menacing music plays, and you know you've got to get out of there, that something bad is going to happen but you don't know what it is yet. If Birdy had started screaming at the same time that Ben needed to pee in the germ-encrusted supermarket bathroom, the world might well have been sucked right into a black hole. As it was, the lights were too bright, and I was working too hard to seem calm and okay, talking to Ben in too high-pitched a voice: "*This* apple? Okay, honey! Super! That's a *super* apple! You sure know how to pick 'em!" Every now and then, Birdy would scritch around a little, and you'd think, from the way my heart pounded, that there was a waking anaconda strapped to my body. How does every mother pull this off like it's so frigging *normal?* Maybe my multitasker is missing a piece.

Birdy didn't even fall apart until the drive home, but by the time we were bringing the groceries inside she was red and sweating from screaming so much. Ben still seems to have some kind of mechanism for tuning her out. "May I please have some almonds and raisins?" he asked in his regular voice, even though I could barely hear him above the din that was Birdy. "What?" I was practically yelling. "What?" When Birdy's crying, I'm incapable of normal interactions. It's like trying to carry on a conversation about the weather while somebody pokes your eyes out with a knitting needle. "Yes," I said finally. The ice cream was melting in the shopping bag and the damp, wailing baby was wedged under one arm, but I managed to dump some raisins into the last of the almonds and hand the bag to Ben. "Um, Mama?" he said, and when his forehead creased with dissatisfaction, I felt every hair on my body rise up in anger. "I wanted to have them *separate*." I told him that that was fine, that he was welcome to separate them out if he liked, but he could hear my impatience, and he ran into the living room in tears. I finished unloading the groceries with the familiar sad-angry feeling like a porcupine in the back of my throat, then I went to find him, lying in a morose heap on the couch. I nursed Birdy and tried to clear my head.

"It's hard, isn't it," I said to him, "when you want something, but Birdy's crying and I get so impatient."

He didn't look at me, but he inched a little bit closer on the couch, still keeping a safe distance from Her Dampness. "Maybe you could talk to me about the nuts," he said.

"You mean about how you wanted me to separate them from the raisins?"

He shook his head. "No. Maybe you could just tell me about all the different kinds of nuts."

"Okay," I said, and then started listing: almonds, peanuts, hazelnuts. I looked at Ben and he nodded, so I continued. Brazil nuts, pecans, cashews.

"Wait," Ben interrupted me, and chopped his hand in the air like an emphatic director. "Cashews are *salted* nuts."

"That's true," I said. "We usually get the salted kind."

"Well," and now he was starting to cry again, "I only wanted to hear the names of the nuts that *aren't* salted." "Aren't" in that utterance was a very long word, like "aaaaaaaaaaaarrrrrrrrrren't." Then he collapsed in a sobbing heap on the floor.

When I told Michael this story later, we were laughing by this point—Michael dubbed the entire fiasco "Salted Nutgate"—but let me tell you, in the moment, there was nothing funny about any of it: groceries perishing on the kitchen floor, a tear-streaked newborn with a yellow-edged diaper, a starving mama who had had to pee for seven hours, and this weeping wreck of a child. This miserable, lost soul of a child who seemed suddenly like the saddest boy on the entire planet. I wished that I had just sorted out the raisins when he'd asked me the first time. I wished that I had hugged him before he'd left the kitchen in tears. I wished that I'd never mentioned cashews. I wished that I had not watched him cry on the floor, that I had not said, with a voice like an icicle, "That's enough, Ben. It's just *nuts*."

Later it was fine again. Ben wiped at his face with his sleeve and said, "Whoof! Was I so sad about the nuts?" And we laughed and put Birdy down to sleep and unloaded apples and oranges into the produce drawer. But I feel like I've crossed a frontier into unkindness, and I just want to go back. I want to pull that crying boy into my lap and brush the hair out of his face and whisper "I know" into his ear. I want never to have be-trayed him in the first place. I guess I'm no different from Ben, really: I want everything—every impossible, contradictory thing—and I want it now.

On some profound level, I swear, I am still deeply re-lieved, every day, that Birdy is healthy and well. And yet I am oddly busy with—and not always grateful for—the workaday world of Ben and his feelings. Our friend Judy—this is "*Memphis* Judy," as Ben aptly calls her, not "*Liz and Judy* Judy"—sent Ben this absolutely perfect, beautifully designed book, *Ask Me*, full of provocative questions and pictures. It's occasioned some greatly revealing conversations around here.

"Have you ever been angry with someone?" one page asks, and Ben looks out the window.

"Yes," he says. "You."

"Really?" I ask him. "When?"

"Every single time," he answers. And when I ask "How come?" he says in this sweetly patronizing way, like maybe I don't speak English that well, "Because of being *mad*, Mama." Duh.

Another page asks, "What are you afraid of?" and Ben mystifies us with his response. "That I'll fly up, up, up into the sky, all by my ownself, without you and Daddy."

"Like in an airplane?" I ask.

"No. Just me," he says, and his hands flutter through the air emphatically, to show me.

"Like *dying*?" I offer, courageously, but Ben shakes his head.

"No. Just flying up alone." We fumble around, reassuring him that we'll keep him safe, but I'm not even sure what from— or, in truth, if we can.

When the book asks "What do you wish that you know could never come true?" I think that Ben won't even understand the question, but he does. Miss Abigail is nursing—guzzling away like a frat boy at a keg—and Ben looks at her. "That I could be a little baby again," he says. "But I know I can't be." *Which would you prefer?* I ask myself, in the book's voice. *Amnesia or a knife to the heart?*

Not all the questions prompt such sad or heavy responses. "What are you investigating?" elicits a question about the meaning of the word "investigating." I'm nursing Birdy again, and so brain dead that, at first, I just keep repeating the word. "You know. Like *investigating*. Like, um, *investigating* something." I finally get it explained, and Ben thinks for a minute. "My pipes," he finally answers. "Your pipes?" I ask. "Yeah," he says. "You know, my mouth and my throat and my lungs. Like 'I think those peas went down the wrong *pipe*.' That's what I'm investigating."

It's actually true—Ben seems to be fascinated by the workings of his upper respiratory tract. One night I'm rubbing Tiger Balm into his chest, and Ben's eyes get big and watery from the fumes. "Whoooeee!" he says, and breathes in. "I can feel that in my hales!" "Your hales?" I ask, and he says, "Yeah, you know, like my *in*hales and my *ex*hales." Ah! I never thought of them collectively as "hales" before. But now I do.

Birdy, for one, has some quite remarkable hales. The other night I lay in bed listening to her breathe—to the beautiful, breathy music of her exhaling—and I tried to think which instrument it sounded like. Because I'm so strange with tiredness, I spent way too long thinking about this. An oboe? No. A recorder? No. Wind chimes? Not really. I finally came up with "dolphins" but then remembered that I had already read that comparison somewhere. Oh well.

It's funny that Birdy's asleep breathing sounds so pretty, since her awake breathing—usually as she's snuffling onto the breast to nurse—makes Michael and me think that "piglet" should rightfully be a verb. We debuted her at Daniel and Pengyew's dinner party, and she entertained everybody with a long and noisy session of nursing, punctuated with gunshot farting and spraying milk. There was a soaked nursing pad up on the dinner table, impersonating a sanitary napkin, and my shirt was hiked up awkwardly, and Pengyew—who is as graceful and elegant as Audrey Hepburn—looked at our damp, rumpled selves before he asked, politely, "Don't they make special clothes for that?" "They do," I said, "I'm wearing them," and Pengyew laughed and hugged us.

Oh, she's such a pigleting piglet, that Birdy! She weighed twelve pounds at her one-month appointment, and she has eleven chins. Plus, she's just starting to smile those first shaking smiles. She looks at me and crinkles her whole face into a little smile, and my eyes fill up with tears every time—even though she looks like she's practicing her acceptance speech for the Alfred Hitchcock look-alike awards. It's so easy to enjoy her—I feel so much less crazy this time, even when things are hard with Ben or when I'm in tears for no particular reason ("But you promised to stop at the doughnut place on your way home," I might say, for instance, before collapsing into a big boo-hoo).

And it would be difficult to overstate how much easier nursing is this second time around. I have, for instance, not once called a La Leche League representative to sob into the phone about how the baby has a "side preference"—guzzling from one breast as if it dispensed pure, molten joy, and shunning the other as if it leaked bong water. I do not secretly want to drop a thousand dollars on a doctor's-grade baby scale to graph the baby's weight against my presumed lactational output. My nipples do not look like abraded UFOs. And I am not constantly scanning the books for more productive positions: The baguette hold? The éclair hold? The Bob Newhart hold? (So far, Birdy and I are pretty happy with the mug-of-coffee-and-a-magazine hold.)

Also, I'm skipping some of the breast-feeding doodads this time, like the nursing pillow I wore constantly when Ben was this age. Even when he wasn't actually nursing, I was simply too tired to remove it. "Cigarette? Cigarillo?" Michael always teased when I staggered by with the pillow strapped around my waist like a vending tray. Now I'm happy to be relieved of my paraphernalia dependence, since by the time you're done with the pillows, the pumps, the pads, and the other milky gizmos, you feel less like you're doing the most natural thing in the world—feeding a baby—than like you have an indulgent and complicated hobby.

For every thing that's different about nursing, though, there's something that's exactly the same. Like the thirst. My God, the thirst! Birdy latches on and, within one second, I'm walloped with a thirst so intense that it's hard to describe. It's like a wave of depression—like I'm so thirsty in that wink of time that I could faint.

It reminds me of the awful way my dad used to get rid of the mice in our house: with a kind of poison that parched them—and they'd die their thirsty deaths scrambling across the floor, searching for water. When I was little, I didn't understand that the thirst was a symptom of the dehydrating poison that was killing them—that they weren't dying from a thirsty *feeling*, as I imagined. (The same way that I imagined it was the locked jaw of tetanus that actually killed you: "Why can't they just *squirt* food into your mouth?" I used to ask, mystified.) But now, I feel just like those mice. "Help!" I yell, nearly every single time I sit down to nurse, thirty-five times a day. "Michael! Help!" Why I never remember to get the water first is a great mystery. It's like a kind of amnesia. Sometimes, when Michael rushes in with the water, there are even a few ice cubes clinking around in the glass, and this makes me feel so grateful that I, literally, weep. "You're so nice," I blubber, and Michael smiles and pats me. "It's just ice, hon," he says. "It's not that big a deal."

So: the thirst is the same as it was last time. And so is the feeling of the milk letting down. "A pleasant tingling" is how most of the books describe it. Really? To me it feels less like a gust of chilled air than like a thick stream of steaming sand scraping its way out. Like pins and needles of the breast. Or like someone is pulling a strand of hot beads from my nipple. Plus, it's not until I feel my other breast—the un-babied one—fill up, spill over, and soak through my shirt that I ever remember about nursing pads. "Michael! Help!"

Allow me to add a note about nursing clothes: skip the nursing clothes. Ironically, their complicated closures and seams draw way more attention to the fact of your nursing baby than a simple half-hiked T-shirt ever does. Either you're wrestling with those useless side slits—threading your breast out like your shirt is a pair of men's underpants. Or else you're unbuttoning a large window in the front, like you're nursing through the seat flap of somebody's long johns. I do own a few items of nursing *lingerie,* sure—all those bras with the baby-come-hither flaps—but otherwise I'm just sticking with plain clothes. I have enough to worry about without caring if a stranger is aghast over the fuzzy top of Birdy's head poking out from under my shirt. Michael always laughs over the "Nursing Tent" that we see in catalogues: "Nothing to see here, folks! Just a harmless person wearing a tent!"

It's true, though, that I'm not a modest nurser. I'd happily nurse naked, outside the Vatican, while the pope waved to me from his little window. The only person who can make me feel furtive and ashamed about nursing is, of course, Ben. Yesterday morning, he rounded the corner into the living room—I could even hear him humming a little something on his way in—then saw me on the couch nursing the baby and stopped short. "Hi, Mama!" he said, without exactly looking at me, and it reminded me of the way you might project a loud, vague enthusiasm when you run into your ex with his new girlfriend at the supermarket. "Hi! How *are* you? Great! That's *great!!!!*" while your eyes scan their cart wildly—*Are those pork chops? Stuffed olives? He hates olives!* But maybe I'm imagining things, and it's really just my own guilt about being such a lactating tramp: first one baby, then the next. Ben, Birdy, I don't care—heck, I'll nurse *any* baby, as long as it's cute.

"Birdy nurses a *lot*," Ben announces regularly, and I want to say, "Oh, kid, this ain't *nothin'*." I want to say, "When you were this age, I was tied to a milky wheel that never stopped turning." (Or, as a friend of mine wrote to me, after her baby was born, "Life rolls along like a pair of twelve-sided dice. With a breast on every side.") I don't tell Ben this, of course. I don't even utter the words "every twenty minutes," but I do laugh and say, "Oh, Ben—you nursed way more than Birdy does!" And we get out the photo album—Ben nursing in the rocking chair, on the bed, in the bath, from the sling; an older Ben standing to nurse while I doze on the couch—and he smiles and seems satisfied.

Then I look through the rest of the pictures by myself, amazed by how different it feels this time around. This new baby has not severed us from our old lives. With the first baby, you can kind of squint at your former self, but it's as if you're parting a heavy, dark curtain to see it: "Was that just last week that we got a slice of pizza and went to the movies?" you think, right after the baby's born. "Who *were* those people?" I remember feeling like my old life had retreated to a dim shape, a blurry thing under layers and layers of wax paper. Now the differences seem more quantitative than absolute. We sit down for dinner, like we've always done, but instead of a plain lap I've got a nursing baby. We read Ben his bedtime stories, same as ever, but Birdy lies, gritching, beside us. We go to a dinner party, and instead of taking turns kneeling over Ben's jigsaw puzzle and relaxing on the couch with a glass of wine, Michael and I take turns kneeling over Ben's jigsaw puzzle and rocking the baby in the sling. With a glass of wine.

The Buddhists describe life as a river: stand in one spot to watch the water rush by, and it will be always the same, always different. When the first baby comes, it's like the sudden boil of the rapids: froth and sound, terror and thrill-a-second joy. The second one feels more like a gentle bend in the water's path. A gentle bend with a boulder or two to keep you on your toes.

I swear, Ben was three weeks old for *years*. Years and years. His newborn period went on for so long that I got way more than my fill. Now I'm stunned by how quickly Birdy is growing up. I just want to press my nose to her fragrant baby scalp and inhale every last molecule of her new yummy being. At least that's what I *think* I feel like. But then, Birdy will be nursed to sleep in my lap, and I'll be doing something really important and absorbing—reading the *Babystyle* catalogue, maybe, or watching *The Spy Who Shagged Me* with Michael—and she'll wake up. I'll catch myself jiggling her absent-mindedly or trying to cram a pacifier into her clenched jaw, just so that I can keep doing whatever boneheaded thing I'm doing. Then I'll happen to look down, and there she'll be—kicking her little legs in the air like she's practicing for the uneven parallel bar finals, beaming up at me the whole time. Doh! I all but have to slap the side of my head to remind myself of the forest for the trees. It will be a real bummer when Birdy asks me about her glorious babyhood, and I remember only that the Crossover Nursing Top came in a color called "persimmon."

When you ask my friend Moira about her most recent vacation, she'll tell you about the kids doing cartwheels on the beach, the sun setting behind them, and then her eyes fill with tears. "I just pray," she always says, and her cheeks pink with passion, "I pray that I will remember every second of this time. I mean, oh my God, they're all driving me completely nuts. But I *pray* that I'll remember this." That's exactly how I feel. Jon and Myla Kabat-Zinn, a pair of groovy Buddhists, wrote this great Zen parenting book called *Everyday Blessings*, and whenever I pick it up, I'm inspired afresh to pay attention—but truly, deeply—to these two kids of mine. They're so *nice*, these Kabat-Zinns, that you can't even hate them for being better parents than you are. Well, you can hate them a *teeny* bit. But if we practiced what they call *mindful parenting*, then "Perhaps," they think, "we would hold our moments differently. Perhaps they would not slip by so unnoticed, so unused, so filled up by us with busyness or diversions."

Exactly. "There is no *after* the snowsuit," I tried to tell my fledgling Zen self all winter, when I would spend a thousand hours wrangling Ben into his long underwear, snow pants, and boots, only to spend another thousand hours peeling them all off—frantically—so that he could pee. Then I'd layer it all back on, Ben looking like a miniature samurai toboggan champion, but by then it would be too dark to go out. "There is only the snowsuit *itself*."

That's how I feel now about changing Birdy's diaper five trillion times a day. There is no *after* the diaper changing. There is *only* the diaper changing, as much a moment to be cherished—albeit a damp and yellow moment—as any other. And sometimes, when I watch her grinning up at the faces on her mobile (one of those Bauhaus black-and-white numbers that we used to refer to as Ben's "real parents"), yelping at them joyfully while I thread her spaghetti arms into their sleeves, I actually believe this.

So, when I locked the keys inside the car at my six-week checkup and had to drag Birdy and her car seat through the sleety rain, back to the OB's office—stepping around the seasonal heaps of drowning worms and thawing dog shit—I tried to be totally Zen about it. I nursed her in the waiting room for the hour and a half it took poor Michael to come and get me. Here, I thought, here I am, now, feeding this beautiful baby bird, which is what I would be doing at home anyways. Here, I thought, here I am, now, holding this peaceful, sleeping baby, pleasantly scanning the Hollywood couplings and uncouplings of *People* magazine. Here, I thought, here I am now, starving, STARVING! Starving so completely to death that I'll be a maternity-pants-wearing skeleton—with Birdy still latched on, no doubt—by the time Michael ever picks me up.

But I was calm again when Michael appeared—grateful, even, and appropriately sheepish. So, my tranquil new Zen self just about broke even with my old anxious, cranky self. Which isn't half bad, if you ask me.

I was, though, so ravenous when we got home that I had to stand at the refrigerator shoveling cold macaroni and cheese into my mouth while Birdy cried and waited to nurse. We call this "putting on your own oxygen mask," after the airplane injunction "Put on your own oxygen mask before assisting others with their masks." It is not uncommon for Michael to come home and find me cramming food into my pie hole while the children wait, with varying degrees of patience and impatience, to be fed. "Putting on your own oxygen mask?" he always asks. Well, sure. I mean, my God, even the Dalai Lama has to eat, no?

At some point, Michael thought to ask me about my appointment. "It was great," I said. "Fine. And we got the all-clear to have sex again!" Michael laughed. They had even asked me what form of *birth control* we were planning to use now. "Um, never having sex again?" I had offered. Because the mere fact of the obstetric thumbs-up is not going to be enough right now to get our erotic wheels turning—you know, light a few candles, put on a little low jazz, and take a crowbar to the boards that someone seems to have nailed up over my libido.

I'm loath to feed into any lame stereotypes about women and sex—about how women suffer sex like an affliction. That's total crap. Women *want* sex. We need it. But these early years, with babies and young children in the house? With breasts full of milk and a mind full of baby talk? Picture a snuffer moving over the flame of a candle. Picture a pair of underpants with the words "Nobody Home." Picture me laughing, "Oh my God, are you *kidding* me?" when Michael looks at me with those glittery, hooded eyes.

Partly, I think it's hormones—a tactful suggestion by your glands that maybe, while you're still nursing one baby, you shouldn't go ahead and make *another* baby. Partly, I think it's that caring for babies and young children is such a bodily occupation: I wipe bottoms and cuddle warm bodies and suckle a gigantic person who looks me in the eyes longingly. When the kids finally fall asleep—after scrambling around on top of me and twisting up in my hair and rubbing my face and tummy, groping me all over—my first thought is not "Who *else's* body parts might I now glom onto my own?" My first thought is usually about a centimeter or two of personal space: a bath, a beer, the latest issue of *The New Yorker*. A fiery round of Scrabble or even a video rated "R" for sexually explicit content. But not so much a game of naked Twister.

And will my breasts ever again be an erotic part of my body? I'm going to have to go ahead and predict "No." Someone might as well just open the refrigerator and caress the milk bottles in there. Besides the fact that by the time I'm done nursing they're going to be about as alluring as empty banana peels.

I have this radical idea that I want to spread around: I think that OBs should scrap the whole "six weeks" thing about sex. Six weeks! I don't even know anyone brave enough to investigate their *own* nether parts six weeks after the birth of their baby. I'm still trying not to even think about what's going on down there—the way you might shield your eyes during a horror movie ("Is my vagina still actually *separate* from my rear end?" is just one of the many questions you might entertain).

So forget six weeks. Here's what I want: I want them to tell you that you have to wait *two years!* That would just totally take the pressure off. You could shrug, disappointed, and say to your partner, "I'm so sorry, honey. Believe me, I'm *dying* to—but the doctor said . . ." Then, if you happened to actually do it during that two-year period, you could feel very naughty and smug, like you had this great burning passion that couldn't even wait for *two years!*

Right?

We've just started reading *Doctor Dolittle* to Ben. And while it's thrilling to be revisiting this favorite from my own childhood, I have to admit that some of it now seems gratuitously bizarre. I remember the great glass snail, sure, but a shady character called the "cat's-meat man"? Not so much. "What's a 'cat *smeat* man'?" Ben asks, half asleep.

"I'm not really sure," I tell him. "Maybe someone who makes food for people's pets."

"Then why does he want to poison all the animals?"

"Um, so that Doctor Dolittle will have more work at his vet practice. But it's a naughty, naughty idea, isn't it?" I'm worried that when we go to read *Little House on the Prairie,* there will be a weird pioneer detail—some unsavory butter-churning incident, something nasty in the woodshed—that I hadn't recalled.

But Ben seems to be enjoying this quirky old book nonetheless. Probably because his imagination, like that of all his friends, is largely consumed by animals. A lot, this just looks like a great fear of dogs—specifically, and somewhat misguidedly, of dogs *licking* him. "Is he not going to lick me?" Ben asks—about Tyla the golden retriever, Daisy the brown Lab, Eloise the miniature poodle—as he leaps into your arms in a panic. "Um, yeah, Ben?" Michael teases, out of his earshot, "Licking is the least of your worries. Have you seen that dog's *teeth?*"

But also, of course, Ben adores animals. Michael's aunt sent him a horse figurine, Midnight, who comes with his own little novella about him and his girl, Amy. Ben loves it. It's a sweet book—not my own personal cup of tea, but totally harmless. Well, maybe not *totally*. There's a strange Harlequin-Romance type interlude, where Amy grooms Midnight for a little too long and everyone seems a little too into it. It's not as unlike porn as you might expect. Here's an excerpt: "After Amy had rubbed Midnight down with a rag, she cautiously approached his rear. She didn't want to take him by surprise and frighten him. She combed his long ebony tail, then rubbed in some baby oil for an added sheen. . . ." If Michael's in bed with us when we're reading it, he licks his lips and casts me lascivious looks, and I have to try not to laugh.

The book's earnest, repetitive dialogue has inspired some truly endless pretend games with Ben. Ben plays Amy and you have to be Midnight, or the other way around. Either way, Ben speaks in the same soft, high-pitched voice because it's his all-purpose Animal Voice—the one he uses to speak both *to* and *as* animals. "Are you Midnight, my horse?" Ben asks.

"Yes, I am," you have to falsetto back to him.

"Am I getting you for my birthday?" he asks.

"Yes, you are."

"And are you maybe a little too powerful for me?" This is one of the book's main plot lines.

"Yes," you have to squeak back, "maybe a little."

"Oh," he says, "I think you are." This continues until you start to feel like your brain is getting pins and needles.

Remember that scene in *Airplane*, with that guy droning on and on about his lost love while the people around him are dousing themselves with gasoline and tying nooses around their necks? It's like that. Sometimes if you're lucky, Ben might mix it up a little. "Did you know that Midnight grew up to fix cars?" he asked us this morning, tapping the hood of a matchbox car with the figurine's hooves. "Ah!" Michael said. "Horse mechanic! 'I think it's your alterneiiiightor.'" (It's like when the Muppets sing about the letter *B* on *Sesame Street*—the fact that it's set to the tune of the Beatles' "Let It Be" is not for the kids; it's simply to keep the parents awake and sane.)

But it's not just Midnight—Ben's a little cloudy on the whole concept of "growing up." As far as he seems to be concerned, adulthood is a metamorphic free-for-all. "When Kepler grows up," he has announced about our neighbor's dog, "he's going to be a little boy. But when *I* grow up, I'm going to be a girl so that I can have a little yoni. *And* a penis." Okey-doke. And yesterday he announced, suddenly, "When I grow up, and Birdy and I are partners, like you and Daddy, then maybe we'll get rings too." *Holy Appalaichia!* as Kathy would say. But I couldn't help smiling. What a sweet thought, in its own strange way. I guess it would preempt the whole problem of in-laws.

How much *do* they understand, these three-year-olds? We were at our friend Carey's house last week, and her son, Josh, Ben's age, came running up to her with an urgent question: "Mama?" he asked, "Am I human?" Carey nodded. "You are," she told him, and Josh went skipping off triumphantly, shouting to his older sister, "Sarah, I *am* human!" It killed us—such a modest goal!

Although, look at Birdy, and you might think that it's not such a modest goal after all. She's still working on the basics, like not whacking herself in the eye with her own fist. Her hands flap around her face like bats. She gains control long enough to claw a red scratch across her cheek or to make a few mysterious signs to the pitcher—one finger up, then two, then knuckles to the lips, *curve ball!*—and then they're off again, roaming indiscriminately through the air. But yesterday she was lying around on her mat, grunting and pumping her legs around, and she actually grabbed the rattle that was lying next to her! She did it kind of on the sly—she never actually *looked* at the rattle—so it was a little like she was shoplifting. Or like a severed hand had grabbed onto a child's toy. But we were terribly impressed. Even Ben—who is not generally moved by Birdy's usual repertoire of pooping and nursing—looked over. "Can you believe she grabbed her rattle?" I asked him, and he smiled and shook his head. "Good job, Birdy!" he said and patted her. "We're so proud of you." Talk about proud! He's only human, that Ben, in the best possible way.

———

Who are these alleged babies who fall asleep the second they're strapped into their car seats? Birdy—like her brother, Ben, before her—is about as likely to fall asleep in the car as she is to stay in the same outfit all day without poop leaking out of her diaper in damp, spreading circles. Which is to say: not likely. Once in a while she'll drop off for a minute or two, but only after she's cried so hard that she succumbs to something like a hyperventilated narcolepsy. Her car seat *torments* her. It's like she's being strangled to death by an octopus, and it makes you think really hard about how badly you want to go somewhere with her. The drugstore for nursing pads and Raisinettes? Unavoidable. Pete's Drive-in to meet Kathy for soft ice cream? A dubious call.

But that's the call I made this afternoon. Birdy was fine for about one minute. Then she started making her little dissatisfied grunts. These are the prelude to the full-on weepy howling that makes me feel like my brain is being fed through a shredder. I sped along, trying to hold the sobbing at bay, but at the first stoplight, we were screwed. I turned up the radio— Fleetwood Mac, "Gold Dust Woman"—and jabbed my foot on and off the brake to rock the car. I sang loudly. Because our air conditioner is broken and it was three hundred degrees out, the windows were down (except, of course, for the broken one that has a garbage bag duct-taped over it). The college kids walking by in their hip jeans all turned to stare at us: Birdy screaming like she was getting branded at a cattle ranch, me belting out a seventies chart-topper and jerking my Ford station wagon back and forth. I must look like a different *species* to them. If I had ever been cool, this would have been a serious setback for the old ego.

It's quite harrowing. And yet, I'm so much thicker-skinned than I was with the newborn Ben. I used to pull over and nurse Ben every time he cried; it took an hour just to drive to the end of our block. In truth, with Ben, the car was the least of my worries. Nothing—none of the bracing how-to books, no dandling of somebody else's sad baby—had prepared me for the experience of Ben crying. If he so much as whined a little in my arms, my heart would start to pound, and by the time he was fully crying—so open-mouthed you could see his uvula shaking in his throat, like a cartoon baby—I would be sweating and frantic. *What do I do? What do I do?* Panic looped through my body like an eel.

I couldn't *believe* that other parents were going through this. When Ben cried, the entire universe seemed to fill with the sound, and I felt, frankly, like I would die. Michael and I scanned the checklists of newborn crying: "A hair wound around his finger or toe?" No. "Clothing too tight or too loose?" We didn't think so. "Diaper dry?" Dry enough. "Hungry?" I would nurse him for the umpteenth time just to check, but no. "There is always a reason," one book admonished, "and you will recognize exactly what it is." I never knew the reason. I was surely the worst mother on the planet. The sobfest tended to start in the late afternoon, and by the time Sam got home from work, I'd hand her my red, tearful baby—red and tearful myself—and he'd fall asleep almost instantly on her chest, like, "Thank God *somebody* is not giving me a total heart attack!"

Looking back, I'm not even sure if Ben cried objectively much or not. I'm guessing *not*. I looked at the clock once, after he'd been crying for unbroken hours on end, and realized that it had actually only been seventeen minutes. But time had become an unfamiliar substance, shifty as quicksand or mercury. When Ben cried, the minutes thickened around us like sap. At his one-month checkup, I mentioned it to the doctor. "He *cries* a lot," I confessed, my voice coarse with the enormity of it, and Dr. Bennet had smiled. "Is 'crybaby' not an expression you've heard?" he asked, and even though he was only teasing, I was struck dumb by the question. A crying baby! What a cliché! The most mundane thing in the world. But my actual experience of it—my panicked, sweating experience—felt so singular. Alienatingly singular, even.

I pressed the issue. "Do you think it's"—and I'm sure I whispered this last part—*"colic?"* Colic! The books fill you with unutterable dread. They make you feel like you might open your door the morning your baby turns six weeks old, and waiting there will be a demonic delivery boy, the parcel in his arms stamped "COLIC." "This is for you," he will cackle before leaving, and you'll be completely fucked. Or that's what it felt like to me, at least. The doctor had shrugged. "I guess it could be colic," he'd said, "but I wouldn't worry too much. It's probably just gas."

Just gas indeed. You spend your life farting or not farting—whatever—and then suddenly you have a new baby, and gas consumes your every waking thought (thanks to the marathon nights, of course, *all* your thoughts are waking ones). If I eat that coleslaw, will the baby writhe in pain all evening? Does his tummy feel hard to you? Is he sucking in air while he nurses? Should I give up dairy products? (My answer to that last question? No. You've got enough to worry about without depriving yourself of ice cream's milky comforts.) We borrowed an infant massage video, in the hopes that we might coax some of the gas from Ben's belly and relax him. But a minute into it, I was devastated. Here were all these babies, lying placidly on their backs and cooing, their capable mothers slicking them with oil, while Ben screamed on the rug in front of me, flailing his limbs like a windmill. I looked at the video and then back to Ben. I felt like I'd been given the wrong materials for the project at hand—like everyone around me was winding colorful yarn around Popsicle sticks, capably completing their God's Eyes, while I fumbled around with a handful of gravel and some rubber cement.

"Three months" seemed to be the agreed-upon endpoint of newborn crying, and I practically sat by the clock, watching the second hand spin around. Comparing those days to the way I feel now, about Birdy crying—it's like comparing the prom scene from *Carrie* with a square dance. I don't even know if Birdy actually cries less, or less loudly, or if it's simply that we've done this before—and that our every last ray of attention is not telescoped in on her, the way it was with Ben. I feel sorry for Birdy when she cries, but it's more like "Poor baby!" than like "Call the paramedics!" Even if there are other people around when she starts her nightly weepies, I don't imagine that they are electrified with horror. I don't imagine that they even notice it at all, really. And I trust that Birdy herself is, in some fundamental if not apparent way, okay.

Luckily, too, Birdy's crying puts Ben directly—and soundly—to sleep. This is the first time he has ever slept soundly in his entire life. We worried so much that her shrieking would upset him, but we always look back to see him dozing peacefully in his car seat while she screams bloody murder. He sleeps like a stone. Like a heavy sack of boy. And it seems like a good coping strategy to me. Even a short trip like this, to get ice cream, and—zap!—he's conked out by the time we get there. Given the chance, I'm sure I would do the same.

And it was all worth it to see Kathy and her kids. Will, her three-year-old, and Ben became entirely sticky and pink (Ben from a large, drippy cherry-dip cone and Will—remarkably—from a single Twizzler), and played hide-and-seek inside the restaurant. Ben is not entirely clear on the concept of hiding games. "I'm going to hide over there," Ben told Will, pointing. "You come with me, okay?" Will wanted to play the normal way—you know, where you don't actually hide *with* the person you're trying to find—so he started counting. "He has to count to 'thirty-fourteen,'" Kathy whispered to me, and I laughed. Ben himself counts only to "twenty-ten."

It's such a funny age for game playing. Yesterday, over breakfast, Ben asked, suddenly, "Where's my juice?" "Right there, silly," I said, "in your cup." "No, no, no," he said like I was being totally dense. "You say, 'I don't know' and then you guess all the wrong places where it is." So we played a few rousing rounds of "Where's Ben's juice?" Is it in the bird feeder? *Noooooo.* Is it in the pepper grinder? *Noooooo.* The heartbreaking part is when Ben gets a little confused and forgets the basic principle of the game he's invented. "Is it in the teapot, over there with your tea set?" I asked at some point, and Ben's face lit up. "Yes!" he said, "I think *that's* where it is!" and he ran over to check. "No," he said, after lifting the lid off the teapot, "it's not in here." "I think it's in your *cup*," I whispered to him, and he laughed and said, "Oh, yeah. Right."

We spent the rest of the morning blowing dandelion puffs. Ben is amazed by the parachuting seeds, the kind of amazement that reminds you why it's a cliché that your kids make you see things as if you've never seen them before. He's amazed by the bright light green of the spring trees. "High yellow," Ben calls it. (We felt like we had some great Southern poet in our midst until it turned out that the derivation is from the neon color of the highlighter pens he thieves from our desk.) "Oooh, look at all these pretty violets!" he said later, and tiptoed to avoid squashing them. The air was so fresh—just walking around outside felt like drinking something cold and tart, but with the sun warming your face. "Is it always spring now?" Ben wondered. I asked him if he could remember what came after spring. "Summer!" he said. "Is summer about as big as a string cheese?" "I don't know," I said. "Is a string cheese big or small?" "Kind of big and kind of small." He moved his hands apart and then together to show me. "Then, yes," I said. "That's summer. Kind of big and kind of small."

But my God—doesn't that describe everything? Kind of big and kind of small. Time with a new baby. Childhood. And life itself.

So Birdy was officially off the charts, weight-wise, at her two-month checkup. A total piglet, as we have long suspected, and I'm glad. I love fat babies—all those munchable dinner roll legs and arms, that vast oasis of cheek and chin. (Of course, if she were a skinny baby, I'd love *skinny* babies: their delicacy and grace, their fairy limbs. *So much more alert and essential than those blobby old fat babies*, I'd be thinking.) But here's the one downside to the scrumptious roly-polies—and I'll write this in a whisper: *stinky neck folds*. Something is festering in Birdy's neck, in a deep fold that's somehow inside three other folds. Michael and I can only catch a glimpse of it when the two of us pry open the concentric layers of her chin, like a set of magic doors. Think Gorgonzola crossed with pond water. It's not good.

I was mortified to tell the pediatrician about it. "Anything else?" he asked, after all the normal measuring and ogling, and I panicked. "Um, yeah, well, we really try to clean her and everything? But I think she's rotting a little bit. In her neck." He smiled at me and helped me jimmy open the folds to look. "Ah!" he said, and scrunched up his nose. "I see. But hey—I've seen *much* rottener babies than this!" Phew! At least we don't have the world's *very* rottenest baby. It turns out she has a yeast infection in her neck, poor kid. We have to wash her neck and *blow it dry with a hair dryer* before putting ointment on it. I worry that someone will look through our window and imagine that what I'm blowing dry is her quarter-inch fuzz of hair. "It's just *impossible* to style unless we blow it out straight," I could explain, shrugging.

But vanity is the least of our worries right now, because yeast has opened a bigger shop of horrors right here in our home. Birdy also has thrush—a yeast infection in her mouth—and a yeast diaper rash. I myself have thrush on my nipples, and also a vaginal yeast infection. We are a pair of very yeasty girls. Put us in a room with a sack of flour and—boom!—bread will be made spontaneously. We now have to swab this milk-shakey banana medicine on the inside of Birdy's mouth four times a day, and then I have to put the same fruity gunk on my nipples. I'll spare you the crass jokes that are getting made around here.

You might think that all this infectious hoopla would di-minish Birdy's zest for nursing, but you'd be wrong. She still manages to chug down her requisite daily gallon or two. And yet, I can't help feeling that she is not quite the passionate nurser that Ben was. He would nurse for hours and hours, like a contestant in his own personal nurse-a-thon. I'd hike up my shirt to offer him a boob, and he'd do that little kicking, impa-tient thing, grunting and whimpering, like this was just the last straw and he really couldn't wait one more second. Then he'd greet the boob like a long-lost friend, all smiles and wide eyes at it, before planting his suckerfish of a mouth. He'd guzzle away for ages, looking up at me every now and then and smiling, like, "Hey! *You're* here too! How nice."

Birdy gets right to the business of *eating*, and then pops off when she's full, milk spilling from her mouth, her head lolling back like a drunk's. And I just don't worry. I don't wish, as I did with Ben, that my boob were see-through, with measuring-cup markings on it so that I could determine how much she was actually getting. I trust that she's getting enough. And—this is the crucial thing—I'm not keeping a nursing log. In the hospital, they try to make you think that if you don't write it all down, then *the baby's not actually nursing.* They're lying about this. If a baby nurses in the forest, but you're not there to write it down, she's still getting plenty of milk. Or something.

I became completely obsessed with the nursing log when Ben was small, and it really detracted from the organic pleasure of breast-feeding. "Start time 3:23," I'd shout to Michael in the middle of the night, like the Indy 500 was revving into action in the glide rocker. "Left side. Write it down! And did you make a note of that last poop? How it was kind of seedy-looking?" Every drop of intake and expulsion was recorded diligently. I kept the nursing log for months, and we developed that recording disorder you get on vacation, where you feel like you have to take a photograph of everything, or it's like you didn't actually *see* it. "Get a picture," you snap, irritated, while a waterfall crashes behind you in miraculous, breathtaking rainbows. "Jesus Christ, I thought you said it was a roll of thirty-six." I remember the nursing log almost as vividly as I remember the nursing itself.

So after Birdy was born, I refused to start again. "There's nothing written here," the nurses would scold in the hospital, shaking the blank chart at me like I was failing algebra again. "But look at her," I want to tell them now. "I think she's getting enough."

Something is up with one of Ben's arms, and we're waiting to find out what, exactly, it is. We have an appointment
at the Shriners Orthopedic hospital at eight tomorrow morning, and I have that squirrelly anxious feeling in my stomach—
like I'm taking a really, really big test, only it's one I can't even
study for. I can sit still for about forty-five seconds at a time.

The truth is that I've been seeing this thing with his arm—
a way that it bulges near the elbow when he bends it, a way that
his wrist looks oddly narrow—for months. It's hard to explain.
"*How* long have you noticed this?" the pediatrician (still not our
beloved one) asked me when I brought him in, like I'd been so
negligent. I felt sick. I may be a lot of things, but low-key about
the health of my kids is not one of them. If I could, I would
bring them in *nightly*, in their jammies, just to get a pediatric
thumbs-up. So I couldn't describe the way I'd see something
out of the corner of my eye sometimes, but then I'd study Ben's
arm closely and it would look fine. Finally, though, we'd been
getting him undressed the other night, and I'd shown it to
Michael and it had definitely looked strange to both of us.
"Does this hurt?" we asked Ben, moving his hand back and
forth, and he'd smiled and said, "No," and wiggled his hips
around to prove it.

We got sent to radiology, where they took a bunch of X-
rays of both of his arms. "Oooh, Mama!" Ben said when I put
my lead apron on, "You look *fancy!*" He'd been so worried that
they were going to swab out his throat again—the poor kid's
had strep twice in three months—that the whole prodding and

X-raying episode was like a tour of the playground, as far as he was concerned. "Do I look fancy too?" he asked and twirled around in his little lead loincloth. The X-ray person kept referring to his "good arm" and his "bad arm," and I tried to give her the *ix-nay* sign—finger across the throat—about saying "bad arm," but she didn't notice. Don't we even get five minutes to figure this thing out before deciding that Ben has a "bad arm"? Sheesh.

On film, the bones of his arm are markedly bowed and not connected into his elbow right—you can see this clearly. The doctor shook her head over the X-rays and looked concerned. I started to feel shaky. "You're supposed to say, 'Oh, he's just double-jointed—all kids are like that!' " I said, but she didn't even smile. She told us that she was going to send us to Shriners. "They may want you to do some blood work first," she said, "you know, to rule out any of the big stuff." My whole head filled with an oceany kind of roar and I could hardly hear myself speak to her. "Big stuff?" I said, and she shrugged and nodded. "Like c-a-n-c-e-r?" I spelled, in a whisper. (Despite the fact that Ben grins and grins at Judy's luscious bald head, I know that the gravity of the disease is not lost on him.) She nodded. "It's probably something congenital, though," she said. "Or he may have dislocated his elbow at some point. They might leave it alone. They might put a cast on it. I'm not really sure."

Later she called to say that the radiologist hadn't seen anything that looked like a tumor. The roar in my head quieted down a little. *Cancer*—I couldn't even hold it still in my mind long enough to get a good look at it. It just flitted around in my brain like a bumblebee. Like a cold wind. We're so barely recovered from our scare with Birdy, I feel a little worn out with fear. But also, I'm worried that we've already used our luck up. "Jesus," Liz said when I talked to her on the phone. "Why so much drama? To remind us that we're all really lucky? That we need to live life to the fullest? Yeah, well, *Uncle*. We get it." Uncle indeed.

I got online to look up "Shriners" and there they were—all of them in their funny little Grand Poo-Bah hats. Who *are* the Shriners? I searched the specialist to make sure that he had a real medical degree (he did) and not, like, a Certificate of Arm Bones from the Medical-style School of Shriners. (Later, my brother was appalled by my doubt. "The Shriners have probably done more for children's health than any other organization," he scolded, and I was appropriately chagrined.) Next I plugged in a bunch of search terms—"bowed radius," "dislocated elbow," "congenital arm disorders"—and read a bunch of stuff I did and didn't understand. "Do you think Ben might be a dwarf?" I yelled to Michael in the other room, and he was quiet for a second. "No," he yelled back. "I don't think so. Hon? I think you should get off the Internet." I only came to links for the Make-a-Wish Foundation twice, but each time my heart skipped fifteen beats.

When I think about kids being really sick, my limbs all turn to bags of sand. A *nuisance* I can handle: a cast, Ben being uncomfortable for a while, Ben's arm having a funny shape. I can already picture the other kids calling him "Curveball," or maybe "Crazy Arm"—although of course I have to picture them saying it affectionately so that it doesn't hurt my feelings. *Good old Crazy Arm! God, I love that guy.* Ben doesn't need to be perfect—just alive and in not a lot of pain.

"Let's hope it's nothing serious," my dad said when I talked to him on the phone, and then he was silent for a second before saying, "My God, that's such a stupid thing to say! What are you going to say? 'Let's hope it *is* serious?' Sorry." But he's right. There's nothing else to say. Let's hope it's nothing serious.

So it *is* nothing serious, this thing with Ben's arm. We are, again, drenched in relief and gratitude. Another healthy child. Hallelujah! It turns out that the bones in his fore-arm are bowed, and this has pulled his elbow permanently out of its socket. A "congenitally dislocated radial head." That's it. It shouldn't hurt him or limit his range of motion, it most likely won't get worse over time, and they're not even treating it. It is what's technically called a "birth defect," although the term seems needlessly derogatory—I'd rather just think of it as a birth *variation:* Ben's curvy arm. "Defect" sounds more like a misshapen jelly bean. A hot-air popper with a leaky butter tray. Not this wildly original kid.

We tried to make the orthopedist at Shriners do scary one-in-a-million worst-case scenarios, but he just kept smiling and shaking his head and telling us that everything would be fine. I had to stop myself from kissing him. I also had to stop myself from asking about the English minor that I happen to know he completed as an undergrad at Penn. ("Just as well," Michael said later. "Nobody's ever too thrilled about creepy Internet stalking.") And the hospital was amazing—great doctors and nurses, excellent unshabby toys, nobody acting gratuitously mean or scary. Plus, it's a charitable organization, so they won't even bill our health insurance for the visit. I am officially in love with the Shriners. Especially the actual Shriner we saw on his tour of the hospital—all glamorous and important, with "Potentate" spelled out in rhinestones on his enormous fez. Totally Village People, in an elderly fraternal lodge kind of way.

In truth, though, the waiting room was a little bit staggering: lots of kids with lots of variations on bodies. Lots of smiling, regular kids with oddly shaped limbs or limbs that were just frankly missing. It was humbling. And also inspiring—all these kids and parents living with so much fear and heartache, but mostly just sitting there, putting together farm animal puzzles, waiting to see doctors—to see what the next thing would be.

I'd like to say that I'll worry less now—I mean, anything could happen, why bother trying to prepare?—but I'm not sure it's true. Because then in the car last night, Ben choked on an orange Lifesaver—went wild-eyed with fear and asphyxiation before managing to swallow it. If we were a cartoon family, then an anvil would have fallen on him just as we were leaving the hospital with our good news. Years are dropping away from my life by the dozen. When we got home, I watched Ben and Birdy sleep, and these waves of love crashed over me, and it was deeply pleasurable, but also entirely overwhelming. My dad has assured me that it will *never* get any better, this life of worry. Poor guy. He had anticipated that maybe having grandchildren would help him worry less—you know, the diversifying of his assets and all—but, it turns out, there are just more and more people for him to add to his roster of concern.

But Ben himself is blissfully *un*concerned by all this drama. If you asked him, he'd tell you that he liked walking around on his heels to show his strong legs off to the doctor. He'd tell you that he's worried that I will never give him another Lifesaver again (indeed, I never will). He just wants to get back to the business of his life. Like riding his new big-kid bike with training wheels. We got the bike secondhand, and it's *loaded*: painted pink and purple, with a basket and a rack *and* handlebar fringe. Totally Pinky Tuscadero. He rides it down the street and does this very cool, grown-up thing, where he says, "Hey, how's it going?" to the neighbors he passes—like it's no big deal, just a regular kid riding by on his bike.

Plus, there's his exhausting job of continuing to pretend that Birdy doesn't exist. She's getting so smiley and outgoing now that this is more of a challenge. And she actually tries to get a hold of him when he's nearby—reaching out her sticky little sharp-nailed grabbers, which just completely disgust Ben. But he actually held her! The inaugural sibling-in-the-lap event. Despite the fact that we had badly wanted to send out the usual second-child birth announcement—the one that depicts the proud older sibling gloating over the new baby—we just couldn't bring ourselves to orchestrate it. "Here," we could have said, "the baby has ruined your life. But hold her— Okay?—so we can get a cute picture." This time it was Ben's idea. Birdy schlumped in his lap for about three seconds, then he handed her back, said "That was nice," wrinkled up his nose, and wiped his hands on his pants. It reminded me of something he once said after our friends had been visiting for the weekend. "Did Andrew give you the Bee Gees?" he asked Michael. I myself did not remember any exchange of the *Saturday Night Fever* soundtrack. "What, hon?" Michael asked, and Ben said, "Did Andrew talk about his root canal and you said, 'Oooh, stop—you're giving me the *Bee Gees*'?" Ah, yes. Birdy seems to give Ben a big case of the screaming Bee Gees.

"There are four of us now," Ben said to me last week while Birdy was nursing, "but really there should only be three." I was in a good mood, and also thinking quickly. "Oh, honey," I said, "but we'd miss Dad so much!" Ben actually laughed. On a different day, if I were feeling less convivial, he would have been subjected to a lecture about Birdy being part of our family now, blah blah blah. I'm happy to have spared him this once. So long as that boy is safe and sound, he can feel however he feels.

***

Rock, paper, scissors. Okay, forget about the rock. There's no rock. But if I had to guess right now, I would say that Ben dreams mostly about scissors and paper. Ben can sit and cut paper the way I can sit and eat pistachio nuts—there's no natural end to the process, it's just a question of somebody else deciding for you that you've probably had enough. Ben has never had enough. Every piece of paper he can get his hands on—including all of his old drawings and most of the notes on the phone table—gets snipped into a heap of odd shapes. These are either dumped into the brown paper shopping bag that's also full of dirty rocks from the yard, or else they're slipped inside the canned-food cabinet, whence they tumble out whenever you go hunting (Good luck!) for something for dinner. "Oh, Mama," Ben says, "those are my e-mails. Please be careful." The scraps might also be stuck to any of the designated major appliances with long tentacles of Scotch tape.

And what is our official Scotch Tape Policy? Ben feels about a roll of tape the way our old cat felt about an open can of tuna fish: he can't rest if he knows it's in the house. And although

Michael and I are staunchly committed to the idea of *consistency* in our parenting, the tape issue keeps us waffling. On the one hand, we want to instill in Ben the value of *conservation:* yes, there is some tape in the house, but we don't need to unwind the entire roll just to adhere an index card to the refrigerator (the issue of whether or not we *want* the index card adhered to the fridge is a separate one). On the other hand, Ben is a person with a vision: he has projects in mind, theories of adhesion to pursue. I, for instance, would go nuts if Michael suddenly said to me, "You can use that pen to write two words, but then *that's it. . . .*" So currently, Ben has his own roll of Scotch tape to use up in a taping binge or to hoard as he sees fit. (He also has his own box of Elmo Band-aids, expressly for treating pretend injuries—our solution to the Great and Tedious Band-aid Debates.)

But back to the scraps. Most are meticulously decorated. He might use pens ("That's not a *pen*," says Mr. Bossypants, with some irritation—usually in response to my asking him to *please pick his pen up off the floor*—"That's a *marker.*") or crayons, and he might make some squiggles and spirals and a handful of fabulously ornate letters. (Why have the N only go up and down and up, when you could have it go back down and up a few more times? seems to be his philosophy.) Then he signs his name on the back—B-E-N or N-E-B, depending on whether he writes it with his right or his left hand. And then the scrap is filed—bag or cabinet—according to a system that is as clear to Ben as it is occult to us.

Everywhere you look, there are scraps and shreds of paper. Cutting up any paper that has adult handwriting on it is now strictly verboten, but I still seem to spend half my life digging among cans of kidney beans to look for important phone numbers, which, even if I find them, have inevitably been snipped beyond recognition. I'd be angrier about this, but it's just so clear to me that Ben can't help himself. He can't *not* cut a piece of paper that he sees—the same way that I couldn't *not* drink a mug of coffee you left lying around, even if you asked me please not to.

Also, I'm really no better when it comes to leaving scraps of paper everywhere. Instead of keeping a normal journal like a normal person, I write down bits and pieces of our lives—funny stuff that Ben says, something new that Birdy has done—on envelopes and bills and magazine inserts, in the hopes that I will one day transfer them all into a beautiful, ribbon-tied book that would be a more likely heirloom candidate than this huge rubber-banded pile of scraps scrawled with my inane observations.

Plus, I tend to write one-word reminders, but I don't always remember what they mean. Over breakfast I saw the word "shrenk" written on the back of our phone bill. I knew it was something funny that Ben has said, but I couldn't remember what. "Honey, what's 'shrenk' mean?" I asked him, and he chewed his cereal thoughtfully. "You know, Mama. Shrenk. Like, 'You have to eat a good breakfast to keep up your *shrenk*.'" Aha! God give me *shrenk*.

But sitting here is another scrap, which says "Birdy is peaking," and I *do* know exactly what that's about: Birdy is peaking! She is achieving the absolute apex of baby yumminess. These days, that girl's just one big drooling, gummy smile with a little fringe of fuzzy hair. If you even so much as cast your eyes on her, her face opens into a gigantic grin, and she kicks her little legs around like a Russian dancer.

And sure, *sleeping* is not one of her finest skills. She seems to be nursing more and more and more in the wee hours. (But, as my friend Anna once said, "If you slept with an open bag of Fritos next to you in the bed, wouldn't you roll over to have one every now and then?") But this does at least spare me the potential agony of *missing* her in the night! A silver lining. Besides, now that I don't lie awake with my heart banging around in some or other terror, I'm happy enough to be up in the night. Truly.

I think I may be starting to relax in a profound way. Various pros and cons attend this relaxing. On the one hand, I'm having a lot more fun. On the other, I worry that I'm opening a karmic window for something bad to happen. I know that's crazy—that the worrying itself keeps nobody safe. But our friend Becky was over the other day, and after she snuck upstairs to peek at the napping Birdy, she came down shaking her head. "I'm so impressed that you let her sleep on her stomach," she said. "I was always too worried to." "What?" I said. *"What?"* And I raced up, and there was Birdy, her face pressed into the down comforter, not one half inch from the edge of the bed. My God! Is there no happy ground between pathological vigilance and gross negligence?

But it's true that I worry less about crib death this time around. I must have woken the infant Ben—accidentally—three times an hour to check if he was breathing. Maybe it's just me and my overdeveloped sense of irony, but I'd inevitably peer my head into the room to check, thinking, "Of course he's fine. I'm just being silly." But then I wouldn't see his chest moving, and I'd think, "Oh my God, he's *not* fine! He's actually dead this time!" And then I'd lean in so close that he'd wake up. "Phew!" I'd think. And "Damn!" while I nursed him back to sleep.

Even though sudden infant death syndrome is something that really happens—and I know it does, because it's how my beautiful baby cousin died—I don't think they should tell you about it. I understand that this is a radical recommendation. But suggesting to a new mother that her baby could die in her sleep at any time, for any reason—and that this death can or cannot be prevented, depending on nothing in particular—is like pulling the rug of sanity right out from under her. It's the worst thing in the world, and it looms over you suddenly, out of nowhere. It reminds me of the signs we used to see on the beaches in California: BEWARE OF SLEEPER WAVES. "What's a sleeper wave?" I'd asked a friend, and she'd said, "Oh, it's a huge wave—like a tidal wave—that lifts itself out of the ocean right at the shore. You can't see it coming." Lovely. "Then does it help to 'beware'?" I had asked, and she'd said, "Probably not much." I dreamt for years that I'd be bent over, examining a starfish or a piece of sea glass, only to look up and see a wall of water towering over my head into the sky. After Ben was born, the dreams returned.

Now, with Birdy, I am less profoundly worried. Maybe I feel more grounded in my identity as a parent—like it's not a thing that will likely be snatched from me without a moment's notice. But I know that it could. I do not forget, for one second of my life, that it could.

News flash: Ben is no longer afraid of things floating in the bathtub! To quote Dr. Seuss: "This may not seem very important, I know. But it *is*. So I'm bothering telling you so." Since the inception of his bathphobia, Ben has responded to all objects afloat in his bathwater like they're just *pretending* to be bath toys—the better to attack him and chew his limbs off. Wolves in tub-accessory clothing. If the shampoo bottle falls in while he's bathing, I scramble to retrieve it while Ben cries, yelling "Get it out, Mama! Aaaah! Get it!" like it's an electric eel. A floating washcloth might as well be accompanied by the sound track from *Jaws*. The origin of this fear has eluded us, but it seems to be related to his sense that anything, at any time, could be sucked down the drain hole. Sure, the drain may *seem* small, but Ben has never been fooled.

So, there he was, doing his impersonation of a fast-forwarding film of someone bathing—he washes lickety-split so he can make his getaway before anything falls in—and his orange fish sponge tumbled off the ledge. Before I could even dive for it, Ben pointed and smiled. "The fish is floating," he said calmly, and I smiled back. "I don't even seem to mind," he said, and tossed his miniature watering can in for emphasis. Then a worried look passed over him and he fished the watering can back out hastily. But he did stay in the tub for the Draining of the Water—a phenomenon that usually sends him fleeing for the safe harbor of his towel—and even watched triumphantly as the last eddy swirled away down the drain.

My big, courageous boy! Although this major accomplishment is tempered, ever so slightly, by a baby step backward—also a bathroom event. The other night I went in to see how the tooth brushing was going ("Uh, not so good" is Ben's usual response as he, say, crouches over a cow-pile-sized blob of toothpaste on the floor), and I found him kneeling in front of the toilet. He stood up immediately, guilt oozing from his every pore, and gave me a strange smile. I thought I could see him chewing, but I couldn't tell what he'd been up to. He stood with his arms stiffly at his sides and shrugged through my interrogation of him—"Nothing. I wasn't doing anything."—so I finally concluded with a little lecture about how it's not such a good idea to play near the toilet, germs can make you sick, etc. A few minutes later, when I went to put him to bed, he held one of his stuffed animals up and imitated my stern look. "Now, Mama, Monkey's going to speak sharply to *you* about eating a little hair out of the toilet!" Bummer.

But Birdy is also hitting milestones left and right—and hers are even somewhat traditional. Like rolling over! I'm proud of her, of course, but secretly I have always found rolling over to be one of the lesser accomplishments in a person's life. Especially since rolling over is inevitably accompanied by grief and weeping over *having* rolled over. My babies, at least, do not enjoy flailing around on their bellies like elderly turtles. I was complaining to my brother's lovely wife about this, specifically about how Birdy now rolls around while she's asleep in our bed, and how I worry about where she might end up. Lori, who is a pediatrician, and amazingly tolerant of our hippie parenting style, nodded and said, enunciating every word like I was not likely to follow, "That's what *cribs* are for." Aha! I had wondered.

Birdy is also working on sucking her thumb: she slurps her whole hand into her mouth and makes so many juicy sounds you'd think she was devouring a mango. Now *this*—thumb sucking—I'm rooting for big-time. Mostly because she won't take a pacifier, and I'm hoping to get a little break from the all-night milk bar. ("Last call," I like to whisper into her downy head at two in the morning. . . .) I lie awake nursing her, feeling like a human pacifier, and then I start to fantasize about a kind of "Give Mom a Break" doll you could invent—life-size, with realistic breasts and nipples that the baby could suck. And then I remember that they already *make* dolls like that—you know, the kind you can buy at an adult "bookstore"—and I'm horrified to have associated my baby, even mentally, with them.

All of which is to say that I'm still a little tired. But not as tired as I was two weeks ago when I was on the phone with the cable company (we're getting high-speed Internet access and, because of my former TV addiction, we're actually paying *extra* not to get cable channels) and I started to cry. Two days in a row they had not come during the two-hour "guaranteed" time slot—I'd been waiting inside with the kids, going slightly crazy—and then when I finally called, they said that they *had* come by but we hadn't been home! Naturally, I became hysterical. I cried and cried into the phone—"We *weeeeere* home," I wailed—until the teenage customer service representative said, awkwardly, "Ma'am? I can hear that you're really frustrated. If I were in your shoes, I'm sure I'd be feeling the exact same thing." Poor guy—he must be a very earnest boyfriend to somebody. "Thank you," I said, and felt a little better.

I'm reminded of the marathon phone calls after Ben was born—after my health insurance company claimed (brace yourself) that my C-section had been "elective surgery." They refused to pay for it. Three weeks after we got home, the morning mail brought an itemized bill for something upwards of $22,000 (FYI, a shot of morphine—$4—is a relatively better deal than a single Q-tip, which costs 75 cents). Already deranged with hormones, I spent the better part of every day talking to a baby-voiced representative whose name was—I'm not making this up—"Joe Boy." Mostly I just got put on hold, which meant listening to a scratchy-scratchy FM rock station—a station that was maybe a third of the way tuned in. "So good-bye yellow brick khhhhrrrrrrrrr khhhrrrr . . . where the dogs of society khhhrrrr. . . ." I wondered if the insurance company had pioneered a technique for reducing claims—if they'd devised a list of ways to break your spirit so utterly that you would just pay the stupid bill yourself:

1) Adopt a bizarre and unprofessional name to dilute the customer's confidence in you.
2) Each time they call, even if it's fifteen times a day, act like you have absolutely no idea who they are or what their problem is.
3) Keep them on hold while you eat your lunch.
4) For the hold recording, use the enclosed audiotape of nails scratching on a blackboard. If this is unavailable, try a radio station that's not tuned in. . . .

They finally paid the bill (this involved my OB writing a letter about the birth in which she insisted, among other things, that we had not exactly "selected" an "out-of-plan" anesthesiologist for the emergency C-section), but not the part that involved the hospital's care of the infant. A week later, we got another letter from them in the mail—a letter addressed to Ben himself. "Dear_____," it started, and "Mr. Newman" had been typed into the blank space. "Because our records indicate that you were not a member of our company at the time of your procedure, we deny claims for payment of your_____." The word "birth" had been typed here. "I feel like I'm in a play about a new mother losing her mind," I had sobbed into the phone to Joe Boy. "He wasn't *born* yet. He had to *get* born *before* he could become a member." "Hm," Joe Boy had said. "Please hold."

All of which is to say: the cable company is small potatoes. I probably should have saved my tears for something bigger—like our running out of cream cheese. But I haven't cried since—a milestone in itself, if you ask me. It's such a wonderful but crazy ride, this whole childbearing thing. And thank God I love the kids I've got, because I don't plan on doing it again.

summer, again

—————

When a child loves you for a long, long time, not just to play with, but REALLY loves you, then you become Real. It doesn't happen all at once. You become. It takes a long time. Generally, by the time you are Real, most of your hair has been loved off, and your eyes drop out and you get loose in your joints and very shabby.

Margery Williams
The Velveteen Rabbit

Sometimes when I go to nurse Birdy, and she's so excited and desperate about it, I like to imagine a cocktail party where everyone would act like a baby. They'd be in their fancy strapless dresses and suits, making grand conversation about politics and the arts, but then the tray of little quiches would come around, and they'd go completely bug-eyed and flap their arms up and down and whimper. And then they'd *eat* a little quiche, grunting over it in a busy way, and then they'd smile a big, drooling smile, with quiche crumbs tumbling happily out of their mouths. Maybe every now and then someone would turn bright red and burst into tears before passing explosive gas and falling asleep.

I can see that these are not the ruminations of a perfectly whole mind.

The thing is, I don't know what it's like to nurse a quiet, discreet baby. I see this all around me—women talking over their Caesar salads with babies calmly in their laps, and you think that the baby's asleep, but then you notice that the woman's shirt is kind of bunched up, and you think: Oh, maybe that baby's *nursing*. With Birdy, you'd never have to wonder. Like her brother, Ben, before her, she enjoys showing off a little. She slurps the milk down like she's sucking the meat out of a crab claw. "Gusto" is a word that might leap to mind. Then she pulls away, grinning, while milk sprays all over the place. And she refuses to let me keep my shirt down over the exposed part of my breast, so I end up engaged in an incessant tug-of-war: I pull my shirt down, and then, when I'm not looking, she hikes it back up, all but pointing to my breast with a flashing neon arrow. She also likes to grope the other breast—just to make sure there's more on deck, I guess. (Perhaps this is not so different from grabbing a second handful of chips out of the bag while your mouth is still crammed full with the first.)

In other words: Birdy's not getting any skinnier. I like to put her in this one terry cloth sleeper that's just a *teeny* bit too small for her, because it makes her look like a plump little sausage. Or, the way the snaps are popping, like Elvis Presley in one of his later jumpsuits.

Ben, meanwhile, is getting more easygoing by the second. You know what I love about three-year-olds? They're just so *flexible*. So come-what-may. Nothing needs to look a certain way or be done in a particular order. They're always like, "Hey, Mom, however *you* want to do it. That's just great with me."

I'm kidding, of course.

Everything has to be exactly how Ben imagines it. (And really—am I all that different?) If you pull off his T-shirt without thinking about it, for instance, and Ben wanted to get undressed *by his ownself*, then he will put the shirt back on just so that he can take it off again. Ben can fall into a fit of weeping despair if you so much as—God, what where you thinking?—*move his cup.* Maybe he asked you to please put some more noodles on his plate and you moved the cup a zillionth of an inch just so that you wouldn't knock it to the floor. The second you're done, Ben will move the cup back exactly where it was, teetering on the edge of the table, and if you're lucky, you can return to eating. If you're not lucky—say, if he's already falling apart with tiredness—then the cup won't look quite right in its new spot. In fact it will never be right again, and everything's terrible, and that's not how it was, and what kind of person would move the cup in the first place? *We might as well all kill ourselves* seems to be Ben's weeping, but unspoken, conclusion.

I find this incredibly trying. I start out with good, energetic intentions to validate his feelings. "I can see you're really upset about the cup, Ben. I'm sorry it's not how you want it." But after a minute or two, I say something like "Yeah, well, I'm kind of done talking about the cup." And a minute after that, I may say something really helpful and loud, like "That's enough, Ben."

I *hate* losing my patience and raising my voice. I always feel terrible about it afterward. Sometimes, when I go to put the kids to bed, I breathe a sigh of relief after they fall asleep, like "Thank God *that's* over with!" I confessed this to Kathy—"I mean, what, exactly, am I looking forward to? *Death?*"—and she laughed and imitated my relief, "Thank God *that's* over with—that pesky old life!"

"Don't wish your life away," my mom used to say when we were impatient as kids. I'm sincerely trying not to.

Birdy went on her first camping trip! Okay, well, not camping exactly: we went with Megan and Andrew and their girls, Ayanna and Carly, to a camping "Resort" in Connecticut, and all eight of us slept in a yurt (imagine a flattened teepee, but made of vinyl, with a deck and molded plastic Adirondack chairs). The campground had all the things I used to be so disdainful of *before* we had kids: lit bathrooms, mini golf, a store offering expensive ice-cream cones and expensive Tampax. We used to be moderately avid backpackers, and in truth, I'm not sure that I *ever* loved all that rigor and schlepping, but now I unequivocally don't. Do you know that Evan Dando song "I Lied About Being the Outdoor Type"? It's like that. Who really wants to be hunched in the wilderness over a rehydrating blob of freeze-dried chicken à la king while the kids throw themselves to the ground from hunger and boredom? Why not just take a dip in the pool before grabbing a cold beer from your yurt's handy refrigerator?

The only thing I wasn't totally crazy about—besides the fact that Ben was the only boy there over the age of six months who wasn't dragging around a toy rifle longer than his own leg—was that it was "Circus Weekend." This meant a pair of bickering old acrobats who can best be described as Connecticut's answer to the Zooquarium: a heavily wigged man and a sinewy, tattooed woman named "Tinkerbell" with terrible posture inside her red leotard and a smoker's cough. The props were awfully shabby—shiny balls with the mirrors all peeling off, an ancient miniature poodle with a hard-on—and there was a great deal of hunched-over juggling. It was, all in all, one of the five or so grimmest things I've ever witnessed in my life. (Later, Andrew saw them sitting by their van, splitting a tin of sardines and a pint of cottage cheese, and he returned to the yurt completely depressed.)

But toward the end of their act, a white balloon popped open on a cruddy brown lunch tray, and a snow-white dove flapped out. "Ooooh, *that's* a magic thing!" Ben whispered, and it was true: something wholly beautiful and inexplicable. I looked at Ben's face—his mouth wide with delight, his eyes so big and bright—and I had to shake my head in wonder.

The rest of our time was spent in and around the lake. Birdy and I swam around together some, but I spent a great deal of time with her in the shade on the beach. "Hey, Mama," Ben would yell, "should I just go ahead and pee in the lake, like you said before?" It's hard to explain to your children that there are some things you do that are not exactly wrong—but you just want to do them quietly, without drawing a lot of attention to yourself. Ben's still dealing in starker moral absolutes. So I had to steel myself to yell back, "That's right, hon!" "But we would never *poop* in the lake, right?" he yelled, past the thronging beachful of swimmers, and I laughed. "Right."

Our lazy lake days were punctuated by much arguing about sunscreen. Megan and I were hardly speaking to Andrew and Michael all weekend, since they took the kids out in a rowboat for, like, a million hours, and seemed to indulge in a little fantasy that the ozone layer had been magically repaired. What is it with men? Is there some gene for sunscreen application that only shows up on the X chromosome? (I'm wondering if it might be linked with the gene that controls your ability to buy wrapping paper.)

In truth, I was happy to be distracted by self-righteousness from my swimsuit-induced torpor. Yes, I know I had a baby relatively recently, but my body still feels like an utterly alien thing. Fat hangs in unfamiliar curtains from my upper arms; the top of my swimsuit cuts into my upper back, where a little droop of flesh hangs over it; my thighs swoosh together amiably when I walk, like they've really gotten to know each other lately. Which they have. I feel like I've been zipped into a padded suit—the kind of thing they might costume you in for a made-for-TV movie about yourself as a binge eater. Hopefully, everybody was too busy staring at my enormous breasts to notice the rest of me. But even as I write that, I laugh. A mom with two kids in her tank suit: I probably wasn't the beach's main attraction.

So I found other things to worry about. I really am a pathological worrier. I mean, there we were, creating some of Ben's earliest and best summer memories—of spacing out by the campfire, woozy with sun and water, a marshmallow drooping off his stick into the flames; of stepping on another kid's marshmallow and the sole of his foot turning into a flypaper strip, dragging around a campground's worth of gravel all weekend; of his sandals getting stolen from the beach; of chasing Ayanna around, the two of them so rosy and full of life. Meanwhile I was running through my Protean roster of worries: the sun, the high-fructose corn syrup, the West Nile virus. The water.

The thing is, last summer we saw somebody drown in a lake. It happened right in front of us: completely surreal and utterly devastating. A kid, somebody's twenty-year-old son, horsing around on an inner tube, then going under, then getting dragged out of the water, dead. Paramedics came with their big, useless heart-shocking machine, and hundreds of strangers stood together on the beach, stock-still and silent. He couldn't swim, it turned out. We will never forget the feeling of that young life dissipating into the air above us. We cried a lot and didn't know what to say to Ben, who was too little to understand. "The water made that person very sick," I told him. "Very, *very* sick," Judy teased me gently, when I told her the story later.

So now, Ben has to wear a life vest if he is within a thousand miles of a body of water larger than a dewdrop. I would keep him continuously in a bike helmet, too, if I could get away with it. Hell, I'd put him in a large tank. Remember that scene in *The Boy in the Plastic Bubble,* where John Travolta goes to the beach in the little portable model of his plastic bubble? I mean, was that really so bad? He still ended up with a pretty girl and everything. I'm like somebody's grandma who covers all the furniture with clear plastic. Sure, you don't enjoy sitting on the couch, but at least you know it's *safe* under there.

But then I try to remember something that Sam once said to me, when Ben was sick as a baby, to help me with my terrible worrying. She said, "It's your job to keep Ben safe, yes. But it's also your job to shepherd him into the world. To help him *live.*" Do you know the Mary Oliver poem "The Summer Day"? I think about it all the time these days. I want so much *life* for my kids. These are the last lines from it:

> *I don't know exactly what a prayer is.*
> *I do know how to pay attention, how to fall down*
> *into the grass, how to kneel down in the grass,*
> *how to be idle and blessed, how to stroll through the fields,*
> *which is what I have been doing all day.*
> *Tell me, what else should I have done?*
> *Doesn't everything die at last, and too soon?*
> *Tell me, what is it you plan to do*
> *with your one wild and precious life?*

———————

Birdy's arms and legs look like tube socks that somebody has filled with flour and then rubber-banded into segments. She's one big dinner roll of a baby. Or one of those animals someone makes at a party by twisting long balloons together. This is vaguely deceptive, though, since when you go to pick her up she's heavy as a sea lion. Which is to say that I was not surprised when, at her four-month checkup, her weight was not plottable on their little graph. "I'll just put the dot up here," the nurse said, and pointed to the edge of the page, "so we get the general idea." What a little fattykins!

Our regular and beloved pediatrician was back from maternity leave, and she and Birdy were *very* glad to see each other. Birdy did her whole wiggling/flapping routine, smiling all the while. She's like a machine with a wiggling/flapping function— and the way you turn it on is by looking at her. It makes for a very fun, very low-tech version of peek-a-boo. "Where's Birdy?" you say, looking off to the side. She lies very still for this part, her eyes wide. Then you look right at her—"*There* she is!"—and the flapping and wiggling commences.

And that's not all she can do—oh no, not by a long shot. She can also put her feet together. I don't mean that they slap together incidentally while her legs are going about their business of having the crazies. I mean she deliberately puts her feet flat together, sole to sole, like she's praying. Then she rubs them together wickedly, like a fly. Like an armless villain, delighting over his devilish plans. It reminds me a little bit of this documentary Michael and I once watched about people whose pregnant

242

mothers had—unwittingly, of course—taken thalidomide. They were missing arms and hands, and they were getting on with their lives—raising their kids, working their jobs—but they were, needless to say, really angry about this drug that had stolen so much from their bodies. But then there was this one guy who was very philosophical and also very animated, in an exuberantly *rabbinical* kind of way—so he talked with his legs and feet, gesturing wildly and expressively with them, as if they were hands, wringing them together or clapping one to his forehead in disbelief. "Oy," he said finally, and shrugged his knees. "What are you going to do?"

Birdy uses her own hands quite sneakily. She's so quick that your glasses are off your face and into her mouth—yoink!—before you even noticed her reaching for them. There is also much dragging of her nails across your forearms, much probing of your molars and gums as she, it seems, studies for her periodontal degree. When she's in the front pack, she'll snatch everything you hold out in front of her—*A dollar bill?* I'll *take that, thank you very much*—before crumpling it up and cramming it into her mouth. I actually had to stop carrying Ben in the Baby Bjorn at her age because he'd become such a kleptomaniac. I remember standing at the cash register in our little natural foods store in Santa Cruz, and the cashier smiled and pointed—"Those, too?"—and I looked to see Ben holding a little bag full of a waxy something or other labeled "Ear Candles." "Um, no thanks."

I'm sure you're already beside yourself over Birdy's accomplishments, but hold onto your hat for this last one: she has two teeth! Two little razor-clam sharpies sprouting their way out of her bottom gums. Ben didn't get teeth until he was seven months old, so we must be *much* better parents now, since, as everybody knows, only the kids of *really* good parents get their teeth in early. Or maybe it's just that Birdy herself is deeply and uniquely gifted. Certainly it's at least one of those things.

"Are they bothering her?" our doctor wanted to know. I'm ashamed to say it, but: I have no idea. Birdy is just not under our magnifying glass the same way that Ben was at her age, when we would notice within minutes a sixteenth-degree rise in his temperature or the onset of a vague ennui. Birdy just tags along, grateful as a stray dog if you so much as look at her for two seconds. Maybe she's been a little fussy lately—she sometimes cries gruntily for a second or two, a little struggling sound, like she's trying to yell through a bandanna that captors have tied across her mouth—but I'm not even sure of that.

But can we all agree that teething is a little overrated? I'm not saying that I wouldn't find it very distracting and maybe even a little painful to have bicuspids poking up through my gums like arrowheads. I'm sure I would drool a lot; I'm sure I would complain. But teething seems to be the PMS of the parenting world—it is invoked to explain *everything*. Friends of mine used to bring their babies to our play group with 104-degree fevers and terrible consumptive coughs, and when I'd look alarmed, they'd just shake their heads: *Teething.* Of course. Teething or, you know, the *Bubonic plague.* It also seems to account for all kinds of unsavory behavior. "Oh, is he teething?" people used to ask sweetly when Ben was, say, going berserk in a parking lot. "Oh no," I used to shake my head. "He's just a bad baby." I was kidding, of course, but isn't it possible that sometimes, maybe, people just act horrible for no good reason?

Birdy's checkup ended with the requisite grand finale of

four ten-inch needles to the thigh. Poor little Birdy—all wiggly and smiling and then: jab, jab, jab, jab, like "*That's* what you get for being so damned happy." She was too heartbroken even to nurse. She just wailed and cried and looked up at me, bereft. Even Ben felt sorry for her. "Oooh, did she get a prick?" he asked, and winced in sympathy. A miniature comrade. I'm glad they have each other.

Ben is trying to understand more about why the world works the way it does. Like words, for example—what's up with words? "Why is where you come out called the 'exit'?" he asks one morning, between slurps of his plum. I tell him that words that start with "ex" usually have something to do with "out," but that language mostly just means what it means because that's what somebody decided a long time ago. "It's largely arbitrary," I tell him, and then spend forever explaining the concept of "arbitrary." I'm in way too deep, and I can't seem to come to a natural stopping place. I've become a horrible robotic explaining machine that's been switched to the wrong setting. Ben listens politely, but is, ultimately, underwhelmed by this little crash course in semiotics. "Oh," he finally interrupts me, "well, *I* think that if you're inside, but there's a little hole to get out, then *that's* the exit, but then it might turn out that it's *not* a way to get out, so you'll think, 'Hmm, I guess I must be home, in my own house.' But then you might see a few things that *aren't* yours? And it turns out it's *not* your house!" He shrugs. "*That's* why it's called 'exit.'" Indeed.

Another day, we're eating breakfast at a diner, and it's as if every single thing there has a question mark pasted to it. "Why?" Ben keeps asking, between bites of his grilled blue-berry muffin. "Why, when you suck milk up the straw, does the milk come up the straw and into your mouth?" "Why, when you chew your food, does the food break apart into little pieces and then disappear inside your body?" "Why, when you click this pen does it click and poke out and then click and go back in?" *Why, when I just want to sit here and drink fifty cups of coffee, are you talking and talking?* Michael and I have not settled on an appro-priate level of explanation. We seem to vacillate—depending on how tired we are—between "That's just how it is" type answers and little lessons in, say, particle physics, all drawn out on a connect-the-dots diner place mat. Ben will surely be some odd combination of a know-it-all and a dimwit.

When we spent the weekend with my family, for instance, Ben had a thing or two to explain to Sam, my brother's older son, who is a whopping six months younger than he is. "When I grow up, I'm going to be a tractor," Sam said brightly one day, and Ben corrected him. "I think you mean 'tractor *driver*.'" This is the same Ben who, just the day before, had decided that he was going to be a little dog when he grew up. "Yes," Sam said obediently, "tractor *driver*."

There is also much identification of the flora and fauna around here. We borrowed some field guides from the library, and now Ben is way into classifying everybody who pauses to snack at our bird feeder. "Ah!" he might say with a mouthful of Cheerios, "A tufted titmouse! Or wait—maybe it's a buck-eyed virio." Are these actual birds? I don't know. "Hmmm," he pon-ders on a walk through the woods, bending over a little purple flower. "A creeping Charlie."

All this I can handle more easily than his terribly dark line of existential questions. "When will the world end?" he asked suddenly the other day. "What do you mean?" I asked him. "I mean, what's after the world? Is it just black and dark and everything's black?" This, frankly, gives me the total willies. "When will all these kids die?" he asks when we read the book *Children Like Me*. "What happens afterwards?"

Recently there was a bee in our bedroom—not just a regular bee, mind you, but a maniac bee, hurtling around the room at a million miles an hour and thwacking itself into everything—and Michael killed it with a shoe. Ben burst into tears and grieved over the bee for hours. It was sad and sweet—one of those times when you feel like your kid is a *much* better, more sensitive person than you are—but also just really hard, this day of weeping angst about the dead bee. "My God," Michael whispered to me at some point. "It's like *The Yearling* of the insect world." But finally Ben had an idea. "Hey," he said, "remember how we made those pineapple juice Popsicles, and you said that if we left them out of the freezer too long, they would turn back into juice? Maybe if we leave the dead bee inside for a while, it will turn back into a bee." "Maybe it will," Michael said dreamily, until he saw my cross look. "I mean, no, honey. The bee can't come back to life."

If we were living in a different century, maybe Ben would be an alchemist—brewing up sulfur and tin into big pots of gold. Instead he will likely have to make peace, as best he can, with reason.

Today, we were cooling off in the sprinklers at the playground, and there was a girl there with two prosthetic legs. She was maybe eight years old, wearing a bright pink swimsuit and clickety-clacking over the cement, in and out of the spray. The sun lit up her hair and her smile, and she cantered around, as glad and frisky as a foal. I am struck, as if anew, with the idea of luck—how relative it is. How lucky this girl's family must feel to have such a spirited person in their midst! I worry so much—about Judy, about the kids, about illness and death—that I can miss the whole point entirely. And the point is *this, now*. It's not about promises of perfection or about the future. It's just this, us, here in the sun, screaming through the spray.

Because I think we're actually doing it—I think this is life with two kids. I wonder if maybe I was dreading it—all those horror stories you hear about your older child turning into Drew Barrymore from *Firestarter*, about the shocking divorce rate in the first year after the second child is born—but it's been okay. And now it's getting good, even. I take Ben to pee, and he skips the whole way, then stops in front of a wheelchair symbol on the bathroom door. "Is this a place to buy a wheelchair?" he asks. "Ah, no," I tell him. "The sign means that this bathroom is easy to use even if you're already *in* a wheelchair." "Oh," he says. "Well, I think it's so that if you get to the bathroom and then realize, 'Oh, it turns out I don't have any legs and I'm tired,' then there's a wheelchair you can buy." Ben's is as good as any worldview I can imagine.

He skips back, and we sit at the picnic table to eat our sandwiches, and even though Birdy is just a bitty thing in her car seat on the tabletop, sucking on a paper napkin, I like the way the energy moves around among the four of us. I don't miss, as I'd thought I might, the way Michael and I used to focus all our attention on Ben, as intense and searing as sunlight through a magnifying glass. You think, after your first child is born, that you may have maxed out your capacity to love. And then the new baby comes, and your heart swells again, like a magic sponge. Here at the picnic table, the breeze ushers in some clouds overhead, and I catch myself feeling happy and—I'm surprised about this—relaxed.

Bad news: Ben has discovered children's music. It's not that we've exactly been keeping it from him all these years, but neither have we gone overly out of our way to expose him to it. I know that this is grounds for bringing us up on charges of Gross Self-Interest, this shaping of his musical taste, but Ben really does love our regular folk music. "Oooh, this is such a pretty one," he'll announce in the car, to our delight, before singing along with whatever women's guitar fave comes on the radio.

All parents secretly believe they've got a musical prodigy on their hands. As soon as the kid can pull to standing and starts to do that bouncing thing when "She'll Be Comin' 'Round the Mountain" comes on, every parent everywhere shrugs modestly and says, "He just really seems to have this great sense of rhythm—we don't know why." This is probably a transhistorical phenomenon: I can picture a little cave baby, bouncing up and down while someone bangs a rock with a stick, his parents shrugging modestly in their mammoth skins. We secretly believe this about Ben, too. I don't doubt that Mozart, by three, was already writing symphonies, not crashing around the house with a pair of maracas and a kazoo, but I'm sure Ben will catch right up.

Or, maybe not, now that the Jig Is Up, music-wise. Now he only likes those CDs where various tone-deaf Pollyannas drone on and on about the alphabet and counting and sandwiches. I have nothing against the alphabet and counting and sandwiches ("Wow," Ben exclaimed, watching *Sesame Street* at a friend's house, "this Billy Joel sure knows his ABC's!"), but the songs make me feel as if somewhere, deep inside my brain, something is liquefying. Sadly, Michael and I catch ourselves humming this stuff too. A kind of collective mania seems to set in at our house, and for days at a time, we'll all be singing the same lines from the same song. But really, *all the time*. There's Michael at the stove, stirring spaghetti sauce and singing, "It's mine but you can have some. . . ." There's Ben, bent over his drawing of a giraffe's long, long neck, singing, ". . . with you I'd like to share it. . . ." Here's me at the computer, singing, ". . . 'cause if I share it with you, *you'll* have some too!" (Every now and then, Ben mixes it up a little, such as when you're eating a malted vanilla ice-cream cone, and he sings, "It's yours but I can have some, from you I'd like to taste it. . . .") Billy Collins has a great poem about this that starts:

Ever since I woke up today,
a song has been playing uncontrollably
in my head—a tape looping
over the spools of the brain,
a rosary in the hands of a frenetic nun,
mad fan belt of a tune.

It's called, hilariously, " 'More Than a Woman.' "

Even when Ben was a tiny infant, we'd finally get him to sleep at something approximating the end of the day, and then Michael and I, alone at last, would sit side by side on the couch, glazed completely over and humming the tinny version of Brahms's "Lullaby" from Ben's mobile.

But now a new kind of music thing is happening to me—and I think it may have something to do with those Mama Weepies that set in during the pregnancy and then last for the rest of time. I'll be driving somewhere, and some kind of ballad will come on the radio—something pretty and lilting, like "Let It Be" or, God forbid, Pachelbel's Canon—and all of a sudden every single thing I see will seem inexplicably moving. I'll drive past a woman kneeling in front of the public library, stroking the frayed head of an old yellow Lab, and it seems so sweet and sad I could burst into tears. A grandfather walking hand in hand with a small child? I might as well put myself to bed for the rest of the day.

Sometimes I wonder whether I would have done this—this becoming a parent—if I had known. You know, known about this love that's like heartbreak. Mostly, and obviously, I think: Of course. Don't be silly. But sometimes my love for these children feels almost like an affliction—like my heart is in the fist of a beast, and I am utterly helpless. Some tiny thing will catch my attention—Ben quietly watching a squirrel at the feeder, or the way Birdy's lips look while she's sleeping—and that love feeling will start to bang around inside my chest like a huge, flapping bird.

Even just last night, I was helping Ben dry off after his bath, and I noticed the pale blue veins that run under the skin of his lower back, like marble. He was babbling away in full color ("Do you think if I mixed vinegar and spices and green oil, I could actually make *peas?*") but just for that second, the sight of those veins—of his blood coursing so visibly through him—made him seem so fragile, and made life itself feel so precarious. Which, of course, it is and it isn't. This love—it's like an ocean of joy, but with an undertow that's something else. Grief, maybe, or fear. In Shakespeare's plays, all those characters who are just stricken with love are always tossing out expressions like "overfond." That's what I feel like.

I think about all the things I must not have understood at all before having kids. Like the Pietà, for example: Jesus, drained of life, hanging limp from Mary's arms. This is not an image that has ever had any especially religious significance for me, but now I can barely look at it. Whatever you believe, there's just no way around a mother with her son dead in her arms. If you're like me, you can only look for a second, and then you have to look away.

Maybe it's because the days are getting shorter again, and I'm filled with the feeling of change. Michael and I were two people, and now we are four. First there is one kind of life, then there is another. I'm a little weepy and nostalgic. I drive by the hospital where Birdy was born, and my eyes fill with tears—I feel such a swelling of gratitude that I want to rush in and kiss all the nurses. "Um, yeah, Cath?" Megan would say. "There are *drugs* to help you with that." It's probably true. But I'm not unhappy. I'm just a little full with something that's not quite happiness.

So I was lying around in bed this morning, staring at the sleeping Birdy, which is definitely one of my new favorite ways to kill a couple of hours. It makes me feel like I'm practicing—you know, in case I ever fall madly in love with a bald, gassy dwarf. But then I had this kind of profound thought: Why is it that we live in a world where you might detest another person—a fully functioning, human-size person, who uses the toilet and everything—because he, say, likes to pray in a differently shaped building from you, but then you would cut off both of your arms—Here, take these!—for a pooping little scratchy-nailed Uncle Fester? Something is seriously amiss.

Because, really, Birdy is just so strange! She lies on her back, watching her fish mobile and screaming at odd intervals. Then she'll stick out her tongue and blow a mischievous little raspberry, pumping her fat knees around. Then she'll lie totally still, grunting a small, low sound like a dreaming dog until her eyes startle wide open and she—bam!—slams both her legs down and flings her arms out to the side: Nadia Comaneci landing a handspring. Sometimes she adds this funny laugh to the mix—a throaty little "huh-huh-huh" like a frat boy laughing at a joke about boobs.

And to think that, just one year ago, Birdy was a mere pinto bean with "limb buds" and I was barfing into a trashcan on the sidewalk! (And Ben was still a toddler, demanding "Read dis *icksinky!*" while he dragged an enormous dictionary over to the couch.) What I should mention again now—now that Birdy's here and I really would cut off all my limbs, you know, just to make her laugh—is that I didn't want another baby.

"Can you *believe* you wanted only one child?" people ask me now, trying to take advantage of my weakness over Birdy. But the short answer is: yes. I *do* still understand why I didn't want more kids. When we arrive at Daniel and Pengyew's immaculate house, and we stagger in with our steamer trunk of a diaper bag and Ben is clomping in his rain boots and announcing his opinions about string cheese and death and Birdy is crying about the yellow poop leaking up the back of her onesie and I have more or less wet my pants in the car and I feel like we actually have *fifty* kids, I understand what I was thinking. When Ben asks me some or other question in a low, grumpy voice—"Can you *fffff stttt* my teeth because I *shwwwww ru*?"— and I can't even hear him because Birdy is crying so loudly, and I am just saying "What? *What?*" while my overcaffeinated heart pounds—well, I understand then, too. This is different from regret, of course. And it doesn't stop me from referring often, and casually, to "my kids" in a smug, happy way. But I can still identify with the self who wanted a more serene life.

Instead, Michael and I have this pair of children who are starting to act like siblings. Birdy idolizes Ben, and Ben largely ignores her. But *politely:* he extends her a funny, formal kind of courtesy. He'll be walking past her bouncy chair and he'll brush against her foot and say, "Oh, excuse me, Birdy, I'm sorry." Or he might weary of her baby antics—say, if her damp person is in the middle while we're reading bedtime books—and he'll say calmly, "Can you please switch places, Mama? I think Birdy's trying to bite my shirt." And I'll look, and her eyes will be crinkled up naughtily, and, indeed, half of Ben's sleeve will be crammed into her mouth.

Two nights ago, we were doing the rounds of bedtime hugs and kisses, and it was as if Ben noticed Birdy for the first time in his life. "I think I'm going to give Birdy a little kiss," he said to me, and I said, "Okay, hon. I think she'd really like that." He bent over her skeptically. She was kicking her little legs, so thrilled that he was looking at her that she couldn't help blowing a long sequence of raspberries. Ben hesitated. "Could you please wipe her mouth with a little cloth, Mama?" he said, and I said, "Sure," and did. Ben bent over her again. "Could you just give her mouth one more last wipe?" I nodded. But the raspberries continued—poor Birdy was probably kicking herself, trying to stop—and Ben, finally, lay back down on the pillows with a sigh. "I don't think I'm going to give Birdy a kiss after all," he said, and I said, "That's fine. Maybe next time she won't be so juicy," and kissed her myself. Such noble intentions! Sure, it wasn't an unequivocal success or anything, but I was so pleased and proud.

And really, we're all changing. I was squatting with Ben by the full-length mirror this morning. He's in a phase of liking to watch himself talk. "Good morning, Mama," he said to me, contorting his features into all these exaggerated shapes while he enunciated each word—big pursed lips, bared bottom teeth, eyebrows knit fiercely together. I was so busy watching his animated face that when I caught sight of my own, I did a double take. Compared to Ben—to the smooth, peachy expanse of his ripe self—I look like I'm made out of a stained paper bag that someone has crumpled up and then tried their best to smooth flat.

When did I get so *old?* My arms, too—they're so freckly and rumpled, like they're made of deflating balloons. I look at teenagers now and can't get over it—how sleek they are, like seals. They're so busy worrying about their invisible blackheads—as I was at their age—that they're missing the whole point about the way their skin actually *fits* them. I know it's happening to my own mom, too. I hand over snapshots of her, of her beautiful, silvery head bent over the kids, and she studies them intently. "I look like a *grandma*," she says, and shakes her head. She's not displeased, just a little surprised. I guess that's how I feel too. I look like a *mother!*

What a year it's been. We just developed this great photo of Judy holding Birdy: they have the *exact* same dark fluff of hair and they're both smiling. Judy looks great and happy now that the chemotherapy is over, and Birdy also looks great and happy now that she can hold her own head up, and I feel like it pretty much sums up our year. If Ben were in the picture too, maybe smiling but also pointing his bossy finger to the place he'd rather have Judy sitting, and if I were in the background, full of gladness and relief but lying on the couch with an ice pack on my head, and if Michael were there too, posed somehow—with wide, calm arms and his gorgeous smile—to communicate the gracious way he takes care of all of us, then that would *really* sum up our year.

I am simply hoping for more. More luck and joy and health—and peace—for all of us.

acknowledgments

I sing a song of gratitude for my lucky life and my happy work:

Leah Hennen edited the original "Bringing Up Ben and Birdy" columns on BabyCenter.com; she has been unflaggingly in my corner, and other things besides: a modest, inspiring editor, a hilarious pen pal, and a true friend. I am in her corner back. And my warmest thanks go to the loyal BabyCenter readers for their loving, anonymous support.

Jennifer Gates, my brilliant and gracious agent, climbed right on board, smiling, and seemed never to look back. Her confidence has been a real occasion to rise to.

The editor of my dreams, Jane von Mehren, offers the unusual mix of freedom and enthusiasm that makes it so pleasurable and unscary to write. Brett Kelly is like Katharine Hepburn playing a publishing superhero: elegant, funny, and smart as a whip; I can only imagine how hard it is to make everything so easy. Bitite Vinklers copyedited the book with meticulousness and zeal.

Cathi Hanauer, Alexandra Kennedy, and Jennifer Margulis each, in different ways, took a chance on me and my writing, and this has made all the difference. And the fabulous editors of *FamilyFun* magazine have kept me afloat all the while.

acknowledgments

I want to thank the friends who have helped explicitly with this book: Andrew Greto, who took the beautiful photograph of Ben and me and Birdy; Becky Michaels, who read the entire manuscript with affection and acuity—and wrote in the margin, one time only, "A little exaggerated, maybe?"; Richard Todd, for untold years of the kind of wry encouragement I can bear; and Katharine Whittemore, who is so generous and funny that I was tempted to write a book of quotations called simply *And Then Kathy Said*.

And then others: Andrew Coburn, Sarah Jain, Sam Marion, and Megan Sanderson, chosen kin; Ali Pomeroy, my oldest friend in the world; Judy Haas, my Memphis angel; Judy Frank, for teaching me to write, and to laugh in the glow of a silver lining; Sue Dickman, Ann Hallock, and Emily Todd for decades of food and friendship; Paul Statt for warmth; Daniel Hall, the poet-boss-godfather at Amherst College, for pleasure. The friends from way back: Kelly Close, Jody Madell, Andrea Martin, Rebecca Morgan, Margaret Muirhead, Jeremy Pomeroy, and Bill Stewart. And the California life support: Gordon Bigelow, Tim Crockett, Carla Freccero, Gail Hershatter, Anita Jain, Grace Laurencin, Anna Paganelli, Ginny Troyer, and the Santa Cruz new mamas, especially Cat Enright-Down, Daleth Foster, Kenée Houser, and Laura LeRoy. On this coast: Nicole Blum, Pengyew Chin, Carey Dimmit, Barbara Findlen, Liz Garland, Moira Greto, Meredith Michaels, Jennifer Rosner, and Molly Whalen. And Ben's Blue Nursery teachers—O paragons of patience and imagination!—for time without worry: Jen Jarrell, Jean Meister, and Katrina Van Pelt.

The extended Newman-Millner clan, especially: Robert and Lori Newman, on-call pediatricians, warm reality-checkers, and a deep source of inspiration; Keith Millner, a true brother and a shining star in the Uncle Hall of Fame; and Larry Millner and Barbara Hunter, my beloved cheerleaders-in-law.

Generation-wise, I am sandwiched by greatness: above are my beautiful, indulgent parents, Ted and Jennifer Newman, who have listened to me so well and laughed at my stories for so long; below are my gentle and sparkling children, Benjamin and Abigail Newman, who have made me so fully happy and human. And right here in the middle with me is Michael Millner. His kindness makes everything possible—it's as simple as that.